Other books by Donald E. Morse:

The Novels of Kurt Vonnegut: Imagine Being an American

*The Irish Theatre in Transition from the Nineteenth
    to the Twenty-first Centuries*

The Delegated Intellect: Emersonian Essays in Honor of Don Gifford

Anatomy of Science Fiction

The Fantastic in World Literature and the Arts

Zones of (Re)membering: Time, Memory, and (un)Consciousness
    by Don Gifford

A Reader's Guide to Kurt Vonnegut

The Choices of Fiction

Worlds Visible and Invisible with Csilla Bertha

*More Real than Reality: The Fantastic in Irish Literature, Theatre
    and Art* with Csilla Bertha

*Silenced Voices: Five Hungarian Plays from Transylvania Translated
    into English* with Csilla Bertha

The Suza Wedding Feast by András Sütő
    translated into English with Csilla Bertha

A Small Nation's Contribution to the World
    with Csilla Bertha and István Pálffy

The Dramatic Artistry of Brian Friel
    with Csilla Bertha and Mária Kurdi

The Celebration of the Fantastic with Csilla Bertha et al

The Mythic Fantasy of Robert Holdstock with Kálmán Matolcsy

*The Theoretical Foundations of Hungarian "lieux de mémoire" Studies/
    Theoretische Grendlagen der Erforchung ungarischer Erinnerungsorte*
    with Pál S. Varga, Karl Katschthaler, and Miklós Takács

The (Web)sites of Memory: Cultural Heritage in the Digital Age
    with Zsófia O. Réti and Miklós Takács

IT'S TIME

Frontispiece: front view of the metal sculpture
The Matter of Time by Richard Serra. Photograph
by R. Polidori (used by kind permission of the artist).

It's Time
A Mosaic Reflecting What Living in Time Is Like

Donald E. Morse

*To Honor
with thanks for many years
of friendship and hospitality.
Hope you have time
for this book,*

Donald 2023

ᴀ **HJEAS** book

Debrecen University Press, Hungary

For Csilla Bertha
and
in memory of Don Gifford

Table of Contents

Preface   xi

Acknowledgements   xiii

Introduction: The Uniqueness of Temporality   15

Chapter 1: Perceiving and Measuring Time   31

Chapter 2: Remembering the Future, Anticipating the Past   77

Chapter 3: Two Time Fallacies:

    Apocalypse Now and Progressing in Time   123

Chapter 4: The Fullness of Time and the Cancer of Time   165

Chapter 5: Time, Memory, and Dementia   199

Chapter 6: Time, the Life Cycle, Immortality, and Mortality 235

Postscript: On the Nature of Human Lived Time   277

Bibliography of Works Cited   285

Index   315

List of illustrations

Frontispiece: front view of the metal sculpture

    The Matter of Time by Richard Serra   iv

Figure 1: The Corpus Clock with"The Chronophage"

    by John C. Taylor   283

HURRY UP PLEASE ITS TIME
——*T. S. Eliot, "The Waste Land"*

Got time on my hands
I've got time on my shoulder
Got plenty of time on my mind
——*Ewan MacColl, "The Lag's Song"*

Preface

This book has been many years in the making incurring many debts along the way—many of which are now impossible to recall or acknowledge. My ongoing debt to my mentor, teacher, and friend Don Gifford will be evident on almost every page as will my debt to Csilla Bertha, who read and helped improve the book over the decades as she has so much of my life.

I would like to thank Kathryn "Kit" Hume for her meticulous reading of the penultimate draft of *It's Time*. Her incisive comments and criticism led me to write a far better book, for which I cannot thank her enough. I would also like to thank Lenke Németh, who generously edited the manuscript, painstakingly correcting mistakes and supplying numerous omissions. My colleagues at the Institute of English and American Studies at the University of Debrecen provided a stimulating and nurturing environment as well as the occasion for many of these ruminations. I wish to especially acknowledge the Institute Director, Balázs Venkovits, who has enthusiastically supported both this book and the whole *HJEAS Books New Series*. My thanks also to Professor Róbert Keményfi, Dean of the Faculty of Humanities, for his strong and tangible support of this book and the *HJEAS Books New Series*.

It's Time has benefited from my numerous conversations over the years with Professor Zoltán Abádi-Nagy as well as his editing of my essays in the *Hungarian Journal of English and American Studies*. This book and the *HJEAS Books New Series* came about thanks to Professor Abádi appointing me to succeed him as editor of *HJEAS*, for which I am most grateful. Much of my thinking about living in time occurred in public in the University of Debrecen graduate seminars on time and I thank the students for that extensive conversation, especially Kálmán Matolcsy, Péter Csató, and Ádám Molnár. A very special thanks to Peter Dávidházi, whose enthusiastic endorsement of this project helped salvage it at a crucial time.

I am grateful to Kálmán Matolcsy for his meticulous copy editing and typesetting. Finally I thank the four evaluators of *It's Time* for their generous, thoughtful assessment: Kit Hume, Christopher Murray, Ildikó Limpár, and W. A. "Bill" Senior. I have been fortunate indeed to know and benefit from their magnanimity. None are responsible for any remaining errors of commission and of omission, as they are solely my own.

Acknowledgements

Portions of chapter 1 appeared in "The Present of Things Future in Fiction," *Focus* (1998), Mária Kurdi, editor, published by the University of Pécs; *The Cultural Influences of William Gibson, the "Father" of Cyberpunk Science Fiction* (Edwin Mellen Press 2007); and "The Simple Magnificence of Bacteria," *Irish Studies Review* 8.1, Neil Sammells, editor, published by Taylor and Francis; and each is reprinted by kind permission of the editors and publishers.

Portions of chapter 2 appeared in "'The Present of Things Future' in Fiction," *Focus* (1998), Mária Kurdi, editor, published by the University of Pécs, and "'Overcoming Time: 'The Present of Things Past' in History and Fiction," *The Delegated Intellect: Emersonian Essays on Literature, Science and Art in Honor of Don Gifford*, Donald E. Morse, editor (Peter Lang 1995), and are reprinted by kind permission of the editors and publishers.

Portions of chapter 3 appeared in "The End of the World in American History and Fantasy: The Trumpet of the Last Judgment," *Journal of the Fantastic in the Arts* 13.1, W. A. Senior, editor, and "'You Cannot Win, You Cannot Break Even, You Cannot Get Out of the Game': Kurt Vonnegut and the Notion of Progress," *At Millennium's End: New Essays on the Work of Kurt Vonnegut*, Kevin Alexander Boon, editor (SUNY Press, 2001), and are reprinted by kind permission of the editors and publishers.

Portions of chapter 4 appeared in "Meaning of Time in Auden's *For the Time Being*," *Renascence* 22.3 (1970), John E. Curran, Jr., editor, and "'Moments for Nothing': Images of Time in Samuel Beckett's Plays," *Arbeiten aus Anglistik und Amerikanistik* 15.1 (1990), and are reprinted by kind permission of the editors and publishers.

Portions of chapter 5 appeared in "Sleepwalkers Along a Precipice: Staging Memory in Marina Carr's *The Mai*," *Hungarian Journal of English and American Studies* 2.2, Csilla Bertha, issue editor, Zoltán Abádi-Nagy, *HJEAS* editor, and "'The Politics of Aging': Frank McGuinness's *The Hanging Gardens*," *Irish Theatre in Transition from the Late Nineteenth to the Early Twentieth-first Century*, Donald E. Morse, editor (Palgrave Macmillan 2015), and are reprinted by kind permission of the editors and publishers.

Portions of chapter 6 appeared in "James Joyce and the Life Cycle," *ABEI (Brazilian Journal of Irish Studies)* 4, Munira Mutran and Laura Izarra, editors; "'All your Life after that again': James Joyce and the Creation of a New Literary Language," *Hungarian Journal of English and American Studies* 3.2, Zoltán Abádi-Nagy, editor; "James Joyce and the Dreamwork of Language: The Book from the Twenty-first Century," *Islands in the Asia-Pacific*, Peter Kuch and Julie-Ann Robson, editors (Colin Smythe 2003); and "'We All Go Away': The Last Moments of Old Age in *The Tragedy of King Lear* and *Three Tall Women*," *"Now You See It, Now You Don't": Hiding and Revealing in Text and in Performance*, Kathleen E. Dubs, editor (Pázmány Péter Catholic University 2006); and are reprinted by kind permission of the editors and publishers.

A personal thank you to the international photographer Robert Polidori for supplying that most elusive photograph of Richard Serra's monumental sculpture *The Matter of Time*. Thanks also to Cathy Neill for her photograph of John C. Taylor's *Chronophage*.

Every effort has been made to trace the owners of copyright materials in this book, but in some instances this has proven impossible. The author and publisher will be glad to receive information leading to more complete acknowledgements in subsequent printings of the book and in the meantime extend their apologies for any omissions.

Introduction:
The Uniqueness of Temporality

> *How could you not be interested in time? It's like*
> *being a fish and not being interested in the sea. It's*
> *where we live. . . . We live in it. We live through it.*
> *It ages us. It changes us.*
> ———*David Mitchell*

Time and space are the very dimensions of our lives. As our body moves through space so our mind moves through time remembering the past, anticipating the future, and experiencing the present. Time is life and our life defines our time. How much time do we have? Very few of us can know the answer and so we tend to go by averages, such as three score years and ten, 65 and out, or the age my parents died, and so forth. Could we have any more time? Could we experience any time other than the years we are living? What is time like for other people? In the midst of the Coronavirus pandemic, American author Joyce Carol Oates tweeted that her experience of time had changed, and changed radically:

> Is anyone else experiencing a distortion of time? Each day feels monumental & tomorrow seems totally unpredictable; one week feels like one month; the future feels foreshortened, like a blank wall just a few inches away. Past crises, like raging wildfires, near-forgotten.

The past, present, and future all felt out of joint to her and with them went Oates's sense of living in time. She and many others around the world became more acutely aware of time. People who have been in prison say much the same thing: that their experience of time changed, in their case it appeared to become stretched, as in the epigraph to this book, where "the lag" (the prisoner) in Ewan MacColl's song—originally written for a television documentary on life in prison—confesses that he has "time on my hands . . . time on my shoulder / . . . plenty of time on my mind." One of the first and most difficult tasks facing a newly arrived prisoner is how to keep track of the passage of time when life has become dominated by an unvarying routine.

> There is no summer nor winter once you land inside here
> Just that old prison grind.
> (Ewan MacColl, "The Lag's Song")

The opposite experience of time is also true: that when events move so fast one after the other, it becomes impossible to absorb them all. Even for someone used to viewing and evaluating dozens of events in time: the Harvard historian Jill Lapore, for example, still experienced a disorientation in time when confronted by what she calls those "monumental events" that rapidly succeeded one after another, such as the several hundred thousand deaths from COVID-19 and at almost the same time the violent insurrection in Washington DC. "These monumental events recede so quickly that it's difficult to get a grasp on anything . . . . I don't normally have that [feeling]. [A]s an historian, I generally feel quite anchored in time" (qtd. in Baltz). Many other people feeling perhaps too anchored in time would, however, like to increase the amount of time they have by somehow slowing it down. At least one character in a novel found a unique way of doing exactly that. He was able to slow down time to a crawl by deliberately joining a long line of people waiting to buy tickets to a popular film but one that he definitely did not want to see!

The Nature of Time

"According to researchers at the *Oxford English Dictionary*, time is the most used noun in the English language" (Sean Carroll, *Eternity* 1), but what exactly is time? How do we experience time whether in a pandemic, in prison, or on more "normal" days? Philosophers, theologians, psychologists, cosmologists, and people generally have for centuries argued and quite often strongly disagreed about its nature. Some have even questioned if it exists. The eminent contemporary experimental physicist, Richard Muller, for instance, who has devoted much of his life in physics to studying the problem of time, confesses that "everything about time I find mind-numbing" (83). Yet Muller persevered in studying time long enough to write *NOW: The Physics of Time* (2016), in which he presents—and in considerable detail, including possible falsifying experiments—his theory of the continual creation of time that as a physicist he sees running in parallel with the continual expansion of space (293).[1] Muller's theory only became possible, however, with a discovery that happened in 1999. In that year Saul Perlmutter and his team at the University of California, Berkeley simultaneously with another research team in Australia discovered to their astonishment that the universe's expansion rate, instead of slowing down, as had been commonly assumed, was actually accelerating, which meant that there could be no tipping point, no collapsing universe, no Big Crunch, and no time reversal, but instead space and time would most likely go on expanding forever. Their finding has since been confirmed by other physicists. For

---

1. For a fuller discussion of Richard Muller's *NOW: The Physics of Time*, see Morse, "Review of *NOW: The Physics of Time* written by Richard A. Muller."

their revolutionary discovery Perlmutter and the Australians were awarded Nobel Prizes in Physics (see Muller 156-57).

Drawing on Perlmutter's discovery Muller then developed what he calls "the cosmological origin of time" (296) or the "*now* theory of time creation" (302). His theory, concentrating as it does on the macro-phenomenon of the expansion of space, offers an alternative to those contemporary theoretical physicists, such as Julian Barbour in *The End of Time* (1999), who reach their conclusions about the nature of time by focusing on the micro-phenomenon of quanta, the basic building blocks of the universe that exist at a level where there is no flow to time, no "before" or "after," and where time remains static. At the quantum level of the universe there is only a continuous present, which led the distinguished physicist David Park to observe that "the strange thing about quantum mechanics . . . is that it does not contain the concept of time" (264). Humans do not, however, live in a micro-scale quantum world but in a macro-scale one. Muller also provides an alternative on that macro scale to those philosophers, such as Craig Callender, who argue "that time fundamentally does not even exist" (Callender, "Is Time an Illusion?" 41). For Muller the "*Now*" of physics instead of being continuous and static—the state of things without any time—becomes dynamic and continuously new. "Every moment the universe gets a little bigger and there is a little more time, and it is this leading edge of time that we refer to as now," he contends (293). His contribution to the discussion of time, coming from an experimental rather than a theoretical physicist or from a philosopher, greatly enlarges that stimulating discussion— which shows no sign of diminishing, much less stopping—by providing a much-needed link between knowledge derived from experiments and knowledge derived from theory.

INTRODUCTION

While physicists, like the philosophers of time before them, debate the existence and nature of time, contemporary writers as diverse as Kurt Vonnegut (1922-2007), George R. R. Martin (1948-), Marina Carr (1964-), and Frank McGuinness (1953-) have attempted to grapple with the problem of time not as a physics experiment designed to reveal a truth or truths about the physical universe or as a knotty intellectual problem to be resolved in philosophical argument but as the way human beings experience their time-bound condition. The great Argentinean writer Jorge Luis Borges (1899-1986), for instance, who spent a good part of his career thinking and writing about time, came to the bleak conclusion that from a human rather than a cosmological or philosophical perspective the problem of time is simply insoluble. He summed up this predicament by saying that "I think the real problem, the problem we have to grapple with, and of course the problem whose solution we'll never find, is the problem of time" ("Borges at N.Y.U." 123). Centuries earlier Saint Augustine in chapter 11 of his *Confessions* put in a nutshell part of the difficulty with time that Borges and most of us experience when he pondered the question, "What is time?" concluding: "What then is time? I know what it is if no one asks me what it is; but if I want to explain it to someone who has asked me, I find that I do not know" (11.14, 267). Centuries later a fictional character in George R. R. Martin's *Dances with Dragons* (Book 5 of "Fire and Ice," which became the *Game of Thrones* television series) in attempting to explain the human experience of time to a young boy reached back to Heraclitus and borrowed his powerful metaphor of time as a river:

> Time is different for a tree than for a man. For men, time is a river. We are trapped in its flow, hurtling from past to

> present, always in the same direction. The lives of trees are different. They root and grow and die in one place, and that river does not move them. . . . Men live their lives trapped in an eternal present, between the mists of memory and the sea of shadow that is all we know of the days to come. (533)

His conclusion that humans are "trapped in an eternal present, between the mists of memory and the sea of shadow . . . of the days to come" echoes Augustine's conclusion to his famous meditation "What is time?":

> It is now plain and clear that neither past nor future are existent, and that it is not properly stated that there are three times, past, present, and future. But perhaps it might properly be said that there are three times, the present of things past, the present of things present, and the present of things future. These three are in the soul, but elsewhere I do not see them: the present of things past is in memory; the present of things present is in intuition; the present of things future is in expectation. (11.20, 273)

When Martin's character describes being "trapped in an eternal present" between memory and the future, he implies what Augustine stated in "the present of things past is in memory"; that is, humans are able to recall events that happened in the past or words uttered in the past only in their "now," in a new present time and this "present of [the] past" will inevitably modify their memory of whatever occurred in the past. Similarly, we may anticipate a future event in minute detail but for that event actually to occur it must not remain in the indefinite future but happen in our present, in our now. "[T]he now, the here, through which all future plunges to the past," as James Joyce once wrote (*Ulysses* 989).

INTRODUCTION

George Lakoff and Mark Johnson in their chapter on "Time" in *Philosophy in the Flesh* (1999) warn those who would define time:

> We cannot observe time itself—if time even exists as a thing in-itself. We can only observe events and compare them. . . . We do not perceive time independently of events. . . . We can only define time to be that which is measured by regular iterated events. . . . We experience only the present. We have to conceptualize past and future. (138, 154, 155)

David Park was even more pessimistic about our ability to define or even to describe time. He once confessed : "I can think of no statement describing our experience of time whose truth must be admitted" (259). All of which may make any or most discussions of time so complicated that many of us will simply give up.

Why is it so hard to discuss time? A good part of the difficulty arises from what contemporary philosopher Nathaniel Lawrence terms "the uniqueness of temporality," which while

> it submits to useful analogy, . . . it simply is different, essentially different, from anything else. To simplify it in behalf of one of its aspects is to declare an ontological position, unwittingly, sometimes half-wittingly. Time is neither just a spontaneity of consciousness nor merely a value for a mathematical variable that can be extrapolated to a zero or infinity. (25)

What makes time so "essentially different, from anything else," as Lawrence outlines in the same essay, is that "temporality permeates . . . [human] experience, so that temporality is part of its texture or structure, rather than an isolatable item in experience. When we undertake to render that temporality into a concept of time, we abstract from our experience certain elements of it while ignoring others" (37).[2] And this becomes a "no win" game. Borges himself cautioned against trying to "solve" this intractable problem. Instead, he recommended attempting to describe and, where possible, to illuminate it through story, for, he maintains, "Our existence in time . . . can only be comprehended through narrative" ("Borges at N.Y.U. 123). Therefore, rather than attempting to define time or to theorize about it, humanists should follow the excellent advice of George H. Ford and "do what they can do well, which is to report on what living in time is like" (141). One of the best means of making that "report" that is both concrete and specific rather than general and/or abstract remains imaginative literature, which, as we shall see, offers "special insights into the experiences of time" (141). But as J. Hillis Miller warns, "This is not easy to do. . . . [R]epresentations of human time in literary works are singular, sui generis, different from all others" (87). Hence this book will discuss a variety of works in several different genres in the hope not of being definitive but of creating a mosaic that will reflect what it is like to live in time, following Borges's excellent suggestion of approaching the problem of the way humans experience time through many different narratives that reflect on that varied experience. Interpreted broadly the narratives discussed here include fiction, drama, and poetry written by an eclectic group of writers among whom are W. H. Auden (1907-1973), James Joyce (1882-1941), Kurt Vonnegut, Samuel Beckett

---

2. For a clear concise history of the representations of time in Western thought, see J. T. Fraser's magisterial volume *Of Time, Passion and Knowledge*, 2nd ed. (1990) and his compendium *The Voices of Time*, 2nd ed. (1981).

(1906-1989), Marina Carr, Ray Bradbury (1920-2012), Emily Dickinson (1830-1886), William Gibson (1948-), W. P. Kinsella (1935-2016), Audrey Niffenegger (1963-), H. G. Wells (1886-1946), and many others. Such narratives, as Borges well knew, unlike life have the advantage of completion; that is, they can offer a nuanced, often complex view of our experience in time whereas individual human testimony and even clinical studies must necessarily remain incomplete or partial and often confusingly reflect the informant's own confusion. Narrative remains the ideal medium for presenting the events upon which our real experience of time depends.

Pieces of This Mosaic of What It Is Like to Live in Time

The first piece, "The Uniqueness of Temporality," is an introduction to this complex and perplexing subject that you are currently reading. It is followed by six discrete but related chapters and a brief postscript, while the second piece of this mosaic, "Perceiving and Measuring Time," delves into the vast shift in the way people have experienced time over the last few centuries from the nineteenth century's spacious present that the nineteenth-century psychologist William James (1842-1910) pictured as a saddleback containing parts of both the future and the past to the late twentieth and early twenty-first centuries, where both the past and the future have shrunk so much that for many the present appears as a knife edge with neither a past nor a future. The chapter also traces the recent history of western views of time from the nineteenth through the twenty-first centuries and describes some of the many ways we have measured it. As the late Irish poet Eavan Boland observed, "one of our human enterprises has been to make time and measure it" (13), which humans have done for thousands of years. We naturally tend to assume that the way we experience time in the twenty-first century is identical to the way our ancestors did and the units we use to measure time today in weeks, months, years, centuries, and millennia is the way people have always done it, but such suppositions are only partially correct. Recently, for instance, much of the world celebrated a new century, the twenty-first, and also a new millennium under the assumption that others before us had also made much of these demarcations. A quick glance into the history of time measurement, however, reveals that of the several measurements of duration these two—the century and the millennium—remain among the most arbitrary of the many that humans have invented as will be discussed at some length. "Perceiving and Measuring Time" notes that historically there have been many different calendars in use and through much of human history there was little or no agreement about their basic features, not even when a new year began.

Similarly, earlier, people did not pay much attention to centuries—neither when one began nor when one ended and a new one began—and even less to millennia. The prime example discussed is the twentieth century as an historical example of humans measuring and marking time as well as our current penchant for giving descriptive labels demarcating centuries. "What might it have been like to live through the violent twentieth century? How should that century be denominated?" The answer to either question is far from obvious.

The third piece of this time mosaic, "Remembering the Future, Anticipating the Past," examines a question posed by both Alice in *Through the Looking-Glass, and What Alice Found There* (1871) and contemporary physicists: why do we remember only the past and not the future? The answer, it turns out, is also not at all obvious. The chapter discusses how we humans experience time including the always-thwarted desire to have more of it either by reliving the past (Martin Amis, *Time's Arrow*) or by being able to live life all over again in future years (Sean O'Faloin, *And Again?*) or by traveling in time. Such discussions were broadened considerably with the publication of H. G. Wells's "invention" of *The Time Machine* (1895), a book that has never been out of print but has always been popular and spawned numerous literary progeny since its publication. Among the many literary and artistic works discussed three contemporary time travel novels by Vonnegut, *Slaughterhouse-Five*, Niffenegger, *The Time Traveler's Wife*, and the eminent evolutionary biologist George Gaylord Simpson, *The Dechronization of Sam Magruder* will explore questions about and implications of travel to the past and the future.

Chapter 3, "Two Common Fallacies about Time," deals with two common mistaken assumptions about time: first, that time will have an end, and second, that time records human progress ever onward and ever upward. Despite the failure of every apocalyptic prediction that the world is coming to an end, a sizable percentage of people in the past and living today, especially in the United States, believe they are living in the End Times, when time will stop. This belief convulsed nineteenth-century America and is one currently held by millions of Americans as reflected in popular fiction, such as Jerry Jenkins and Tim LaHaye's spectacularly popular Left Behind series of sixteen novels. Similarly, despite all the evidence to the contrary, many believe that history is the record of human progress, which while true about technology and our knowledge of the natural world becomes less demonstrable when discussing human society and world affairs. Whether the pandemic and other catastrophes caused by drastic climate change will also challenge people to shift their beliefs only time will tell.

The second part of the chapter on the notion of progress begins a series that explores various aspects of the experience of lived time by focusing primarily on time as depicted in the work by a single author as in this chapter, which concentrates on the fiction of Kurt Vonnegut. In many ways Vonnegut is *the* representative American writer of the post-World War II years including his rejection of the popular notion that history is the record of human beings progressing in time. He remarked repeatedly to the effect that "I don't have the feeling we are going anywhere" and in novel after novel set out to demolish clichés of human progress in time from the old General Electric slogan "Progress is our most important product" to the erroneous belief that humans are the pinnacle of evolution or creation.

Chapter 4 and the fifth piece of this mosaic, "The Fullness of Time and the Cancer of Time," begins from the premise that every world religion has had to contend with the problem of time. The first part of this chapter discusses some of the numerous nineteenth and twentieth-century Protestant theologians, who devoted much of their preaching and writing to the problem of time. The poet W. H. Auden drew on several of them for his religious long poem, *For the Time Being* (1944), in which he explores a facet of contemporary Protestantism's grappling with the problem of time. The second part is devoted to Samuel Beckett, who spent much of his career writing about the problem of lived time in his prose, poetry, and plays, yet unlike Auden he did not conclude that "[t]ime is our choice of how to love and why," but instead and more starkly affirmed that he found time a cancer that eats away all that is valuable in and to human life. Much of his writing attempts to "articulate, and perform, finitude—of lived time" (Mihálycsa 176). At the end of his life one of his very last works sums up his experience and belief with the motto "make sense who may" (*Complete Plays* 476). Because Beckett continually worried the problem of time throughout his writing career, the discussion will be necessarily limited in scope to his early plays and their images of time.

The sixth piece in the mosaic of what it is like to live in time, chapter 5, entitled "Time, Memory, and Dementia," explores the interrelation between time and memory along with the consequences of their erasure in those suffering from dementia. Is it possible to hold onto or to recapture time through memory? For instance, could an adult woman understand the mystery of her parents, especially her now dead mother's seemingly inexplicable—from the child's perspective—suicide and the equally unknown motivation for such a violent act? Most parents have a life together that remains forever unknown to their child since it occurred before the parents had any children or at least before the children became aware of their having more to their lives than as their parents. This situation remains true even for the many children who survive their parents by years or even decades, since in all cases both the child and the parent have only a fixed percentage of their lifetimes in common. Only through fantasy, as in W. P. Kinsella's *Shoeless Joe* (1982), or by piecing together shards of memory as Millie does in Carr's *The Mai* (1995) might a child overcome even partially this unyielding time constraint and begin to understand how and why a parent acted in such a seemingly inexplicable way. The second part of this chapter explores some of the terrible consequences of experiencing dementia, which robs people of their time-past through loss of memory and time-present through loss of words, and those losses lead in turn to a loss of any time-future.

The final chapter and penultimate piece of the mosaic, chapter 6, "Time and the Life Cycle, Immortality and Mortality," examines the end of lived time in the Life Cycle, while also considering the chimera of immortality and the consolations of mortality as time runs out as it must for all humans. Almost alone among writers in English William Shakespeare (1564-1616) and James Joyce aimed at giving readers nothing less than all of human life lived in time. Most writers work by exclusion but both Shakespeare and Joyce practiced inclusion; that is, they "put it all in," as Joyce proclaimed in *Ulysses*. Few writers in English have illuminated the cycle of human life as extensively or as clearly as James Joyce. The first part of this chapter examines how through his novels and short stories he presents all of human life as lived in time from infancy to death. The chapter also examines three stories by Petronius (27-66), Jonathan Swift (1667-1745), and Oscar Wilde (1854-1900), which powerfully depict the dangers of immortality or of life lived in endless time. The chapter continues with an extended discussion not of immortality but of mortality as depicted powerfully in Shakespeare's *King Lear* (1606) and Edward Albee's (1928-2016) *Three Tall Women* (1991).

The greatest of Shakespeare's tragedies, *King Lear*, presents an uncompromising view of the world steeped in injustice and fratricide, and over all is the ubiquitous smell of mortality for "time must have a stop" (*Henry IV*, part 1; 5). Like the biblical Book of Job, upon which Shakespeare drew so extensively, the good and the innocent suffer while the evil appear to prosper. Age and mortality also enter the tragedy as Lear's options narrow, his world flies apart, his time runs out, and events do indeed race downhill like the Fool's justly famous "Great Wheel" (2.4, 69).

Rather than *Lear's* apocalypse of last things or Beckett's world under threat of erasure, Albee's *Three Tall Women* shares with tragedy the focus on last moments as the time of the Tall Woman's life runs out and her life moves towards resolution and affirmation. In act 1, the three women embody three reactions to the process of aging over time that leads to death. In act 2, the three women embody three of the seven ages of the Tall Woman as Albee employs unusual theatrical means to atomize effectively and to illuminate in a surprisingly affirmative way an individual at the end of her life's time.

The final and relatively small piece of the time mosaic, the Postscript "Life Remains a Blessing / Although You Cannot Bless," explores the implications for lives lived in time inherent in Auden's lyric poem "As I Walked Out." The poem juxtaposes a romantic lover's hyperbolic pledges to overcome time itself and thus defy mortality with the inevitable physical and emotional effects of time's passage. Yet, despite time's inevitable conquest, the poet is still able to affirm that "[l]ife remains a blessing." Taken together with this postscript the six chapters of *It's Time* form this mosaic—this "report on what living in time is like" that describes human beings' existence in time from a variety of perspectives that range from the desire to escape from a time-bound life and the various attempts to overcome human mortality and finitude, to the time-destroying problems of faulty memory and dementia, and, finally, to a necessary acceptance of human mortality as the natural end to a life lived in time.

Chapter 1
Perceiving and Measuring Time

Time is Nature's way of keeping everything from
happening at once.
———*John Wheeler*

[I]n the past the time-span of important change
was considerably longer than that of a single
human life. Thus mankind was trained to adapt
itself to fixed conditions.
   To-day the time-span is considerably shorter
than that of human life, and accordingly our
training must prepare individuals to face a novelty
of conditions.
———*Alfred North Whitehead*

How people experience and measure time has changed
dramatically from the late eighteenth to the early-twenty-first
century.[1] At the approximate mid-point in this two-hundred-
plus-year process, late in the nineteenth century, William James
concluded that for most people

> the practically cognized present is no knife-edge, but a
> saddle-back, with a certain breadth of its own on which we
> sit perched, and from which we look in two directions into
> time. The unit of composition of our perception of time is a

---

1. I am drawing upon Don Gifford's *The Farther Shore: A Natural History of
Perception* (1990), where he meticulously documented the considerable
shift in perception of how people experience time using first Gilbert
White's experience at Selbourne, England in the eighteenth century
recorded in *A Natural History of Selbourne* (1789), then Henry David
Thoreau's experience at Walden roughly a century later (*Walden*, 1854),
and finally his own in late-twentieth-century western Massachusetts.

duration, with a bow and a stern, as it were—a rearward- and a forward-looking end. (Vol. 1, 609-10)

James designated his saddleback of duration as the "specious present"—a term he borrowed from E. R. Clay to denote what is commonly called "the present" but usually refers to something that is both part of the past and part of the future. James devoted much of his work in psychology to ascertaining exactly how people perceived events in time and space. Out of these experiments and observations he developed his trenchant metaphor of the present, as perceived by most people, as a saddleback of duration inextricably connected both to the immediate past—the rearward end of the saddleback—and to the immediate future—the forward-looking end rather than, say, only a metaphoric knife-edge of the present.

This view of the present as duration informs literature of both the nineteenth- and the twentieth-centuries as it becomes an important component of the moral vision of nineteenth-century poetry, such as that of Gerard Manley Hopkins (1884-1889), as well as of early-twentieth-century fiction, such as that of James Joyce. In Hopkins's poem "Dun Scotus's Oxford," for example, the poet walks the streets of the city fully aware that even the air he inhales—"The air I gather and release"—is air the long-dead philosopher Dun Scotus "lived on." In his journals for 1872, Hopkins remarked on the omnipresence of Scotus (1266-1308) in his experience of Oxford: ". . . just then when I took in any inscape of the sky or sea I thought of Scotus" (221). Hopkins's "rearward" portion of the saddleback of time stretches into the past for over 500 years and intertwines with his present vision. Similarly in his poem "Spring," his celebration of "all this juice and all this joy" of spring includes knowledge of its transience, that it will all too soon "cloy." His model for the arrival and the passing of spring is the biblical story of the Creation and Fall: "In the beginning / In Eden garden." Anticipated loss also invades this celebration of spring, however, for in the future innocence shall be lost through "sour with sinning," which in turn creates an imperative to immerse now in "innocent-minded Mayday." Thus the present moment of welcoming spring expands to hold thoughts of the past going back to the Creation and subsequent Fall, but also the present contains knowledge of the past and present and—most importantly for Hopkins—future redemption through the "maid's child" destined to become the Christ. All of which is present in Hopkins's saddleback of the present.

The quintessential novel embodying James's notion of the "specious present" as a saddleback of duration, however, may well be James Joyce's *Ulysses* (1922) with its protagonist, Mr. Leopold Bloom, who cannot even walk down a street without recalling some incident from his past while also anticipating future events. He observes that he feels so very different in the present from how he felt in the past and that leads him to reflect on what he calls "the stream, of life" and to reflect on himself speculating if he is still the same person he was then: "Happy. Happier then" (155). "I was happier then. Or was that I? Or am I now I? . . . Can't bring back time" (168). While Mr. Bloom knows he can never return to a previous moment in time, he is nevertheless able to call up memories from those happier days and by bringing them into his present—a present that is proving increasingly difficult as the day goes on—lessen his anxiety about the immediate future when he anticipates that his wife, Molly, will commit adultery. His present thus includes a painful anticipation of the near-future but, more importantly for him, the consoling memory of the joy of making love for the first time to his future wife on the Hill of Howth in Dublin (175-76)—a very spacious saddleback of present time. (See chapter 6, "Time and the Life Cycle," for an extended discussion of time in *Ulysses* and in Joyce's fiction in general.)

Evolving Time

Over the course of the twentieth century William James's metaphor of the saddleback of present time became more and more attenuated, however, until today it appears as merely a quaint wish for another "simpler" time. The homey metaphor James chose to illustrate the nature of experiencing present time, being perched on a saddleback of duration, which would have been a nearly ubiquitous experience for people in the nineteenth century, would become during the twentieth century first exotic, as the group of people experiencing sitting in a saddle shrank until it was more and more limited to the rich, and then in the twenty-first century it would become simply obscure since by that time few people would encounter a horse and rider, much less themselves ride a horse. But more importantly, during those hundred or so years, there occurred a fundamental loss of exactly those very connections to the past and future in individual experience that had led James to formulate his metaphoric image. As a result of this loss, by the end of the twentieth century the experience of the present had far more in common with James's rejected image of the thin knife-edge of the present than it did with his more spacious saddleback. Gone from the late-twentieth- and early-twenty-first-century experience of the present is an awareness of any historical continuity within which events occur along with any appreciation of the human community stretching both backwards and forwards from the present moment. This loss led Don Gifford to describe the United States at the end of the twentieth century as "a nation without history inhabited by a history-blind people. The present as moral-duration is reserved for those who, in the continuing media coup of the 1980s [and well into the 2010s and 2020s] are dismissed as wimps by those who stand tall in the saddle-back of the historyless present" (122). He concludes:

> The duration-block of present time expands, and the bow and the stern of William James's metaphor fade into the mist. . . . [The result is] a profound change in our sense of what constitutes an event and the timespace in which it occurs; thus a profound change in our perception of that succession called time; and thus a profound change in what was once assumed to be a sequential web of cause and effect in human affairs. (122; see also 173-213)

The considerable shift away from that "sequential web of cause and effect" to the knife-edge of the causeless present will become more immediately comprehensible if considered in the light of an example, such as how remarkably the vicarious experience of war has been transformed historically from mid-nineteenth-century to early twenty-first-century America.

The perception of the American Civil War (1861-1865) remained within the "sequential web of cause and effect," yet even here there began a process that would result in the continual shrinking of the present. That Civil War was the first war to be reported in photographs as well as in text. As a result those far away from the battlescape no longer merely read about events after the fact but now could more immediately encounter war's appalling reality through photo-graphs in magazines—most notably Matthew Brady's in

Harper's Bazaar. A little less than a century later, World War II's violence became even more vivid and more immediate through newsreel images accompanied by a graphic soundtrack that were shown serially from 1931 to 1945 (when the war ended) in movie theatres under the rubric of "The March of Time." Each showing began with announcer Westbrook Van Voorhees's stentorian intoning of "Time Marches On!" In those newsreels, Van Voorhees would each week describe events pictured on the screen in a voice appropriate for Dooms Day. While in the nineteenth century readers might wait weeks for Brady's photographs of people and events to appear, audiences in theaters of the 1940s would see dramatically presented newsreel action footage, such as the D Day invasion, sometimes within days but, at most, a couple of weeks after the events took place. Moreover, those images were experienced by most people in the audience as brilliantly, immediately real which helped negate the saddleback metaphor by closing the gap between the past when the event happened and the present when a record of it was seen on the screen.

In contrast to World War II, the Vietnam War became commercially sponsored home entertainment as audiences watched incidents usually within a mere forty-eight hours of the event itself first on their small black-and-white screens and, later, on the larger screens of color television sets. Although the time between the event and its viewing was reduced dramatically, the reduction in the size of the images occasioned by the relatively small TV screen, as compared to the World War II movie screen, often made it difficult for an audience to equate such images with the violent reality they pictured.

During the 1990 Gulf War, however, images of the bombing of Baghdad appeared simultaneously with the events themselves as cameras filmed and concurrently broadcast them in color or at least in the grainy green of night-vision cameras. "[A] war on TV with real-time play-by-play. What could be more modern than to watch news all the time, coverage of events happening in any corner of the world, what must have once required days, weeks, months to reach you?" (Phillips 258). This almost simultaneous occurrence of events and the worldwide broadcasting of those same events reached something close to perfection with the 2003 War in Iraq. The distance between the occurrence of events on the battlefield and the viewing of those same events within the safety of the home narrowed to seconds or fractions of seconds as audiences witnessed them as they happened. Often in the United States, the war appeared on large screen color television sets where, ironically, the very immediacy of the images often produced an effect of unreality since those images on the television screen, as opposed to those of World War II on the far larger movie screen, appeared indistinguishable from the images of various interactive computer games. This impression became heightened by the sanitized US television broadcasts that avoided images of war's carnage in contrast to what the rest of the world witnessed on their television sets.

Thus in less than one hundred and sixty years, the distance in time from events taking place on a battlefield to someone on the home front viewing images of them became reduced from weeks to days, then to hours, and finally to only fractions of seconds. Moreover, because so much of the War in Iraq was carried on over long distances (miles high above the Earth for the high-altitude bombing and miles horizontally distant for artillery shelling, and, thanks to their incredible equipment and training, even a half mile or more for sniper killings), the resulting images on television often appeared not as if captured from real events but as if taken from the all-too-familiar simulacra of computer games and/or advertising. "Right at the very heart of news, history threatens to disappear" to be replaced by advertising (Baudrillard 6, 23). Thus the viewed images themselves went from horrific to familiar, from mirroring reality to reflecting unreality, from being part of the saddleback of duration to being part of the causeless present. The War in Iraq may have been the first war whose images were simultaneously witnessed all over the globe. As Jean Baudrillard wisely observes: "No event can withstand being beamed across the whole planet. No meaning can withstand acceleration" (2).

Much of this shift from reporting events to disseminating images occurred because of now ubiquitous television. Baudrillard warns of the deadly quality of TV when he asserts that "[t]elevision inculcates indifference, distance, skepticism and unconditional apathy. Through the world's becoming image, it anaesthetizes the imagination, provokes a sickened abreaction, together with a surge of adrenaline which induces total disillusionment" (61).[2]

---

2. Compare Kurt Vonnegut's lament that "TV is an eraser" (*Timequake* 193) to that of Thomas Frick, who cautions against

> the insane and dangerous deviance of TV's seamlessly constructed counterworld, its darkly hermetic consistency, its manic paucity of human feeling and response . . . . [I]t appeared truly remarkable that we willingly installed such agents of insidious madness in our living rooms and bedrooms. We might as well be agreeing to neural implants by aliens . . . . We've allowed it to destroy our politics, our neighborhoods, and our common sense by sucking our attention up into its ubiquitous reification of the world as view, not of any particular thing but as such. (210-11)

Television's ephemeral, constant stream of images along with its instant events or instant-replays of events replace and erase history, art, and literature, damaging both individual and collective memory.

The end point of this shift in perception from event to image was captured by novelist William Gibson in *All Tomorrow's Parties* (1999), with the street urchin Boomzilla's prosaic description of "this butt-naked girl, black hair, maybe Chinese, Japanese, something, she's long and thin" (268) who appears suddenly out of the Lucky Dragon store's super-fax machine. An absolutely incredible event but, for him, an event devoid of meaning. The Lucky Dragon security TV camera records the girl leaving the store and instantly shows the image unmediated on its screen as do all the security cameras on all the Lucky Dragon screens simultaneously all over the world: "every last screen, [showing her] walking out of every Lucky Dragon in the world" (269). While Boomzilla, the street-wise kid contemplates briefly and only for the time it takes him to smoke a cigarette the multiplicity of images, the event itself quickly recedes from his consciousness to be replaced by his indignation over the store being out of his favorite "muff-Lette" (269).

This apathetic way of perceiving a startling event in time and space has important implications, for if life is experienced as being lived only on the knife-edge of the present—or in Boomzilla's succession of images each of no special import—then Darko Suvin's well-known "feedback oscillation" between the fantastic and the mundane cannot exist, as any line dividing the imaginative from the real will be erased ("SF and the Novum" 148.) All events become equally forgettable once they register in present time. Rather than fading gracefully into James's "mist," events simply and abruptly disappear to be replaced by another event of no more and no less importance and that event in turn becomes replaced by yet another undifferentiated event and so on and on and on.

Giving voice to what many living in the twenty-first century experience daily as a loss of any time-future because of the brevity of the present moment, a character in Gibson's *Pattern Recognition* (2003) observes that

> [f]ully imagined cultural futures were the luxury of another day, one in which "now" was of some greater duration. For us, of course, things can change so abruptly, so violently, so profoundly, that futures like our grandparents' have insufficient "now" to stand on. We have no future because our present is too volatile. (57)

A critic somewhat disingenuously claims that "Gibson . . . is not writing about the present, about the past, or about the future. He is writing about the Sprawl, and its laws are lies: untrue to us" (Dunn 77).[3] But so we might claim of all fiction. All fiction by definition is lies and much of fiction, including Gibson's fictional Sprawl, may be metaphorical and, as such, reflect our present and our past and—unless things change dramatically—it may also reflect our future.[4] Gibson himself

---

3. Carl Freedman notes that "[t]his physical landscape [of the Sprawl] has its supplement and analogue in the less tangible mean streets of cyberspace, that hallucinatory terrain that exists only electronically but in which computer cowboys like Case have exciting, dangerous adventures" (196). As often with Gibson, there is a basis in fact for his fiction. For instance, since 1970 Chiba City has been a sister city of Vancouver, where Gibson lives. As Ian Lancashire observes, Chiba City was designated as the country's research center for high-definition (now "high-vision television" (341). Lancashire's notes on Chiba City and Gibson's invented Ninsei Street are extensive and uniformly illuminating (341-46).

4. Patrick Parrinder warns that

> science fiction as metaphor tends to imply a post-structuralist "conventionalism" or "anti-foundationalism" denying or downgra-

believes that "almost every science-fiction novel is about the time during which it was written" ("The Digital Way of Life"). Gibson's Sprawl itself is an almost classic illustration of extrapolation, that staple of twentieth-century and twenty-first-century speculative fiction, which may help account for its repellant fascination. As John Pierce observes, "we live in a dynamic, evolving society and culture whose current trends really can build into a future that seems an exaggeration of the present—not always, of course, but often enough to justify satirical science fiction that seems at once fantastic and disturbingly close to reality" (192). While Gibson's work is rarely satiric in Pierce's use of the term, it is "at once fantastic and disturbingly close to reality."

Because his fiction remains so "close to reality" that it provokes a shock of recognition, much of what disturbs readers results from Gibson's attention to that knife-edge of the present where his characters precariously perch: this is the instant where everything happens. Since "there is no there there" (*Mona Lisa Overdrive* [1988] 48) interpreting events for characters such as Boomzilla becomes inessential, a waste of time, or meaningless.[5] Unlike James's saddleback that invited or even required events to be placed into a historical context and then interpreted, in the world of Gibson's characters there is no historical context and nothing to interpret. Everything occurs instantaneously in "the historyless present" (Gifford

---

ding the referential aspects of fiction. In this view, statements no longer have a truth content, so that it would be absurd to judge imagined futures [such as Gibson's] by their potential correspondence with any 'real' future. (28-29)

5. All references are to the first edition and not to one of the various paperback reprints.

122). Perhaps the most vivid example remains that "butt-naked girl, . . . walking out of every Lucky Dragon in the world, wearing that same smile" (*All Tomorrow's Parties* 268-69). Each of those smiling girls is a discrete event occurring simultaneously at different points all over the globe—yet each event mirrors all the others and all occur at exactly the same moment. Here, thanks to yet another technological revolution in communication and media, the experience of time and space appears dramatically altered. Not only has that experience moved away from James's saddleback of duration, but at the very end of the twentieth century when Gibson writes *All Tomorrow's Parties*, it also has turned its back on Heraclitus's river of flux and change. Events occurring in time become part of an instantaneous chaotic simultaneity of non-events "photoflash[ed]. . . far too wide" (Joyce, *Finnegans Wake* [1939] 583). Simultaneously all over the planet that girl "unfolds sort of" and appears out of a machine. In this version of James's "knife-edge" present, that present by definition can contain nothing but this ephemeral event. Though the moment appears almost indefinitely replicated across the globe, there remains no room for Heraclitus's spacious moving river into which one could not step twice—because both river and person were in flux. Instead, there is only the tyrannous, omnipresent knife-edge of the ubiquitous present. In this sense, István Csicsery-Ronay, although speaking of an earlier Gibson novel, also accurately describes *All Tomorrow's Parties* when he contends that "in each paragraph, the narratives depict the process in which autonomous technology of the futurist future severs the links with the historical past" (238). To which I would add: "and with any connected future."

The girl, this miracle of nanotechnology, appears in that most trite of all contemporary—and perhaps future—settings:

that of the wonderfully misnamed "convenience store." Gibson's Lucky Dragon is, however, the ultimate in such convenience stores. Modeled in part on the United States' contemporary 7-11s, the now globalized Lucky Dragon comprises a huge, worldwide chain. "There were Lucky Dragons all over America, all over the world . . ." (9). For a future world committed to images rather than life there could be few more fitting symbols than that of the appearance of life being created out of a machine, rather than the reverse of live humans creating a machine. Moreover, the creation occurs within a machine devoted to processing and transmitting information—the Lucky Dragon Nanofax. The girl becomes a super-fax sent everywhere at once. When the image walks among humans on an equal or, perhaps, superior footing, that completes the reversal of humans creating the machine to the machine creating humans.

By appearing simultaneously in every identical Lucky Dragon located in identical nameless Sprawls around the world, the "girl" or the image of the girl powerfully reflects the nature of Gibson's urban landscapes. These urban sites have been deprived of any local identity and appear easily swapped one for the other (East Coast United States, say, for Tokyo). *All Tomorrows Parties* takes place in "the technologically scarified landscape of postcolonial cyberpunk" (Apter 229) that almost by definition fails to retain historical memory (232). Multiple instant identical events, such as the nanofaxed girl, can produce no historical memory as such. This paraspace oddly presages that of the embedded reporter in the 2003 War in Iraq who eagerly described events and interviewed soldiers as he crossed "the river Ganges" or, as he later said, having been apprised of his error, "you know, one of those biblical rivers"

(Massing 18).[6] Instead of a series of discrete contemporary events in the War in Iraq, each taking place within a definable, identifiable, and incredibly ancient landscape, there was this reporter's instantaneous reporting of non-events occurring nowhere—"you know, [at the edge of] one of those biblical rivers." Such loss of collective memory, similar to that in *All Tomorrow's Parties*, appeared all too vividly real both in Boomzilla's instantaneous forgetting and in the conspicuous failure of US troops to protect Iraq's and humanity's invaluable, ancient treasures—those relics of ancient history, such as the irreplaceable Summerian tablets, destroyed or vandalized during the War in Iraq End Game.[7] Similarly, the girl pops out of the machine everywhere, yet she appears to

---

6. "In cyberspace, Gibson provides an electronic manifestation of a science-fictional paraspace, 'an alternate space, sometimes largely mental, but always materially manifested, that sits beside the real world'" (Samuel Delany, qtd. in Bukatman, *Terminal* 157). Elsewhere Bukatman notes that "paraspace is always constituted as an other space for the characters and exerts tangible effects upon them. It is the space in which the character's language, rationality, and subjectivity are broken down and deconstructed" ("Amidst These Fields of Data" 214). Something similar happens to their sense of time, as this essay demonstrates.

The ignorance of American reporters covering the War in Iraq became legendary. Perhaps, even more unfortunate was their indifference to geography or history. The assumption that "you can talk to any cabdriver [in Doha] and he'll tell you everything you need to know" made for very poor reporting. Of course, the fact that "most of the cabdrivers in Doha are from India and Pakistan" did not help (Massing 18). For a succinct critical overview of the failure of the American press to cover the War in Iraq, see Massing. For a brief analysis of some of the worst Newspeak used during that war, see Russell Smith.

7. For the probable extent of the loss, see Holmes and Randerson, who believe that "the consequences will be devastating" (8). Fifteen months later, their prognosis was again confirmed (Liu and Dickey 45).

exist nowhere in particular—the Ganges, the Tigris, the Potomac, Heraclitus's spacious rolling stream—"you know, one of those biblical rivers." Such loss of memory, such banishment of Mnemosyne, dooms all human arts as it does all human history. Moreover, the girl out of the nanofax machine is the Idoru of Gibson's earlier novel (*Idoru* 1996) translated through technology into three-dimensional reality.[8] As such, this nanotech-constructed Idoru in *All Tomorrow's Parties* becomes the counterpart of the various ROM characters constructed within the computer in Gibson's earlier fictions. When Casey, for instance, in "The Winter Market" inquires whether the debilitated Lise, now a computer construct, is identical with Lise, the woman he knew in life, his friend Rubin replies, "God only knows" (*Burning Chrome* [1982] 141).

Such constructs and their setting give rise to intriguing, if familiar, questions about time and the timeless. Gibson's early fiction does offer, however, an alternative to the con-temporary frenetic flutter of instantaneous, often-unreal images in the—at least partial—timeless world of virtual reality found inside the computer.[9] In *Neuromancer* (1984) and *Mona Lisa Overdrive*, "the megalopolitan near-future" proves, as Nicholas Ruddick astutely remarks, "at once literally and figuratively a multileveled information field" ("The Bits" 91)

---

8. The reader is left to resolve whether she is actual flesh and blood or an ingenious simulacrum. Perhaps the answer resides in the eye of the beholder.

9. Thomas M. Disch rightly advises that "[t]he problem with virtual reality as an SF concept is that it is so protean as to allow any phantasmagoria to be passed off as science fiction" (216). He illustrates his point by citing "Kathy Acker's *Empire of the Senseless*, in which the author simply incorporates into her own work those chunks of Gibson's *Neuromancer* that have won her special approbation" (216). Fortunately, I am dealing with the original and not a borrowing.

operating within the spacious present. That information field, located indefinably within the computer, offers by contrast an apparently timeless world of pure data without "the flesh the cowboys mocked" (*Neuromancer* 285). Some characters are forced to become part of that world of data, while still others, such as Lise, are constructs within it. Dixie Flatline exists only within virtual reality in the form of "a construct, a hardwired ROM cassette replicating a dead man's skills, obsessions, knee-jerk responses" (*Neuromancer* 76-77). As Ruddick contends, this "is a human reduced to the sum of his 'useful' information. But 'reduced' is a loaded word: in fact, if the future is an information field, then Dixie Flatline may be better adapted to wander it than the human computer jockey hero, Case, who is trapped in the 'meat' of his flesh" (88). And what of the Idoro in *All Tomorrow's Parties?* Has she abandoned virtual reality for the "real" and if so on what terms? And, under what conditions? As a character in "The Gernsback Continuum" asks: is it "possible to photograph what isn't there"? (Gibson, *Burning Chrome* 6).

Case's desire to become part of the matrix Ruddick accurately assesses as a wish

> for a uterine space and is therefore a regressive desire for undifferentiation—though the matrix, as its etymology suggests, is also potentially a place of creative conception and development. For Case, the matrix's most seductive offering is . . . an artificial and timeless landscape that is the last chimera of entropic development. (90)[10]

10. P. A. Hancock forcefully reminds those fascinated with virtual reality as an alternative reality that although "[t]he opportunity seems almost without limit . . . [, u]nfortunately, the present state of development does not match these expectations. . . . Much still needs to be done to make the   promise a reality or even a virtual reality" (146). Clearly, Gibson is writing fiction rather than predicting events, yet, as Amanda

Instead of time-bound "meat," cyberspace seductively offers a timeless quality experienced almost incidentally by characters that attempt to move within it. For instance, the lengthy cyberspace confrontation between Case and Wintermute in the shape of Deane takes place almost instantaneously in "real" time: "It was only a few seconds . . ." (121). Amy Novak maintains that "[w]hen the 'semiotic ghosts' of Case's experience in cyberspace enter the linear narrative movement of the text, they resist linearity and causality and instead create an alternative narrative space that requires us [as readers] to constantly renegotiate our construction of the present" (70) and our assumptions about time. Such movement between the narrative and what Novak labels "the present" may also have the effect of forcing readers out of the spacious present. Characters themselves, however, in order to more immediately and more vividly access the world of virtual reality—what one character in *Mona Lisa Overdrive* calls "this France that isn't France" (258)—ignore all bodily functions in their present time and some will physically connect their brains directly to a computer via a surgically implanted shunt thus creating cyberspace, "a consensual inner-spatial realm accessed by brain-computer interfacing . . . a very 1980s concept" (Ruddick, "the Bits" 84). But one with high risk. Forgetting Gertrude Stein's warning that "there's no there there" and yielding to the ultimate temptation to imagine that "to live here is to live. There is no difference" (*Neuromancer* 305), the more extreme are prepared to trade their life in the physical time-bound world for a non-human presence in timeless cyberspace. But as Keith Booker points out, "immortality achieved via

---

Fernbach observes, his "imagery of the womb-like computer spaces within which his cyber jockeys thrive continues to circulate in recent films like *The Matrix* (1999)" (142).

computer may be bought at the price of a process of dehumanization that converts the empowered and even immortalized humans into computer artifacts themselves" (156).[11]

In *All Tomorrow's Parties* a reverse process occurs, in which the world of virtual reality invades the world of actuality. When Berry Rydell leaves the San Francisco Bay Bridge, he thinks:

> The bridge behind him now, perhaps forever, is a medium of transportation become a destination . . . . He has glimpsed the edges of a life there that he feels is somehow ancient and eternal. Apparent disorder arranged in some deeper, some unthinkable fashion. Perhaps he has been too long in the pay of the company of those who order the wider world. Those whose mills grind increasingly fine, toward some unimaginable omega-point of pure information, some prodigy perpetually on the brink of arrival. (273)

This alternative—"the omega point of pure information"— becomes the actually imagined as in Case's ultimate temptation in *Neuromancer* that occurs when he finds that he could overcome time by trading his body and mind for a reunion with

---

11. To which Booker adds: "this sort of encroachment of the technological into the human is, of course, a classic dystopian motif" (156). BB in Dan Simmons's *Hyperion* (1989), for instance, interfaces through just such a built-in neural shunt. His body has been modified to better access the machine (393). The reverse process, whereby virtual reality invades actual reality, is difficult to conceive of, much less actualize, but a central character in *Hyperion*, John Keats created by the AIs (artificial intelligences), is somewhat human and somewhat machine and somewhat an artificial intelligence, all packed together in a cybrid; while in *The Fall of Hyperion* (1990), readers learn that humans have become the ultimate computer in the service of the AIs (see especially 410-15). Gibson's girl out of the nanofax machine is, perhaps, a clearer example.

his dead ex-lover, Linda, within the matrix. Like Odysseus facing Nausikaa in Homer's *Odyssey*—that last and most human obstacle to his home-coming—Case is tempted to abandon his quest at the very moment when, if he is not within sight of his goal, he is at least closer to it than ever before. For some of Gibson's characters, this futuristic choice of staying in the timeless world of cyberspace, when voluntary and positive, becomes reminiscent of those more ancient mythological choices confronting humans who choose to escape from this visible, impermanent time-bound world in favor of an invisible permanent one.[12] Brian McHale locates this act as somewhere between "dying the death of the organic body . . . [and] dying into the half-life of cyberspace" (171), "some middle state beyond or outside biological life—not a state of non-being, not death" (169).[13]

W. B. Yeats makes a similar distinction between "dying the death of the organic body . . . [and] dying into the half-life" not of cyberspace but of an immortal land. In the Irish myth of the Sidhe (the all-powerful Little People) such choices by humans

---

12. Case opts out and eventually creates a life in this world that includes a family of four children (*Mona Lisa* 137). Bobby and Angela, however, physically die, but in cyberspace they marry and live in a simulated castle: "They have come to live in this house: walls of gray stone, roof of slate, in a season of early summer. The grounds are bright and wild, though the long grass does not grow and the wildflowers do not fade" (256). For an extended discussion of these characters and their choices, see Weiss, especially 73-77.

13. In one of the most often quoted passages in *Neuromancer*, Case laments that having "lived for the bodiless exultation of cyberspace, it [his being deprived of cyberspace] was the Fall. . . . the elite stance involved a certain relaxed contempt for the flesh. The body was meat . . . the prison of his own flesh" (12). N. Katherine Hayles comments perceptively that this "view . . . parses virtuality as a division between an inert body that is left behind and a disembodied subjectivity that inhabits a virtual realm" (290).

were invariably fatal as Yeats illustrates in various poems and plays, but perhaps most clearly and most directly in the early play, *The Land of Heart's Desire* (1894). While the settings are vastly different—the mythological Irish Other World and cyberspace—the plots of *The Land of Heart's Desire* and Gibson's *Mona Lisa Overdrive* run parallel to a remarkable degree in their twofold dramatic crux. In both works, forces from the invisible timeless world—the land of the fairies in Yeats and the world of cyberspace in Gibson—invade the actual world. Also, in each work, one of the characters makes a fatal choice, in spite of and in opposition to well-meaning advice, and chooses "the land of heart's desire" in Yeats's play and the matrix in Gibson's novel over the quotidian, every day, time-bound world. But the crucial differences between the world in Yeats's play at the beginning of the twentieth century so clearly rooted in the Irish oral tradition and that of Gibson's novel at the end of the century rooted in the new information technology lie not so much in those structures and motifs their authors borrowed either from oral cultures or information technology, but in the nature of the world the characters are escaping from and the one to which they flee. Yeats's Land of the Little People or Tír na nÓg is older than Christianity and its inhabitants wield enormous power over nature and human destiny; Gibson's cyberspace is a recent invention, has no power over nature but itself requires electric power for its operation, and has considerable sway over humans, especially in its Artificial Intelligence manifestation. Yeats's invisible world intersects with this one at the edges of religion, art, and poetry; Gibson's intersects with this one at the edges of super computers, the Infobahn, and Artificial Intelligence. Yeats's play postulates a world freed from human time partaking of eternity in some mysterious way. Gibson's novel invents a cyberspace world also freed from human time, linked to other matrices in the Centauri system (*Mona Lisa Overdrive* 259; compare *Neuromancer* 316), and partaking of the timeless within the confines of a battery-powered computer located in a piece of junk sculpture—one of his most brilliantly ironic dystopian images.[14]

Finally, although both works embody the desire for a timeless land, their assumptions about human time are quite different and reflect the huge shift in the experience of time that occurred in the twentieth century. In *The Land of Heart's Desire*, the hunger for eternity appears juxtaposed to a partial world whose time is clearly imaged in James's saddleback of duration, while in *Mona Lisa Overdrive*, desire for total absorption in the timeless becomes juxtaposed to a fragmented world whose time is imaged in James's knife-edge. Both works share with each other and with all such fantasies their attempt "to replace cultural life with a total, absolute otherness, a completely alternative self-sustaining system" (Rosemary Jackson 60).[15] For both, that "completely alternative self-sustaining system" becomes located in a timeless world. Both worlds are located within but are not part of ordinary human experience whether that of the Little People inside the Faery Mound or that of the virtual world inside the computer within the junk sculpture. Those not initiated will see only the outer appearance, the container—the Mound or the junk sculpture—

14. For a quite different reading of the place and value of the junk sculpture, see Palmer, especially 238-39.

15. Rosemary Jackson is speaking here of the "Dracula myth . . . in its countercultural thrust " (60). But what she says about this important myth applies equally well, I believe, to this myth of the other world, the better place of truth and absolutes which replaces this one of compromise, lies, and frustration.

and remain completely unaware of the marvelous reality hidden inside.

The desire for liberation from Gibson's *Blade Runner*-like decimated urban landscape—what Scott Bukatman calls the "kinetic liberation from the very limits of urban existence" (*Terminal* 146)—is as familiar as that embodied in Yeats's play and may be equally as dangerous.[16] Those who leave this world for the more perfect, timeless one of Tír na nÓg subject themselves to its time frame, its dream logic, its non-human values. Similarly, fleeing into the timeless virtual reality of cyberspace means fleeing into the non-human dream of perfection. Thomas A. Bredehoft is surely correct when he characterizes this flight as dangerous nostalgia for it may convince us "to mistake escape for liberation and . . . wishful thinking for reality" (261). No matter how solipsistic or absorbed computer hacks may become, they must at some fundamental level remain aware that "there is no there there" or face the prospect of going mad or starving to death. The alternative is to leave the body behind completely and become a construct within the timeless world of data as others earlier went with the Sidhe into their ancient timeless world:

> *Come away, O human child!*
> *To the waters and the wild*
> *With a faery, hand in hand,*
> *For the world's more full of weeping than you can*
> *understand.*
> (W. B. Yeats, "The Stolen Child" 20)

---

16. For a different reading of this possibility as implicating a person "in the sinister totalitarianism of the Gernsback Continuum," see Bredehoft, especially 260.

But humans learn to live with their lack of understanding and to accept the "weeping" in life as due to their tragic nature. Only the gods are comic because immortal and living outside time.[17] Humans are tragic because they pay a real and terrible price for their mistakes and at their end when they have no more time they disappear from Earth. To imagine a way around this problem or a direct route to immortality whether by going with the Sidhe into the fairy fort or disappearing into the datumplane or creating and sending a nanofaxed image is to deny one's humanity, to become supremely comic. Yet the temptation has always been there: to substitute perfection for living, image for reality, timelessness for time.

Gibson's novels thus reflect that "profound change in our perception of that succession called time; and thus a profound change in what was once assumed to be a sequential web of cause and effect in human affairs" (Gifford, *Farther Shore* 122). In the late-twentieth- and early-twenty-first-century world, that "life-world of effaced nationalism, blunted characters, and psychic extremes" (Apter 232) with its instant replicated events in the knife-edge present, the temptation to escape may acquire new urgency and more immediacy than when time flowed like Heraclitus's river and the present appeared more spacious as in William James's saddleback. Yet, for all their urgency, such temptations remain dangerously similar to those described by Yeats in *The Land of Heart's Desire*. The more things change, the more they remain the same—even in

---

17. The gods are essentially comic because there can be no consequences from their actions and they are never in danger of dying unlike mortal humans, for whom the world is often a dangerous place and death—when they have used up their time—a certainty. Therefore human life is tragic but the gods' existence is comic, as Rachel Bespaloff demonstrated so convincingly in *On the Iliad*.

William Gibson's world of nanofax technology precariously balanced on the knife-edge of the present.

Measuring and Marking Time

> *The first great discovery was time, the landscape of experience. Only by marking off months, weeks, and years, days, and hours, minutes and seconds, would mankind be liberated from the cyclical monotony of nature.*
> ——*Daniel Boorstin*

Whether a knife edge of the fleeting instant or a more spacious metaphor, time as the medium of human life—what Daniel Boorstin termed "the landscape of experience"—remains inescapable. Measuring and marking time even with such simple questions as "What's the date today?" or "What time is it now?" reflect a common assumption that there will be one single answer no matter where on planet Earth we may find ourselves. We in the West, for instance, measure time by seconds, minutes, hours, by days weeks, months, by years centuries, millennia, but how uniform or universal is this? The quintessential human preoccupation with measuring time has taken and still takes many different forms that often produce quite varied results. Calendars may be "the back bones of history," since "without them there would be no structure to what happens apart from sequential order" (T. Bowersock 29). But the history of calendars and their making reveals many processes both convoluted and fascinating that have led not to uniformity but to variety. Almost all ancient calendars were "primarily lunar," which created huge problems as they were based on a year that varied considerably because of the 28-day lunar month (for details see Fraser, *Time, Passion and Knowledge* 50). Moreover, the year began in almost all ancient calendars not on the first of January but with the vernal equinox that now occurs on our current calendar on the first of March. When Julius Caesar replaced the lunar with the far more accurate solar calendar in 46 BCE, he moved the beginning of the year from March to January first. This Julian calendar also included a leap year every four years thus ensuring accuracy. To this day most religious calendars have not become solar but remain lunar. Having two or more very different competing calendars has often led to conflict or at least caused uncertainty in dating the same events both in sacred and secular history.[18]

During the Middle Ages the first of the year reverted back from Caesar's January first to the vernal equinox in March as most if not all economies were agriculturally based where the most important date was the one that indicated when it was safe to plow and plant. There—in March—the first of the year stayed until Pope Gregory introduced his calendar that once again shifted the beginning of the year away from March to January first where it has remained—at least in the west.

Of the several units by which we measure time the century might appear the most clearly defined—one hundred years from the first day of the first year to the last day of the last year, but exactly which year was the first and which year was the last in any given century has often been contentious as has

---

18. For a detailed discussion of the creation of the Western (Christian) calendar, see Gustav Teres's fascinating, detailed, and complicated discussion of the role of Dionysus Exiguus, who attempted to reconcile solar accuracy with lunar liturgical dating. The western chronology's "strength is the universality it achieved around the world through the industrial and scientific revolution" (Fraser, *Time, Passion and Knowledge* 53). For a lively account of the transmigration of the first of the year, see Racoma.

the issue of exactly which day begins a new year and which day begins a new century. In 1582, for example only Catholic countries adopted the new Gregorian calendar and so only those countries celebrated together the advent of the seventeenth century on the same day and in the same month. One hundred years later when the European Protestant nations agreed to follow the new calendar beginning in 1700 both Protestant and Catholic countries celebrated together the arrival of the eighteenth century as later they also celebrated the arrival of the nineteenth century. Russia still lagged behind, however, since it did not adopt this innovation until 1918. One unexpected result for Russians was that the October Twenty-Fifth Revolution that occurred in 1917 became something of an anomaly since it would be commemorated according to the now-common calendar not in October but in November! Still, in the year 2000 much of the world's population celebrated on the same day both the arrival of the new century and the advent of a new millennium.[19]

The twenty-first century is, therefore, the first century where all of Europe and Russia plus all of the Western Hemisphere, Australia, much of the African continent, and some countries in Asia joined to celebrate the advent of a new century on the very same day. Unlike the last millennium that happened with hardly anyone noticing, this one arrived in an orgy of media hype, Y2K anxiety, and stage-managed event.[20] The time-induced anxiety produced by the approaching new millennium spread so far and so fast in October 1998 that the United States Congress passed and President Clinton signed the "Disclosure Act" that provided 300 billion dollars to

---

19. There does exist, however, a vocal minority of true believers and Arthur C. Clarke fans who awaited the millennium in the authentic year of 2001.

20. "Y2K" became media short hand for "the year 2,000."

upgrade "computers and application programs to be Y2K compliant," according to the *Encyclopedia Britannica*. Many predicted the millennium bug would precipitate chaos in computers and computer networks around the world. Computers used in finance and in government were seen as especially vulnerable. Other individuals and groups of people fervently believed that time would stop and the world would come to an end on December thirty-first 1999 or if not, then perhaps at dawn on January first 2000. Such end-time beliefs have come to naught in the past (see chapter 3: "Two Common Fallacies") as they did with this new millennium.

Rather than the dawn of a New Age or the sunset of the End of Time in this new century our notions of time, space, and the universe may well be challenged again as they were in the twentieth century. The further we look into space, the further we are able to see back in time. In the first decade of the twentieth century what we saw in space was limited to the Milky Way Galaxy—that incredible river of stars once visible everywhere on the planet before light pollution forced it to fade into oblivion except where no or few humans live. Until the 1920s, the whole known universe, all the time and all the space humans conceived of was contained in that Milky Way Galaxy. Then in the 1920s astronomers with their new telescopes discovered first one other galaxy then another and then another all out there somewhere beyond our own. As the century wore on with so many new tools for probing deep into space and therefore deep into time, such as high powered telescopes and the new radio telescopes, the billions of galaxies in this universe proved beyond reckoning—a fact that would probably astound a nineteenth-century astronomer. Our knowledge of time also increased exponentially in the last few decades thanks to the Hubble telescope and other such innovations. We are now able to look far, far back in time beyond the formation of the galaxies and back to the very creation of the stars to see the "moment only a billionth of a second after the big bang" when the universe began (Rees, "Our Place" 58). This new knowledge in turn prompts new questions. Twenty-first century cosmologists rather than speculating on the existence of other galaxies as they might have done at the beginning of the twentieth century now began contemplating the possibility of the existence of other universes. We might live not in an isolated or solitary universe but possibly in one of a multiplicity of universes or what the science-fiction writers have dubbed, a "multiverse." And that prompts other questions: Where did all these universes come from? Do they share our experience of time or does time behave differently in different universes? Within the next fifty years, cosmologists may well discover where and how such universes begin. (At the moment most speculation centers on fairly simple models. It could be within a few years that someone somewhere will accidently or on purpose start a brand new universe—an act that would revolutionize our notions of time and space, but such speculations are beyond the subject of this book.)

Back in the eighteenth century when Newton defined space as increasingly vast and vaster, our comfortable home here on planet Earth became just a bit more precarious. Later, at the end of that same century, geologists led by the Scot James Hutton examining the fossil record discovered that time stretched far beyond human comprehension.[21] In the twentieth

---

21. "The oldest evidence of temporal awareness may be a marginal case. There is a bone of about 30,000 years ago, on which are marks that could be tiny pictures of the sequential phases of the moon" (Lawrence 30; for a full discussion see Lawrence 30-31).

century John McPhee "coined the term 'Deep Time' to distinguish geological time from the scale of time that governs our everyday lives. . . . The intervals of geological time are too long to be readily comprehensible to minds used to thinking in terms of days, weeks and years" (Henry Gee 2).[22] Attempting to deal with millions then billions of years we must employ analogies and/or symbols in our efforts to understand such vast stretches of time since cosmic time frames have proven far beyond human comprehension. One of the most arresting contemporary analogies may be seen in the magnificent Rose Center for Earth and Space that opened in New York on 19 February 2000. There, a cosmic time walk encircles part of a huge sphere eighty-two feet in diameter that houses various exhibits. Visitors stroll along this 360-foot-long (appr. 110 m) cosmic time walkway that has been proportioned in relation to each major cosmic event in what scientists postulate as the almost fourteen-billion-year history of the universe from the initial Big Bang to the present. As a visitor walks forwards, millions, billions of years pass until after traveling most of the cosmic walk at last the Age of the Dinosaurs appears—an event that occurred almost nine hundred million years ago. Those huge beasts ruled the Earth for about six hundred million years until wiped out by some—possibly cosmic—cataclysm, such as a comet or asteroid colliding with Earth, or possibly by a cataclysmic climate change. Continuing on the tiny bit of the cosmic time walk left, the visitor comes at last upon the human record. Those who designed the time walk for the museum were hard pressed to find exactly the right symbol, some satisfying icon that could adequately reflect all the time

---

22. The term "Deep Time" first appears in McPhee's book *Basin and Range* (1981). For an exceptionally clear and helpful discussion of "Deep Time," see Henry Gee, *Deep Time* (2000).

humans have been in the universe in relation to the complete time walk that represents the universe's thirteen-and-eight-tenths-billion-year history. Finally they hit on an ideal image: all human time from the first records of human culture to the present, when seen in proportion to the total life time of the universe, is represented by the width of one single human hair! That's how long we humans have been here relative to the age of the universe—if the time of the universe is represented by 360 feet, then all human history recorded and unrecorded occupies only the width of a human hair. Human beings are hardly a blip on the cosmic scale. So how significant can we be?

Once we thought the whole universe revolved in beautiful crystalline spheres around us here on planet Earth, which itself was assumed to be only a few thousand years old. Later, the universe became limited to the mighty complex of stars that make up the Milky Way. In the twentieth century cosmologists, having looked back in time to within a tiny fraction of a second after the birth of space-time itself, almost to the very beginning of this universe, began to ask once more about the probable end of the universe but within a new context. In the last years of the twentieth century, many—perhaps most of them—concluded that the very universe we call "home" may not be going to have an end either in a bang or in a whimper but instead may be in a never-ending accelerated process of expansion. As discussed in the introduction, "The Uniqueness of Temporality," rather than a universe that begins with the Big Bang then expands until it contracts back to the Big Crunch, we are more than likely living in a universe that, while it did begin with a Big Bang, will go on expanding and expanding and expanding more and more rapidly forever (see Introduction). Everything rushing away from everything else until there remains just silence, emptiness, darkness.

If this ever-outward expansion appears likely, then where exactly are we in space and time in these early decades of the twenty-first century? We obviously no longer exist in a comfortably small bright universe created just a few thousand years ago, nor do we live in one doomed to retract into a fiery apocalypse. Rather, we find ourselves in a universe that appears infinite, continually stretching apart, whose components and make-up are stranger than we could ever have imagined. Humans themselves here for barely a tick on the cosmic clock inhabit a dust speck in a small solar system on the outer edge of a minor galaxy that appears to be condemned to race away forever from every other galaxy, every other body in the universe until "nought nowhere was never reached," as James Joyce so poignantly phrased it in *Ulysses* (699). I find this kind of mega-strength existentialism projected over an infinite amount of time unnerving, even bleak. Yet such observations about our terrestrial home and the possible future of the neighborhood could make us realize how privileged we are as sentient beings, as well as how increasingly alone we may become.[23]

Twentieth-century science radically altered our view of the space and time of the universe in which we live by providing us with more information about its nature and origin, while twentieth-century technology like nineteenth-century technology—at least in the West—also radically altered the

---

23. The possibility that we are alone in our galaxy has been explored in great depth by the physicist John Gribbin in *Alone in the Universe: Why our Planet is Unique* (2011) and in a brief and more limited synopsis in *Scientific American*, "Why We Are Probably the only Intelligent Life in the Galaxy" (2018). The opposite assumption that we are not alone in the universe has led humans to mount the extensive SETI (the Search for Extraterrestrial Intelligence) project to find other intelligent life within our immediate neighborhood.

way we live in that universe. The various revolutions in medicine and transportation are prime examples. Small wonder that

> [t]he whole of the nineteenth century in Europe but especially in England under Victoria became a time of economic and social progress that people assumed would continue forever—or at least into the new century. From 1855 to 1900 the British National Income tripled from six hundred and thirty-six million pounds to one billion, seven hundred and fifty million pounds. . . . As a result of rising affluence and a belief in progress the population increased by 55%. (Cook and Stevenson 216)

Technology that so challenged and improved people's living conditions also helped create that dangerous illusion of progress in other non-technological areas even including human development. To imagine that because we can jet to London from, say, Budapest after breakfast and get there in time for lunch we've progressed as a society rather than succeeded in creating a technological marvel that shrinks time and space may be to delude oneself. Henry David Thoreau (1817-1862) tried to keep his focus on the end to which technology was being put rather than being distracted by the newness and novelty of inventions. Thus he questioned not whether a telegraph could be constructed from Maine to Texas but to what end it would be put when constructed: "We are in great haste to construct a magnetic telegraph from Maine to Texas; but Maine and Texas, it may be, have nothing important to communicate" (36). Thoreau also questioned the social cost to America of its highly prized railroad for he knew the dangerous working conditions of those who were building it: "We do not ride on the railroad; it rides upon us" (63). He described himself as "a sojourner in civilized life" (1); that is, he saw himself not as a permanent feature of the landscape but as only temporarily present and as such asked, What is the best use of these great inventions? What is the best use of the time I may have left? Similarly, Ralph Waldo Emerson (1803-1882) questioned the price tag in human health of much technological "advancement" when he wryly observed in the mid-nineteenth century that "the civilized man has built a coach, but has lost the use of his feet" ("Self-Reliance" 279). Whatever would he or Thoreau say about us today with our planes, trains, and automobiles? Such inventions may have greatly increased human comfort, safety, and even longevity, but they have failed to improve humanity itself, nor were they designed to do so. Moreover, as we living in the west know all too well, technology itself by inducing climate change and enabling pandemics is now a major threat to life on this planet. Also, when such technology combined with social immaturity, moral infantilism, and political tyranny, it helped create the twentieth-century police state.

The relatively pessimistic conclusions drawn from contemporary cosmology of the ever-expanding universe as well as those drawn from the realization that advances in technology often result in environmental and human disasters deviate radically from our contemporary bias inherited from the nineteenth century that as time moves onward all things become progressively better. That bias now appears so ingrained that we find it in everything from science, technology, and history to art, literature, and society (see chapter 3). Since we often see only what we are prepared to see, wherever we look in human history or human activities we tend to find progression and progress. The history of art offers a vivid example of this human belief in progress over time in the view of ancient cave paintings as becoming increasingly sophisticated. Until very recently art historians analyzing cave painting found in caves of Southwest Europe that flourished some 10,000 to 35,000 years ago saw an ever-increasing complexity in technique and theme within a "25,000-year continuous artistic and cultural tradition" (Snyder 36). Studying these remarkable cave paintings

> it came to seem that cave art began with hand stencils and crude engravings about 40,000 [years ago] . . . and progressively evolved through time to an artistic climax at the Lascaux cave . . . discovered during World War II. It is generally felt to contain the most remarkable and lovely of all the world's cave art. The polychrome paintings are dated at around 17,000 [years ago] . . . (37)

And the chronicle of progress continued: "a sort of Lascaux style is then perceived as coming down in other, later caves, excellent work up to the Salon Noir in the Niaux cave in the Ariège, dated about 9000 [years ago]" (Snyder 37). So the story went until 1994 when the Chauvet cave was discovered with its "fifty-foot-high chamber and a quarter mile of passageways of linked chambers full of magnificent depictions that were the equal of anything at Lascaux" (37). There was only one problem: carbon dating revealed these wonderful paintings to be 33,000 years old! That is, "16,000 years older than those at Lascaux—almost as distant in time from Lascaux as Lascaux is from us" (Snyder 38). Once again we had fallen into the trap of trying to impose our vision of progress over time upon people remote from us in time. We need to recall that "There is no progress in art." As the American poet Gary Snyder affirms, "Art that moves us today can be from anywhere from any time" (38). Rather than reflecting continuing human progress, art provides continuity in human experience.

Emerson believed that "[n]othing is secure but life, transition, the energizing spirit" ("Circles" 413). In science, "transition" and "the energizing spirit" may be seen in the efforts of the human intellect to comprehend the physical universe through science that—as knowledge expands and measurements become more precise—inevitably results in discarded partial descriptions, negated hypotheses, and revised theories since as observations become more refined, knowledge increases and new theories evolve. This same transition and energizing spirit appears in art and literature not as progress but as the attempt by the human spirit to comprehend the universe which in turn often results in a series of partial likenesses, broken images, and revised metaphors as writers and artists reflect on their experiences in lived time bringing more art and literature into being. Science and technology, art and literature each consistently, importantly adds to human understanding and insight. While science attempts to provide us with the most accurate description of the physical world including where we find ourselves in time and space, literature and art attempt to provide us with the most accurate picture of our inner world, where we assimilate new knowledge and insight and attempt to assess its value, all of which includes our experience in time.

Marking Time

If the story of how we came to celebrate a new century and a new millennium holds its own fascination, that story tells us little about what it may have been like to live in the time of the century recently concluded. For that we need to turn to literature. As Emerson contended, "The use of literature is to afford us a platform whence we may command a view of our present life" ("Circles" 408). Two plays that "afford us [such] a

platform" are the very familiar *Ubu Roi* [King Ubu] (1896) by
the French *enfant terrible* Alfred Jarry and the less familiar *The
Electrocution of Children* (1998) by the Irish playwright Chris
Lee.[24] Together these two plays bracket the twentieth century
from 1896 with the first Paris production of *Ubu Roi* to 1998
with the Dublin Peacock Theatre premiere of *The Electrocution
of Children* at the Abbey Theatre. Both offer insight into what
it was like to live through the time of the twentieth century.

When *Ubu Roi* was first performed in 1896, the audience
rioted and later the press joined those who were present that
night in outraged condemnation of the production. Jarry
accounted for the riots attendant on this and on subsequent
productions of *Ubu Roi* by saying that the public's anger "arose
precisely from its recognition of itself" (qtd. in Beaumont 105).
While the play's importance in the theatre is difficult to under-
estimate, for Jarry did succeed in his "deliberate attempt to
revolutionize totally [the] theatre" of his day (Beaumont 86),
it may be even more important as a cultural document; that is,
as a vision of what became over the course of the twentieth

---

24. Chris Lee was born in Dublin and now lives and works as a Social
Worker in London. Among his many plays produced in London are:
Hummingbird (1996), *The Optimist's Daughters* (1997), *Eat the Enemy*
(1999), *On the Line & Paranoid in the Sentimental City* (2000), *Vermillion
Dreams* (2004), and more recently, *Ash Boy* (2006), *Shallow Slumber*
(2012), *The Knife* (2016), and *A Small House at the Edge of the World*
(2018). RTÉ (Radió Telefís Éireann [Irish Radio and Television])
recorded his radio play *The Parallax of Jan Van Eyck*. *The Electrocution
of Children* shared the Stuart Parker New Playwright Bursary Prize for
1998. In 1999 Lee was chosen as the Writer in Association at the Abbey
Theatre for the 1999-2000 season. *The Map Maker's Sorrow* was
commissioned by the Abbey Theatre for the Peacock Theatre's entry in
the 1999 Dublin Theatre Festival. Much of this discussion of *The
Electrocution of Children* is taken from my essay "'The Simple
Magnificence of Bacteria': Chris Lee's *The Electrocution of Children*,"
published by the *Irish Studies Review* in 2000.

century the charnel house of Europe. It is here that the play interrogates politics, the social sciences, and philosophy. If most commentators and historians looking back at the nineteenth century saw there an unending story of human progress and achievement, Jarry did not. For him, that century illustrates only sinking and collapse. He saw the world as a blocked up sewer—to believe otherwise, he thought, was simply self-deception. In *King Ubu*, Jarry offers what Keith Beaumont calls his "version of Everyman—an embodiment of the greed, the gluttony, the brutality, the treachery, the cowardice and the stupidity of Mankind as a whole" (114). This is Everyman preoccupied with destroying the world and himself in it—the ultimate suicide and a stunning image of the twentieth century as the century of war. King Ubu can never be satisfied with simply acquiring more and more, but must accumulate all in order to be able to reduce those very acquisitions along with everything else to garbage, excrement, offal. His world is a world in ruins. Jarry has proven to be the great prophet and Ubu the great icon of the whole twentieth century. "That such a conception betrays a particularly bleak and pessimistic view of the world is undeniable" (Beaumont 114). People may wish to believe otherwise, but Jarry asserts they merely deceive themselves. For him Ubu remains the only true Everyman.

This vision of all life reduced to offal resonated so powerfully throughout much of Europe that Jarry's play has been produced again and again in numerous European countries throughout the twentieth century as if each new generation had to experience his vision for itself. In 1998, for example, the ninth Hungarian production in thirty years— almost one production every three years!—played at the Csokonai Színház [the Csokonai Theatre] in Debrecen,

Hungary that spring while a new version appeared in London that summer and so on and so forth across the former World War I and World War II European battlescape. "Come, come Lord Ubu, kings aren't supposed to behave like that. You're butchering the whole world," protests one observer in the play. But that is precisely Ubu's clear and announced intent. "With this system [of inventing and collecting massive taxes on everyone and everything], I'll soon make a fortune; then I'll kill everyone in the world, and go away" (45). "I'm off to the war and I'll kill everyone," boasts Ubu (49). Like Caligula, who wished that all mankind had but a single neck so he could cut off its head with one whack, Ubu will and does decapitate the whole world, although it takes several well-aimed blows of his axe to do so.

His best stroke was war—that most efficient pre-nuclear device for creating *merde* out of living flesh and blood. War leaves behind carrion and offal and excrement. It leads to the desiccation of the world as brilliantly interpreted in that Debrecen production directed by István Pinczés. So "Long live war, three cheers for the war" (47). And war may well be the ultimate childish act indulged in by adults. Part of Jarry's genius lay in portraying the cruelty and stupidity of the adult world using language and imagery from the playground (Beaumont 130). Here is the child's love of dirt, excrement, and naughty words combined with the child's single-minded focus and cruelty. "In all directions there is a vista of burning houses and the sound of our people's groaning under the weight of our phyance [those huge taxes]" (Jarry 45). Ubu is the ultimate vindictive, cruel, stupid child wielding total power as an adult. The result is a terrifying vision of the Earth as one vast desert littered with carrion—a vision witnessed again and again in the twentieth century. If the character King Ubu is an Everyman at home in the new twentieth century of War, then the play as a whole is Jarry's perceptive, if extremely disturbing, reflection on philosophy, society, and politics at the end of the nineteenth century, which led to the devastation in the twentieth. Few plays have ever been as prescient as *Ubu Roi* has proven to be. At the end of the twentieth century, the play continued to illuminate the nightmare of humans using their time not to communicate with one another or down through the centuries but to complete King Ubu's vision of a world filled with excrement.

One hundred years after the first performances of *Ubu Roi*, Chris Lee's *The Electrocution of Children* debuted in 1998 at Dublin's Peacock Theatre without riots but before a very uncomfortable audience witnessing a contemporary version of dehumanization from a perspective disturbingly similar to Jarry's. Like the characters in *Ubu Roi*, the characters in *The Electrocution of Children* often appear to be wayward children for whom "the rules of logic and propriety simply do not (or do not yet) exist" (Beaumont 118). Such unbridled action results in the ubiquitous death and excrement in *Ubu Roi*, while a similar, if smaller, series of corpses—the immolated Gordon and his murdered father, the still warm body of Gary, and the anonymous Man—litter Lee's stage. Although no one blatantly boasts, like King Ubu, of killing everyone and anyone, life in *The Electrocution of Children* has almost as little value as it does in *Ubu Roi*. The play's central dramatic situation is the randomness of violent events or "change through catastrophe," in Lee's quotable phrase. This violence appears mirrored in each individual scene, culminating in a last speech from God. In the Dublin production, God appeared on stage addressing humanity from a modest television set lowered precariously on wires. The effect was as if CNN were bringing humanity the latest message from its god—a sort of fireside chat by the Creator Himself—a most appropriate image for the end of the twentieth century when all information arrived prepackaged for the small screen. Moreover, God's final word about the Earth and its human inhabitants proves appropriately ironic. "A slight error," he confesses. "A minor, but none the less significant oversight on my part which has grave consequences for you. . . . in the year 2003, a giant asteroid . . . will crash into central Europe and knock the Earth off its orbit. . . . it will result in, well frankly, the end of everything. I'm terribly sorry." God may be somewhat apologetic for this coming event, but that will not prevent it from happening precisely as all the play's other equally disastrous incidents have occurred, inexorably, inevitably. This macrocosmic, central, catastrophic situation of God's "mistake" is repeated in the microcosm where a killer makes an arbitrary choice of which victim to spare and which to kill, a young man immolates himself while another murders, and a doctor kills rather than saves her patient.

The impending end to all human life on Earth because of God's "slight error" relates to but is distinct from the possibility of humanity committing suicide through ecological destruction and/or bringing on nuclear winter. Life on Earth has always been precarious, but in the late twentieth-century humanity discovered with a shock the important role that random, extra-terrestrial events may have had in determining its fate. One reputable theory declared that humans most probably owed their origin to an asteroid that crashed into Earth wiping out the dinosaurs thus creating an opportunity for mammals to develop. (In much the same way, life itself may possibly have arisen thanks to a passing comet's gift of water to the planet.) What happened to the dinosaurs could obviously happen to humanity as, in the opening scene of Lee's play, God Himself testifies. "One chance encounter with a comet, and for humans at least, it's goodnight." That "chance encounter" or an equally chance encounter with a careening asteroid is not only plausible but is now recognized as highly probable. As if to substantiate Lee's point as *The Electrocution of Children* neared its opening night, newspaper headlines in March 1998 proclaimed that an asteroid was hurtling towards Earth to destroy all human life early in the new millennium. More complete calculations released a few days later indicated it would miss Earth by a fair margin.[25] But humanity's collective sigh of relief had to be tempered by knowledge of the similar probable cause of the dinosaurs' demise. The serious effects of such an encounter had been vividly illustrated in July 1994, when a fragment of the comet Shoemaker-Levy hit the planet Jupiter sending up clouds of debris as big as planet Earth. Any such fragment from a similar comet or, alternatively, any meeting between Earth and an asteroid measuring a mile wide or more would mean the end of humanity. The cliché "Love thy neighbor" took on new ironic meaning when acknowledging Jupiter as our neighboring protector planet. Working to save humanity from destruction, the planet Jupiter is, as God suggests in *The Electrocution of Children*, the best friend Earth has.

---

25. Those new predictions about Asteroid XF11 failed to create front-page headlines. Similarly, the discovery of two interstellar space rocks hurtling by Earth at incredible speeds that led statisticians to estimate that such rocks strike the Earth "about once every 100 million to 200 million years . . . over the eons several billion tons of interstellar material must have crashed into Earth" (Jewitt and Moro-Martin 41). For a full discussion of the possible role of comets and asteroids in seeding life on earth, see Bernstein et al. 26-33.

Much like Jarry's *Ubu Roi*—where "Everything depends on what you can get away with" (Shattuck 10)—*The Electrocution of Children* holds a mirror up to our frantic anonymous world in which people have forgotten how precious the gift of life and the gift of time is and how fragile human beings are. Humans, "here by chance" and as "glorious accidents of an unpredictable process" (Gould, *Full House* 216) squander their opportunities to be creative, turn their backs on relationships, fail in their attempts to communicate, and prey upon one another. Produced on the cusp of the new millennium, *The Electrocution of Children* in its disquieting and often unnerving portrait of an atomized humanity in a catastrophe-prone universe yields a new way of seeing ourselves and our world. It enlarges the stock of available reality as did *Ubu Roi*, and it does—to return to Emerson— "afford . . . us a platform whence we may command a view of our present life, a purchase by which we may move it" ("Circles" 408).

These two plays, one from the beginning and the other from the end of the twentieth century, form a pair of lenses through which to view that century and to attempt to understand what it might have felt like to live through some of those one hundred years. Although many believed that the twentieth century would continue the great work of the nineteenth by becoming the Great Century of Progress, that Century of Progress ground to a muddy halt in the chaos, confusion, boredom, and gas of the trenches of France in World War I. Others thought the twentieth century would fulfill Woodrow Wilson's dream of a World Made Safe for Democracy, but that dream died a quick death with the failure to establish the League of Nations. Still others believed with Henry Wallace that this would be the Century of the Common Man, but the

American vice-president's vision of a post-war world with "an egalitarian society of common men and women of all nations seeking common interests" (qtd. in Donald W. White 8) died in the frost of the Cold War.[26] And then there were those such as Henry Luce, the publisher of *Time* and *Life* magazines, who championed the twentieth century as the American Century. "America's first century as a dominant power in the world" trumpeted a *Life* editorial (February 1941, qtd. in Donald W. White 8). But the American Century came to an equally abrupt stop in the jungle and rice-paddies, the cost and disgrace of Vietnam.[27] Perhaps President Harry Truman best expressed the hopes of most people for the twentieth century when he announced, "We want it to be humanity's century" (qtd. Donald W. White 9). And so it was. But not humanity dedicated to democracy or the common man or America or human values but humanity dedicated to war. For the twentieth century really acquired its rightful name in the forties when it became apparent that Yeats's "blood-dimmed tide [was] loosed" all over the world ("The Second Coming" 5). This was indeed King Ubu's Great Century of War. Perhaps it is as fitting as it is terrible that this century should have ended almost where it began with Sarajevo, Bosnia, and Kosovo.

Human beings, who aspire to discover the innermost secrets of the universe and are able to predict whether or not an asteroid or comet will hit the Earth, still fail to end social isolation or individual immolation. Their spirit, which creates such incredible monuments as the great cave art, still cannot

---

26. What may prove its greatest legacy, Aaron Copland's wonderful "Fanfare for the Common Man" does live on, however, in the concert hall, from downloads and on CDs.

27. See especially Donald W. White, "Part V: The Decline of a World Role," 339-426.

keep them from slaughtering one another, as if carrying out King Ubu's orders. Yeats's "rough beast, its hour come round at last," may have already slouched "towards Bethlehem" and been born (21-22). Simply trying to survive in the twentieth century proved extremely difficult if not impossible for far too many people. C. M. Clark, the distinguished Cambridge historian, reflecting on the mass killings that went on throughout the century concluded that "[i]n the twentieth century . . . violence and destruction achieved such intensity that they broke the boundaries of the visions that had given rise to them" (60). The century's geopolitical events amply illustrate—perhaps more clearly than ever before—Emerson's contention that "Society never advances" ("Self-Reliance" 279). Still, Imre Kertész (1929-2016), the Hungarian Nobel Prize winner for literature in 2002, warned us: "It is so easy to condemn and reject our century, which teems with apocalyptic events; it is all the more difficult to live with it and in a brave effort of the intellect to say: this is *our* age, and in it our life is reflected" ("My Speech about the Century" 25; English translation qtd. in Kemper). Or to adapt the famous aphorism about a book, a century is a mirror: if an assassin looks into it, don't expect an angel to look out.[28] Luckily, we humans are both assassins and angels and, let us hope, a whole lot more besides. We look in the mirror of the twentieth century and see reflected there the horror of its wars. But we can also see the most astonishing explosion of knowledge about the physical universe. We look in the mirror of the twentieth century and see reflected there the increasing isolation of individuals and the increasing atomization of society. But we can also see the eloquent testimony in art and literature to the human spirit—to the many new ways of seeing ourselves individually and together from the ancient

---

28. "A book is a mirror: if an ass looks in it, don't expect an apostle to look out." A favorite oft-quoted aphorism of W. H. Auden.

caves in France to the contemporary stage. That's Emerson's "platform whence we may command a view of our present life, a purchase by which we may move it"—if we have the courage. The twenty-first century has barely begun and, as John Dryden (1631-1700) said of another century, "it's time to begin anew" (146).

Chapter 2
Remembering the Future, Anticipating the Past

The universe does not look right.
——*Sean Carroll*

The discovery in 1999 of the rapidly accelerating expansion of the universe led many scientists and philosophers to rethink how they viewed the fundamental nature of both time and space since both now appeared to be potentially infinite (see "Introduction"). Before that Nobel Prize-winning discovery there was a consensus among physicists and many philosophers that rather than time having a past, present, and future there exists instead what physicists call a "continuous present." In other words, there is only a continuous now with neither a past time nor a future time—a condition that appears to obtain in the universe at the quantum level. Yet the question persists that if time exists as such a continuous present, why is it that in life—as in literature—we remember the past but not the future?

In *Through the Looking Glass*, the White Queen upbraids Alice for having "a poor sort of memory that only works backwards" (248), to which Alice responds, "What sort of things do you remember best?" The White Queen replies somewhat airily, "Oh things that happened the week after next" (248). The nature of memory and what humans are able to recall from the past depends to some extent on the kind of world in which they find themselves. In Looking Glass House time and space are mirror images of our world—or at least they appear to be. Time does run backwards for the White

Queen and space—as the Red Queen demonstrates—why, space is to be negotiated: to arrive at any designated place one must first go away from it. Nevertheless, the chess game in the story does progress in time, beginning with an opening move and then several moves later enters the end game; Alice does move forwards across the chess board, square by square in chapter after chapter until she reaches her opponent's first rank and becomes crowned as Queen Alice.

Time and Space in Looking Glass House thus appear almost paradoxical, but what of the time and space of our universe? A major reason for the odd appearance of the universe, according to cosmologist Sean Carroll, lies in our experiencing a progression in time from the past through the present into the future. This notion of progression, as he elucidates, contradicts those "microscopic laws of physics that underlie the behavior of the universe [and which] do not distinguish between past and future" (48). According to the laws of quantum physics, we should be able, like the White Queen, to remember the future, but all our observations from the most amateurish to the most sophisticated and all our experience both brief and extensive suggest we cannot. We are stuck with our "poor sort of memory"—we humans remember only the past and of that past we may recall only a fraction of events or words that occurred earlier. Fully replicated memory exists only in fiction, as in Jorge Luis Borges's short story "Funes the Memorious," where the protagonist, Ireneo Funes, is cursed by total recall of everything thanks to his "infallible . . . perception and . . . memory" (63).[1] Should Funes wish to

---

1. New research reveals that at least four humans have something approaching Funes's ability to recall in detail past events and scenes. One person, for instance, "recalls in detail most days of his life, as well as the day and the date of key public events" (Elias). Yet, despite their prodigious—by human terms—memory, none is cursed with Funes's

recall and review an incident from, say, his life as a ten-year-old, then, unlike you or me, who are able to recall such incidents within seconds, he would have to allot to the memory of the past event an amount of time equal to the amount of time that the incident occupied when it originally took place in his time-past. Where we constantly modify an event whenever we recall it, Funes is powerless to change even the smallest detail because his memory remains identical with the event itself. Yet not even Funes can recall the future, for, like each of us, including cosmologists and physicists, he lives in a universe that appears to have changed and continues to change—one that began billions of years ago as "hot, dense, homogeneous"; that is, "completely different from today's [universe, which is] cool, dilute, lumpy" (Carroll, *Eternity* 26). Sean Carroll summarizes this movement as "[t]he universe start[ing] off orderly and . . . getting increasingly disorderly ever since" (26). In other words, according to Carroll, in our universe we observe an arrow of time where none should be—an arrow that moves from hot to cool, from dense to diluted, from homogeneous to lumpy, from the past to the present.

Our felt universe is indeed asymmetrical with the Laws of Quantum Physics; thus instead of remaining constant in an omnipresent "now" with no past or future, time in our universe—the one we experience—changes: events that happened in the past may or may not continue in the present and on into the expected future. Change does occur in lived time: the future—that great unknown—becomes the present

---

total recall. Researchers studying the four human subjects believe that "larger areas . . . [of the brain] almost certainly explain [this] . . . rare gift" (Elias). Oliver Sacks reports on musical savants one of whom knew "more than two thousand operas, as well as *The Messiah, The Christmas Oratorio*, and all of Bach's cantatas" ("An Auditory World," *Musicophilia* 163).

and then moves into the past. Such an arrangement leads, perhaps inevitably, to attempts to know what cannot be known; that is, to know about the future before it becomes the present. It was this desire to explore "the future of the human race" that motivated H. G. Wells to create his metaphorical vehicle, the time machine, and it was, at least in part, this desire to know what cannot be known that helped catapult his novella *The Time Machine* to popularity in 1895—a popularity that still shows no sign of diminishing.

Wells's novella is both highly original and reflective of its age. The intellectual currents of nineteenth-century thought were roiling with the impact occasioned by the discovery of geological time in the previous century—a discovery so startling that it took nearly a century for thinkers to come to grips with its major implications. Then Charles Darwin produced his *On the Origin of Species* (1859), perhaps the single most influential scientific book ever published, and initiated an intensive debate over the nature, past, present, and future of humanity.[2] At the end of the nineteenth century, in 1891, four years before Wells finished *The Time Machine*, mathematician and physicist William Thomson [Lord Kelvin], unaware of nuclear reactions and, therefore, basing his calculations upon internal combustion plus gravitational contraction, estimated the life of the sun at five million years with another few to go at which point the sun would simply go out leaving the now frigid solar system in utter darkness (Ferris 247).[3] Wells with his keen scientific interest speculated

---

2. For a survey of the scientific discoveries in the nineteenth century that challenged the century's received wisdom bringing "all in doubt," see Tibor Frank, "'Dogma and Science': Patterns of Victorian Unbelief."

3. To his credit Lord Kelvin added a parenthesis to his calculations: "(I do not say there may not be laws which we have not discovered)" (qtd. in Ferris 248). In *The Time Machine*, a possibly last remnant of life appears

about the implications of such discoveries for the future of humanity and wrote several essays with the ominous word "extinction" in their titles. Essays such as "On Extinction" (1893) and "The Extinction of Man" (1894) are clear forerunners of the last chapters of *The Time Machine*. Moreover, in another earlier essay, "The Man of the Year Million" (1893), Wells affirms that "it is not what man has been, but what he will be, that should interest us" (176); hence in *The Time Machine* the Time Traveller heads off into the future rather than into the past. Wells drew directly on Darwin's theory of evolution as he quotes approvingly from a "great unwritten volume . . . by one Professor Holzkopf . . . at Weissnichtwo"— that is, "Professor Wooden Head at the University of Don't-Know-Where": "Evolution is no mechanical tendency making for perfection according to the ideas current in the year of grace 1892; it is simply the continual adaptation of plastic life, for good or evil, to the circumstances that surround it" (177). Wells believed that such adaptation would lead to an increasing emphasis on the mind; hence the physical expansion of the human head at the expense of the body that we find in his novels, such as *War of the Worlds* (1897), and in various essays.[4]

The Time Machine retains Professor Wooden Head's evolutionary assumptions, but with a twist. The Time Traveller in the far-future year of 802,701 encounters the

---

in the repugnant shape of a black ball with tentacles "hopping fitfully about" in the shoal near a deserted beach (148).

4. Wells's speculations about the future of a big-brained humanity evolving into a large head and shrinking body became popular, especially in later science-fiction stories, but had no basis in science. Peter Ward, the well-known paleontologist, biologist, and astrobiologist, speculating on the future of homo sapiens, says flatly: "The big-brain vision has no real scientific basis. The fossil record of skull sizes over the past several thousand generations shows that all our days of rapid increase in brain size are long over" (54).

diminutive Eloi, who he discovers to his horror are a cattle farm for the monstrous Morlocks.[5] Biology has triumphed over culture, as Nicholas Ruddick observes ("Introduction" 33). When, thanks to his promiscuous use of fire, the Time Traveller escapes from the eight-hundred and two thousand something year to plunge still further into futurity, he arrives at a time after humanity has disappeared and been replaced by giant monster crabs (146). The *New York Times'* nineteenth-century reviewer labeled these concluding chapters "a pessimistic business" ("Speculative and Pessimistic" 263). Clearly, Wells's pessimism violated Victorian notions of progress towards perfection, but he did not back down and consistently defended his position: "The long roll of paleontology is half-filled with the records of extermination; whole orders, families, groups, and classes have passed away and left no mark and no tradition upon the living fauna of the world" (Wells, "On Extinction" 174). Later, in his *Outline of History* (1920), he would summarize his belief that "[n]ot only is Space from the point of view of life and humanity empty, but Time is empty also. Life is like a little glow, scarcely kindled yet, in these void immensities" (8; qtd. in Parrinder 40).

Like Wells's contemporary example in "On Extinction" of the Western plains of the United States, which were once covered in bison but now remained devoid of the huge herds (175), the Time Traveller encounters not a single "human mark or tradition" in a future where huge crustaceans rule the world. Even the green Museum at Kensington, which survived

---

5. The Morlocks are a variation on Professor Wooden Head's concluding portrait of humanity living deep underground "with their boring machinery ringing away, and artificial lights glaring and casting black shadows . . . . Humanity in dismal retreat before the cold, changed beyond recognition" (181).

over eight hundred thousand years, is gone. Barely avoiding becoming crab dinner the Time Traveller again hurls himself into the far-future world of "30 million years hence" (Wells, *Time Machine* 147)—a world permeated by "the sense of abominable desolation" (146) which Wells elsewhere describes as "a chill of solitude[,] . . . the awful solitude . . . almost beyond the imagination" ("On Extinction" 175). Encountering this late-Earth in the throes of Lord Kelvin's predicted Heat Death of the Sun, Wells has his Time Traveller flee from this "abominable desolation" of the Sun's last days as darkness, oxygen-depletion, and bone-chilling cold over-spread the Earth (148). He beats a hasty retreat and, reversing his course in time, returns to his warm, snug Victorian English home and the dinner party that awaits him (148-49).

It is difficult to over-estimate the incredible popularity then as now of what Wells called his "invention."[6] When Patrick Parrinder organized an academic conference on the occasion of the 100th anniversary of the publication of *The Time Machine*, he expected a handful of specialists in the field of popular culture to turn up. Instead, over two hundred academics from a variety of disciplines appeared. Similarly, Wells's book remains in print long after it gave him his much-needed economic independence. His "invention" spawned a strong sub-genre as well as a highly profitable marketing niche. In modern physics Einstein's special theory of relativity validated the possibility of time travel to the future but not to the past. Much later physicist Richard Feynman (1918-1988) argued for travel to the past. Today, a fair number of physicists are immersed in the math and physics of time travel,

6. There were no handy labels in the late nineteenth century such as "science fiction" nor did today's ready-to-hand niche marketing of various forms of fantasy exist. Wells, therefore, coined his own label of "invention."

publishing articles and books on the subject—many inspired by Wells's novella. At least one physicist, Ronald L. Mallet, credits Wells's book with motivating his career-choice to do physics (see Mallet and Henderson, *Time Traveler* [2006], especially 13-18, 169-74, 186-89, 195-97). As physicist and science writer Paul Davies observes, "It was actually a work of fiction that triggered the only systematic investigation of time travel in the history of science" (*About Time* 245).

A little over a half century after Wells's publication, both that sub-genre of time travel novels and stories along with theoretical physics had, however, accepted time travel not only to the future but also to the past and even established rules for and conventions of such travel—many rooted in the cause and effect of Time's Arrow. One of the most prominent, the "Butterfly Effect," became a law in physics but a convention in time-travel fiction. The term gained currency in popular literature and journalism through the success of Ray Bradbury's now classic science-fiction story, "The Sound of Thunder" (1952), in which a rich, adventurous, if not too bright, time traveler goes on a safari some 60,255,000 years in the past to hunt and kill a Tyrannosaurus Rex. Despite all the verbal and written warnings about never to leave the metal path especially built for Time Travelers, he falls and accidentally steps upon a small black and gold butterfly. When he and the rest of the expedition end their hunt and travel back through the millennia to their own world and time, they find that world visibly, linguistically, and politically changed. As a character had warned earlier: some incident in the past, such as killing a butterfly, is "a small thing that could knock down a line of small dominoes, then big dominoes and then gigantic dominoes, all down the years across time."[7]

A second law of time travel postulated by contemporary physics, the "Grandfather Paradox" features in many novels and stories and even became the subject of a film, *Back to the Future* (1985; Dir. Robert Zemeckis). The "Grandfather Paradox" poses the question: What would happen if a time traveler went back in time and performed some operation or had some accident that resulted not just in her world being changed because of the "Butterfly Effect," but also in her not being born? (Deutsch and Lockwood 68-69). In *Back to the Future*, the young man must act to bring together his future parents or he will simply cease to exist either in the future or in the past. In the film, everything turns out all right as his parents-to-be do romantically entwine thanks to their future son's ingenuity at that most sacred of all American rites of passage, the high school senior prom. He thereby prevents his own erasure—a Hollywood Happy Ending. Physicists tackle the paradox somewhat differently in that they use the Butterfly Effect to cut the Gordian Knot of the "Grandfather Paradox" by theorizing that were someone to go back into the past, that is, to a time before they existed, and act in such a way that would prevent their being born, then they simply would not be present either in the past or in the present (Deutsch and Lockwood 68-69). QED. Problem solved.

Wells's novella demands the reader's active participation in thinking about the very nature of time, for "The Time Traveller and the reader are engaged in the same activity: they

---

7. I wonder if Henry Kissinger read this story when young and borrowed his domino theory from it. "The Sound of Thunder" appeared originally in *Collier's* magazine, 28 June 1952, then in several collections of Bradbury's short stories, and was made into a movie in 2005. It has the distinction of being "the most republished science-fiction short story of all time," according to Wikipedia.

try to understand the nature of temporal contrast presented
and then to discover connections" (Huntington 2). (Compare
the discussion of time in *Time's Arrow*, which follows.) The
theme of time travel may well be, as Arthur C. Clarke noted,
difficult "to take . . . very seriously," but at the same time, as he
also argued, it is "one of the most fascinating—and sometimes
the most moving—in the whole of literature" (xiv). Three very
different novels bear out Clarke's opinion: Kurt Vonnegut's
popular and critically successful *Slaughterhouse-Five* (1969),
Audrey Niffenegger's best-selling popular fiction, *The Time
Traveler's Wife* (2004), and the great evolutionary biologist and
paleontologist George Gaylord Simpson's relatively unknown
and posthumously published *The Dechronization of Sam
Magruder* (1996).[8] Vonnegut uses time travel as a means of
exploring the nature of evil, the issue of free will versus
determinism, and the implications of unmerited suffering.
Niffenegger takes time travel as a test of fidelity in a love
relationship buffeted by unexpected, forced absences, while
Simpson uses it to explore utter, existential aloneness, what
Wells termed "the awful solitude . . . almost beyond imagination" ("On Extinction" 175). The first two novels limit time
travel to the person's own timeline between birth and death or
slightly beyond. Neither Billy Pilgrim in *Slaughterhouse-Five*
nor Henry DeTamble in *The Time Traveler's Wife* travel
hundreds of thousands of years into the future or the past.
Vonnegut begins his account of Billy and his World War II
experiences with the now-famous sentence: "Listen: Billy
Pilgrim has come unstuck in time" (20). He does indeed "come
unstuck in time" but, more specifically, he comes unstuck on his

---

8. The history of Simpson's novel is now impossible to reconstruct.
Written at some point during his lifetime, his daughter, Joan Simpson
Burns, found it among his papers long after his death and saw it through
publication.

timeline, and while he may be arbitrarily thrown either backwards or forwards, he remains always on that life's same timeline. For instance, Billy has seen his death many times but treats it as only one moment of many so does not dwell on it but moves back to other moments when he is alive. Davies in *About Time* describes such movement as Billy's being tossed into the future or back into the past as a "sort of immortality . . . restricted to a fixed set of events" (41).

In Vonnegut's novel, when Billy comes unstuck in time, he always becomes the age he was or will be. For example, when he is with Montana Wildhack in the Tralfamadorian zoo, he suddenly goes "time traveling again" to New York City, where he becomes the Billy of his past who once was in Times Square; that is, he becomes that age and experiences only whatever he experienced at that earlier time (179). Yet, at the same moment as he is in Times Square he is also in the Tralfamadorian zoo as the time-traveling trip takes no time from the zoo present. Rather than multiple Billys, each existing at different points in time, Billy exists in a continuous present where all his life at every moment resides on his lifeline much like those plot lines for *Slaughterhouse-Five* Vonnegut drew using various colored crayons on a roll of wallpaper (5).[9] It may be a measure of the popular acceptance of time travel as a concept since Wells's initial book that Vonnegut is able to assume Billy's physical presence both in the present in which he time trips and simultaneously in the time-when to which he travels.[10] But does this assumption beg the question of the

---

9. In Wells's continuous present the Time Traveller travels to a future far beyond his lifetime, which then becomes as much a part of his timeline as his life lived in Victorian London.

10. Both the Time Traveller in *The Time Machine* traveling to the distant future and Sam in *The Dechronization of Sam Magruder* traveling to the distant past remain the age they were before their trips began.

time-traveling person's corporeality? If someone time traveled back into his or her own past, would he or she do so as the person s/he was when the trip began or as the person s/he is during the trip? If I, say, at forty years of age, traveled back in time to when I was eight, would I be my forty-year old self visiting, that is, co-existing with my own eight-year old past self already present there or would I be—like Billy Pilgrim—the me I was at eight?

Audrey Niffenegger in *The Time Traveler's Wife* (2005) sets out to explore exactly this first intriguing variation on the Grandfather Paradox, which might in this instance be renamed more appropriately "the Child is Father of the Time Traveler Paradox." In her novel, the Time Traveler does corporeally travel to and exist in whatever time period he arrives at even if that means co-existing with his earlier or later self as in the episode where Henry DeTamble at twenty-seven appears to his young nine-year-old self and undertakes to introduce him to the wonders of the Art Institute of Chicago. Clare, the wife of the novel's title, meets time-traveling Henry first when she is six. He, at various ages, visits her repeatedly through the years from her childhood to her old age. By the time she is in her teens she knows she will marry him sometime in their future. When he visits her on her eighteenth birthday from his future where they are married, she seduces him, although on her time line she has not yet met him. (A case of her future husband cuckolding her future lover.)[11]

---

11. Clare, like Henry, has her own time line on which she meets him for the first time when she is six years old and the last time in her eighties. She has, therefore, known Henry "all her life" (141). Henry, on the other hand, will meet her on his timeline for the first time some fourteen years later when she is twenty. Mirroring this phenomenon, much of the book takes place after 2004, its date of publication. Henry dies on 1 January 2007 and visits Clare for the last time in 2053.

The Time Traveler's Wife is a story of true love and true lovers that becomes extremely complicated by Henry's unpredictable, abrupt time traveling. Both Henry's and Clare's past become so intertwined with their future as to create powerful tides of confusion in almost any of their present moments, yet they—to borrow John Donne's famous lines from "A Valediction: Forbidding Mourning": "endure not yet / A breach, but an expansion, / Like gold to airy thinness beat" (21-23). Much of Niffenegger's novel reads like a novelization, a time-travel version of John Donne's famous compass metaphor in "Valediction," where the poet compares his lover to "the fixt foot [that] makes no show / To move" of a compass—the kind used to draw geometric figures—while the speaker of the poem, presumably male, is compared to the other foot of the compass that "must . . . obliquely run" (31-32, 38).

The Time Traveler's Wife is, however, no metaphysical love poem but a thoroughly contemporary twenty-first-century novel, and so Niffenegger, like Wells before her, gives her readers a plausible scientific explanation for Henry's odd ability—an explanation only slightly ahead of the curve of then-current psychological experiments involving gene sequencing. Henry consults a research doctor who clones his odd genes, snips out the suspicious DNA, and inserts it into a mouse embryo. With a lot of work and much patience, the doctor using Henry's genes eventually comes up with mice able to time travel. Based on his research, he hypothesizes that Henry is "a new kind of human" (126) with the ability to travel in time but with no ability to control or to choose when and where he will go. Like Billy Pilgrim, Henry slips and slides through time but only rarely welcomes the experience of being suddenly hurled to another time of his life. He also pays an appalling price for his trips in physical danger and verbal abuse since he always arrives "from nowhere, naked . . . . No clothes, no money, no ID" and, therefore, must "spend most of [his time] . . . acquiring clothing and trying to hide" (3). He is often arrested and/or beaten-up, has accidents and becomes injured as he tries to steal or borrow what he needs. The rigors, unpredictability, and sometimes the torture of time travel take their toll and he dies at forty-three—old before his chronological time. His daughter, Alba, however, having inherited the same genome sequence, appears to have more control and is less the plaything of whatever impels the time traveler to travel.[12] The daughter as the next step on the evolutionary ladder comes to see time travel as a great adventure. "Sometimes I can go when and where I want," she boasts (376). "Can you not go at all if you don't want to?" asks her father plaintively, clearly weary of being tossed wherever and whenever (376). Whether Alba represents a new improved level of evolved humanity, some variation of Arthur C. Clarke's post-human from *Childhood's End* (1953), or is simply a "prodigy" or evolutionary sport caused by one slightly odd sequencing gene, only time or another novel will tell. Putting aside the scientific or pseudoscientific explanations, we do live in an age that appears to accept time travel, at least as metaphor if not as a coming physical reality. *The Time Traveler's Wife* remains compelling both as an Einsteinian thought experiment and as a poignant tale of great love sustained over a lifetime that includes presence and absence, gain and loss.[13]

Billy Pilgrim and Henry DeTamble as involuntary Time Travelers whose travel appears limited to their lifelines, or in

---

12. The various explanations given to him are far from satisfactory.

13. This may help account for *The Time Traveler's Wife* becoming a bestseller.

Henry's case slightly beyond, with no control over where and when they travel may not be the best advertisements for time travel, unlike Wells's original Time Traveller, who at least had a machine that could be programmed and controlled. Could contemporary scientists and engineers design and build such a machine? Paul Davies in *How to Build a Time Machine* (2002) offers a blueprint for such a device that appears grounded in current scientific knowledge—yet may pose some difficulties for the amateur mechanic. His basic plan begins: "Take one black hole and place it . . ." So apparently anyone could make a time machine, if that person only knew how to maneuver that black hole. Still, even if we made such a machine, there remains the nagging question that George Gaylord Simpson raises in *The Dechronization of Sam Magruder* as a challenge to Wells: how could any Time Traveler, whether Wells's, Vonnegut's, Niffenegger's, or Davies's travel to what by definition does not yet exist? Wells's Eloi and Morlocks will not come into existence until 802,693 years after the Time Traveller paid his visit to them. Billy Pilgrim experiences his death by assassination not once but several times. *The Time Traveler's Wife* concludes with Henry visiting Clare in 2053 when she is 85 years old, and he has been dead for decades (517-18).

Simpson will have none of such scenarios, for he argues quite convincingly that the only place to which anyone could travel in time would be to somewhere or somewhen that has already come into existence; that is, to the past. His narrator, the Universal Historian forcefully argues that "[d]uration demands . . . existence in . . . the time-dimension universe, or, to speak very loosely, in the past. It follows, of course, that the future does not exist and has no reality in any sense of the word" (12). "[Y]ou can't go traveling to the nonexistent" (13). End of argument. Like Wells, Simpson offers his own plausible theory of time as a dimension: "Even intuitively, we feel that existence and reality demand duration. Yet the world of our senses, that in which we have our subjective beings, is the present, only, and is without duration" (12).[14] The protagonist of his novel, Sam Magruder travels, therefore, to the past, to the deep past, back to the Age of the Dinosaurs—a "Crusoe of the Cretaceous," to borrow Arthur C. Clarke's phrase (xix). But Magruder confronts a far more difficult situation than Robinson Crusoe in that he faces his hostile environment stark naked with no tools or material to be salvaged from a convenient nearby shipwreck and with no hope of rescue. He has absolutely no way of escaping from the past in which he finds himself trapped. Nor does he have even the remotest possibility of finding human companionship since human beings, including Man Friday, will not even appear as humanoids on Earth for millions and millions of years. He is utterly, inescapably alone.

His becomes an extraordinary tale of Emersonian self-reliance as Magruder goes about constructing an island of human habitation in the Age of Dinosaurs with only his "bare body and brains" (Simpson 46) and with no hope of a Friday to assist. "My reality," he decides, "is unbearable" (90), yet bear it he does as he struggles to survive in a supremely hostile environment. But Magruder does more than merely survive, for he also struggles like Job to understand who and where he is. The conclusion he draws in the Cretaceous millions of years in our past is similar to the one Job reached a couple of thousand years ago sitting on his dung hill, though Magruder's comes filtered through the theory of evolution. Much like

14. Compare to Wells, who bases his concept of time as the fourth dimension upon a current new mathematical theory by Simon Newcomb (see Wells 223).

Gertrude Stein, who on her deathbed is reported to have first asked those gathered around, "What is the answer?" but then hearing no reply she laughed and tried rephrasing, "What is the question?" Magruder similarly concludes that "the questions *are* the answer" (94). And being a scholar, thinker, researcher, once his survival becomes assured, then and only then does he devote much of his time to thinking: "You do not do much fancy thinking while you are still fighting an apparently losing battle for bare survival" (100), he wisely notes. But once he succeeds in establishing "a routine for survival" (97), he sets himself the dual task of trying "to understand, and [then] . . . writ[ing] my reactions to this world. By a million-to-one shot, I might even leave them to posterity. That, at least, is something only a man could do" (97). What consolation he finds lies not in his personal survival per se, which he comes to realize "no longer seems very important even to me" (101). "[L]ost in the wilderness of time" (101), he comes to identify himself with the long course of evolution that will result in human "culture and civilization" (101). In this, the longest of stories spanning millions of years, Sam Magruder, like each of us, plays only a miniscule role, but nevertheless his is a part of the Grand Human Narrative miraculously preserved in Jurassic mud.

Ursula K. Le Guin once remarked that "an improbable time will give rise to an improbable literature," and it surely is no accident that after the publication of Wells's *The Time Machine* there occurs an explosion of twentieth-century improbable and fantastic literature. Looking back from our vantage point in the twenty-first century, we observe the continual expansion of science fiction since Mary Shelley's initial thought experiment in femaleless parturition, along with the growth of both serious and popular fantasy culminating in James Joyce's attempt to grasp and recreate in writing the world of the unconscious in *Finnegans Wake* (1939) and J. R. R. Tolkien's great epic of renunciation in a grossly acquisitive age, *The Lord of the Rings* (1954–1965).[15]

"Literature is," as Ezra Pound proclaimed, "the news that stays news" (Ch.2) and the same may be said for painting, sculpture, or any of the arts. The Guggenheim Museum in Bilbao, for instance, commissioned Richard Serra's highly original, monumental sculpture *The Matter of Time* (1997) (frontispiece), a series of huge steel constructions weighing a total of 1,034 tons. Perhaps cosmologists, such as Sean Carroll, could encounter the symmetry of time for which they search by going to Bilbao, where inside "The Matter of Time" they could experience a journey without a beginning or an end but rather a continuous present.[16]

Where Serra utilizes cutting-edge technology to create a sense of the timeless, the inventor John Taylor invested millions of British pounds in a time-keeper, the Corpus Clock, whose imagery embodies the sensation of being trapped in a time-bound world. Installed at Corpus Christi College in Cambridge (hence its title) and unveiled by physicist Stephen

---

15. A similar point is made by Andrew Blake in his stimulating reading of the Harry Potter phenomenon: "The worldwide welcome for Harry [Potter] builds on this irruption of the fantastic. . . . This is a literature that attempts not to report, accurately and often valuably, on the way we live now, but to deal with the fundamental questions of human existence" (99), which is exactly what each of the three discussed time-travel books also attempts to do.

16. "Band," a typical Serra construction, consists of a "70-foot long unfurling ribbon—but its shape is not apparent from inside the exhibit. With no distinct interior or exterior, it creates four separate spaces. 'Nothing repeats,' Serra says. 'There is no beginning, no end to the band.' As with all his works, they give viewers a fresh perspective on the meaning and uses of space" (Patel 64).

Hawking on 19 September 2008, the Corpus Clock creates an overwhelming sensation of time being consumed (Figure 1). The clock has no hands or any digital readout, but tracks the passing seconds by having an ugly insect-figure mechanically grab and pull them along. This all-black, vaguely menacing, and highly unattractive creature is based on John Harrison's Grasshopper Escapement (ca. 1722) that made possible the first mechanical clocks. The figure with its needle teeth is far more menacing than Harrison's escapement formed of wood pieces or any natural grasshopper, which it resembles. Nor do any comforting sounds, such as a grandfather's clock's tick-tocks accompany this image of time, for when the hours are struck, their number is told by the sound of the requisite number of links of chain dropping into a coffin! The sight and sounds create a kind of ultimate image of industrial timekeeping.

Rather than bemoan the loss of time or lament human mortality as the Corpus Christi Clock suggests we should, contemporary writers of time-travel tales—much like artists, such as Richard Serra—reveal people using time to assert the worth of the individual human life as well as the value of seeing oneself as a part of human history, as Simpson does in Sam Magruder, or to warn of the danger of human arrogance when confronting evil, as Vonnegut does in *Slaughterhouse-Five*, or to celebrate the "miracle of love across time," as Niffenegger does in the *Time Traveler's Wife*. There is a fundamental urgency in these stories. They do not merely record the "happy hours" as the old sundials once did, but neither do they demonize time in chronophage images as the Corpus Clock does. Instead, such art and stories assert the uniqueness of all human experience in time and the uniqueness of each individual human being, confined though each may be to one asymmetrical timeline of experience stretching from the "unknown to the known through the incertitude of the void" (Joyce, *Ulysses* 697).[17] As Richard Serra reminds us, "Nothing repeats" (qtd. in Patel 64), thus guaranteeing the uniqueness of each life and each work of art. Perhaps it is in literature and art that the human answer may be found to the cosmologists' dilemma posed by the asymmetry of time: the universe may not look right but it sure feels right to those of us who believe with Sam Magruder and Gertrude Stein that "the questions *are* the answer." Like Sam Magruder and unlike Billy Pilgrim, humans may still make the effort to communicate in novels, art, lectures—recording "our [unique] reactions to the world"— that is, something a human could do. Reconciling this basic human achievement in time with the ungainly appearance of the universe may be a job best left to future cosmologists.

"The Present of Things Past"

> *Time is so fundamental to our experience of the world . . . [that] [o]ur very notion of personal identity . . . is closely bound up with memory. . . . To be an individual implies a continuity of experience together with some linking feature, such as memory.*
> ———*Paul Davies*

To say that humans live in Time is to affirm that we live in the present moment but a present moment that includes remnants and images of our past that we carry with us into the present as memory. The past itself, however, by definition must

---

17. The narrator of *Ulysses* records that Leopold Bloom "as a competent keyless citizen . . . had proceeded energetically from the unknown to the known through the incertitude of the void" (697).

be over, finished, which means that all events previous to *now* have receded beyond the knowledge of those of us living in the present. As St. Augustine wrote in his *Confessions*, "I can confidently assert that I know this: that if nothing passed away there would be no past time" (11.14, 267).[18] Yet often when referring to past events we make the false assumption that an account of the past written in our present is somehow an account of what actually took place "back then." In Augustine's terms this would be the knowledge of "the past of things past." Scholars, such as Hayden White in *The Content of the Form* (1987), have warned against such assumptions: "How else can any past, which . . . comprises events, processes, structures, and so forth, considered to be no longer perceivable, be represented in either consciousness or discourse except in an 'imaginary' way?" (57). White's statement implies that "history is first and forever a form of storytelling," as Brian Attebery maintains (42). And both of those terms, "'imaginary' way" and "a form of storytelling" are synonyms for Augustine's "the present of things past."

Once an event has happened or a person leaves the world stage, they go down the stream of time to lodge forever in the past of memory. Literature offers many instances of humans who find this truth so difficult to accept that they will attempt by various means to circumvent it or even to overcome it. The most vivid of these efforts may well be the age-old human fantasy of beginning again, living life all over again, or of being given another life to live—fantasies that re-present the past as a way of reliving or of somehow extending it into the

---

18. Augustine's meditation in chapter 11 of his *Confessions* is a foundational text for this and, I suspect, most humanistic discussions of time. For an in-depth authoritative discussion of this chapter, see Gábor Ittzés, "'What, Then, Is Time?': A Reading of Book XI of Augustine's *Confessions.*"

present; fantasies that refuse to bow before the completion, the finality of what's past; that refuse to admit that it can no longer be perceived in the present.

Within contemporary popular culture in English this desire to bring the past forward into the present, of being able to re-live life, comes in a variety of forms ranging from the bizarre, such as the use of past life regressions to discover the authentic accounts of the "lost years" of Jesus, to the popular spate of revenant tales and films where the sons and daughters of Count Dracula, though dead, continue causing trouble in the present. In *Dracula* (1897) itself, Bram Stoker (1847-1912) suggested several possibilities for overcoming the limitation of what is "no longer perceivable"—a life lived and ended in time. Stoker's vampire, Count Dracula, drinks others' blood so that he may continue to exist as the Un-Dead, while the madman Renfield believes that "by consuming a multitude of live things . . . one might indefinitely prolong life" (234). Another such method of prolonging life invented by the fifth earl of Goinister in Aldous Huxley's *After Many a Summer* (1939) enabled him to live to be more than 201 by consuming a daily dose of a most revolting potion made from the guts of carp (249).

The heroes of Mark Twain's *A Connecticut Yankee in King Arthur's Court* (1889) and Ford Maddox Ford's sequel, *Ladies Whose Bright Eyes* (1935), do not extend life on their timelines but do add to it through being catapulted back in time to the medieval era, where they live for many years. Hank Morgan, Twain's ingenious Yankee, brings with him his extensive knowledge of guns, explosives, barbed wire, rubber, electricity, and other "useful" inventions that he employs to "modernize" the past, which leads ironically to his creating a barren landscape of death and decay where there had been flourishing vibrant life. In contrast, Ford's Mr. Sorrell discovers how very little practical knowledge from his own time he actually has but simultaneously recognizes, appreciates, and does not attempt to change the humane values of the earlier period when land was less crowded, people less materialistic, and heroism—even when unintended—more possible. Sorrell concludes by wishing that such values could be appropriated by his contemporary world. *Connecticut Yankee* on the other hand, which begins as a dream of escaping from the confines of one human lifetime, very soon devolves into a nightmare, a cautionary tale warning of the dismal future humans living in Twain's own time face given their propensity for violence coupled with the irrevocability of the past.

In Thornton Wilder's *Our Town* (1938), Emily Webb having recently died cannot escape to any past since she has no more time. She is, however, given a single day in which to visit her former life. Rather than escaping from time and the condition of being dead by reliving part of her past, she instead experiences how fleeting human time really is: "It goes so fast," she laments. "We don't have time to look at one another" (88) as events and people move from the present to the past to become "no longer perceivable." Only after death does she realize how terribly precious lived time actually was or is—a feeling which those in the midst of life including her younger self appreciate only sporadically if at all.

Billy Pilgrim in Kurt Vonnegut's *Slaughterhouse-Five*, unlike Emily, does truly escape from the confines of unidirectional time by coming "unstuck in time" when without willing it he may slide backwards to experience once more events now in his past or he may be flung forwards to preview events that will occur in his future as discussed earlier in this chapter. Forced to view all his life non-sequentially he appears to have overcome the limits of a human life lived in time and so is able to adopt a godlike or Tralfamadorean perspective concluding that "everything was beautiful and nothing hurt" (84). Such a cosmic perspective is, however, forever denied his fellow humans with their vision limited to now and for whom "the 'normal' condition . . . in this world is not good health and good feeling but bad health and pain" (Driver, "Via Dolorosa" 16).

But what if a person were able not just to visit but to relive their past? Seán O'Faolain's *And Again?* (1979) and Martin Amis's *Time's Arrow* (1991) have heroes who do live their lives again, although in quite different ways. In *And Again?* the gods trick James Younger, an old man aged 65 and about to die, into accepting their offer—made through a letter bearing the unlikely return address "Department of External Affairs, Olympus, Timeless"—to live again but with certain conditions, such as:

> he will live backwards for sixty-five years, growing younger
> . . . until the ripe age of zero. His memory will be severely
> limited to his professional skills and small details of his
> previous life but with no recollection of any intimate
> relationships. (8)

Under such circumstances Younger obviously will not have the opportunity to solve the same set of problems life may present "all over again." Instead, his "second time around" proves radically new; so new that he may not even be James Younger, but his twin brother, Robert Younger, of whom he believes he had never heard of much less known in his previous 65 years of life! As the rest of the world moves forwards in time, he travels back in time in the sense that his body instead of aging continuously grows increasingly young until, he imagines, he will eventually metamorphose into a moth—a symbol of the fragility and evanescence of human life and also, perhaps, of the specific danger of being too attracted by the flame of this opportunity to live again and thereby have twice as much time as ordinary mortals. But such a symbolically satisfying picture proves not to obtain. Instead, in his own peculiar way he, too, moves forwards on the stream of time in every sense but the one of physically growing old as instead he continually grows ever physically younger. His experience in this second lifetime becomes a model of a well-lived life in that he consciously, actively strives to retain memories this time and to participate actively in life rather than letting it slip unacknowledged through his hands as it appears to have done in his first sixty-five years. What is gone is gone, he discovers, never to be recovered, since "[i]n life nothing happens twice," whether the person lives his life once or twice (7; compare Heraclitus's river). His grandson, Bob Two, not understanding this reality, spends all his time assembling "facts," such as the dates when events happened, trivial and now meaningless souvenirs of times forgotten, and in the process neglects to live in the present.

Younger cannot avoid his present as he grows physically younger, while living for one hundred and thirty years or twice the length of what would have been his traditional "three score years and ten" (the expected biblical 65-year life span). His present often turns cruel as, for example, when he must separate from his wife, whom he deeply loves, because his "youngering" is becoming an embarrassment to her: how could he, who appears to be a twenty-year-old husband of a forty-eight-year-old woman, have a sixteen-year-old daughter? In two years the father and daughter will appear the same age! He realizes that he dares not risk their even being seen together in public. He must, therefore, go into exile returning only after his daughter moves to another country. When he at last is able to return, it is to his love, which truly transcends time and physical limits. In his last years he moves backwards through puberty and beyond to become an infant again—the former lover and husband now physically a baby but emotionally and intellectually a one hundred-and-thirty-year old man able to crawl and scrawl one last three-page entry in his memoirs. Unlike most humans, he knows with complete certainty which day will be his last on Earth, since his death will occur on the exact Mirror Day of his birth: 1900-1965-2030. As he approaches his end he does not metamorphose as he had expected, but instead grows smaller and smaller. His wife, Nana, describes his end:

> He dwindled and dwindled until he became as tiny as a clothes moth, though still talking like a man. I had long before stopped feeding him with a spoon as small as a snuff spoon or with milk from a rubber teat. At the last I was cultivating him like a silkworm in its pupal stage, except that he was not moving onwards from larva to imago but, as all his life he had been, backwards towards his final condition of becoming his own spectre. The last night I saw him, a ghost in a padded match-box, he was as beautiful as a scarab. . . . When I came back the next morning, his birthday, to look at his beauty again the box was empty. (285)

What exactly then was the nature and objective of this gods' radical experiment with human lived time? The Secretary to the Department of External Affairs wrote: "our interest is solely to decide, once and for all, whether what you humans call Experience teaches you a damned thing" (6).

Whatever the gods may have decided, Nana concludes, perhaps too hastily, that "most of the purpose of the experiment of making Younger grow younger and younger was to demonstrate mockingly that no gods' amount of experience teaches us mortals a damned thing" (286). Yet her verdict may well be too harsh, for Younger's second venture at living life does show how a life may be lived in full awareness of its limited time span, yet with a sense of leisureliness and calm in contrast to Emily's sense of speed and urgency in *Our Town*. By accepting his lot—strange as it might be—and by entering fully into the gods' experiment Younger discovers that a human life becomes complete not simply by filling time-present but by also reworking or remapping time-past in present memory. "I need to remember," he confesses, "Only the immortals can live forgetting" (5). In the very last months of his life, he realizes that he has spent his second life re-acquiring what he had lost of his first although, like everything else, he of necessity does so backwards. At last as an infant he knows the joy of having actual memories of childhood and babyhood rather than guesses, suppositions, or gossip: ". . . what a . . . joy it was for me . . . to recapture after my lifelong thirst this vast gulf of infancy" (283), he writes four months before his end. Without complaint or objection, this time he accepts his end as fitting for a life in which "I have lived, loved and learned" (285). Having "chanced life-at-any-price" (282), his reward is a full life—a life come full circle to fulfillment and completion, and his last words are those of thanks to his wife, through whom the memory of his mother and his infancy and childhood were restored to him: "Thank you for all you have given me, above all for not being an abstract philosopher with me, for feeling with me, for opening my past to me, for being a fool with me, for being one with me in love" (285). Having acquired his past, he becomes free to leave life with no regrets.

The Arrow of Time Reversed

In Martin Amis's *Time's Arrow*, the river of time appears to reverse itself to flow backwards not from the future into the present but from the present into the past carrying the main character, Odilo Unverdorben, with it. Since *Time's Arrow* confronts both the difficulties of reversing time in order for Odilo to live life again and the problems of representing past-time in memory through the writing of history and in imagination through the writing of fiction, I shall discuss it at length. While it is never clear exactly who narrates the tale, it appears safe to assume the narrator is Odilo's soul, conscience, or spirit—whatever embodies all those values and opportunities that he rejected in life in order to dedicate his life fully to evil. The narrator finally puts the matter to rest by labeling himself with the bitterly ironic pejorative "parasite" (72).

In contrast to Younger's acquiring a past, Odilo loses his past bit by bit as he moves backwards in time. Instead of puzzling over the meaning of events and his own identity as in *And Again?*—is he James Younger or his twin brother, Robert Younger?—in *Time's Arrow* a nameless narrator puzzles over both the movement and nature of time raising questions about his and Odilo's nature and identity. Knowing only duration and mistakenly assuming that Odilo has just begun to live rather than having just died, the nameless narrator continually misreads signs and misinterprets events including such decisive ones as death and birth as well as mistaking essential distinctions, such as backwards and forwards:

> I moved forward, out of the blackest sleep, to find myself
> surrounded by doctors . . . They are life's gatekeepers. . . .
> Time now passed untrackably, for it was given over to
> struggle . . . and the sense of starting out on a terrible
> journey, towards a terrible secret. What did the secret have to
> do with? Him, with him: the worst man in the worst place at
> the worst time. (11-12)

Some of his crucial errors here about time include the use of "forward" to describe backward movement in time, "sleep" to describe death, and "starting out" to describe his end. While he correctly labels the doctors around his deathbed as "life's gatekeepers," the label becomes ironic when a reader recognizes the accompanying misperception of the nature of the gate. Rather than a gate of birth and beginnings, his is a gate of death and endings. All action in *Time's Arrow* takes place within the flow of time. Ironically, Odilo moves through this ceaseless change erroneously assigning events to time-future, time-past, and time-present and crucially doing so without any will of his own, since all events have previously occurred.

The narrator's ignorance of time's direction creates irony in much the same way that Oedipus's ignorance of his past creates irony in *Oedipus Rex*. In Sophocles's play the king laudably tries to rid his land of plague by publicly decreeing banishment for whoever is responsible for it without knowing that person's identity. Later, when he discovers to his horror that the source of the country's illness lies in past events of which he himself was the cause, he is then powerless to change either the events themselves or their cause. Similarly, Odilo in *Time's Arrow* remains condemned to replay his life, for, like Oedipus, it is far too late and now absolutely impossible for him to change any past event. He must, therefore, run backwards on

his timeline until the moment when, as he anticipates,
"[m]y father . . . will come in and kill me with his body" (172).
After that he will divide into sperm and ovum which in turn
will be re-absorbed harmlessly into his parents' bodies. His
awareness of his end—in much the same way as Oedipus's
dawning awareness of the truth—only adds to his torment:
"Odilo knows this that he will perish upon his father entering
his mother and feels this too" (172). Earlier the narrator had
admitted that "[h]e is travelling towards his secret. Parasite or
passenger, I am travelling there with him. It will be bad" (72).

At the beginning of the novel Amis capitalizes on the
comic effects created by treating literally a life being lived
backwards: "it is the garbage people [moving backwards] who
bring me my reading matter" (20). The first human conversation appears in the novel in reverse printing:

> "Dug. Dug," says the lady in the pharmacy.
> "Dug," I join in. "Oo y'rrah?"
> "Aid ut oo y'rrah?"
> "Mh-mm," she'll say, as she unwraps my hair lotion. (14)

Readers will quickly reconstruct the conversation by reversing
the words: as "Dug" which reverses to Gud or good; "Oo
y'rrah?" reverses to harr'y oo or how are you?; and "Aid ut oo
y'rrah?" reverses to Harr'y oo tu dia or How are you today?

Amis does not continue using this reverse spelling—the
joke might quickly wear thin—but still continues to indicate
time's running in reverse by inverting the order of sentences
within each conversation. This technique forces the reader to
participate in this backwards-running world since only by
reconstructing conversations through reversing their order in
time can the reader affirm the normal temporal order. Every
word that Odilo speaks backwards is obviously predetermined

since he has said each one before. But then everything in his world—gesture, emotion, action—is completely and fully determined. "I speak without volition," says the narrator, "in the same way that I do everything else" (14). For humans, as J. T. Fraser maintains, "[e]xpectations, memory and conscious experience—elements of the mental present working together—make us aware that our potentialities are greater than our possibilities. This awareness is manifest in a feeling that has a special name: it is called free will or human freedom" (167). Odilo surrendered his free will; that is, he gave up his human freedom in order to serve evil more fully as a Nazi doctor in the death camps, especially in "fiercely coprocentric" Auschwitz (132).

Erich Kahler argues that those Nazi doctors such as Odilo, "professionally attending to the most gruesome activities, seemed to act only with a certain part of their being, while another part was left behind, remained in the background." He continues noting that this Nazi "split in the personality reaches into unfathomable depths, it is total, it is consummate schizophrenia . . . . The part that commits atrocities seems wholly impersonal and, accordingly, inhuman in the literal sense of the word; indeed, we should rather call it a-human" (*The Tower and the Abyss*).

In *Time's Arrow*, the part "left behind . . . in the background," whether conscience, soul, or animating principle—is continually negated by Odilo's actions. What remained of him was, therefore, reduced over his lifetime to the inhuman or a-human. The kind of negation he practiced involves surrendering human freedom and ultimately all hope. As Dante emphasized in the motto he chose for Hell's gate, "Abandon All Hope / Ye Who Enter Here": those who forfeit all choice and freedom in effect choose Hell—where by definition there can be no further choice because there is no more time, hence there can be no further hope. This utter lack of choice, this lack of possibility once an event or person moves from the present to the past becomes Amis's theme, while his narrative method of moving literally backwards through Odilo's life allows him to "attend to the most gruesome activities" of this "life that is unworthy of life" (Amis 154).

Ivan Karamazov in *The Brothers Karamazov* (1880) confronted a world where "everything is permitted" and recoiled from its implications, for such a world has little room or reason for compassion and mercy. A century or more later Eliot Rosewater in Vonnegut's *Slaughterhouse-Five*, who "found life meaningless, partly because of what [he] . . . had seen in war," remarks to Billy Pilgrim: "everything there was to know about life was in *The Brothers Karamazov* . . . 'But that isn't enough anymore' . . ." (70-71). It is not "enough" not only because the twentieth century witnessed a terrible increase in the scope of violence, but also because of the radical increase in state-sponsored terrorism against individuals and groups. There appears no end to madness on a massive scale from the crude Turkish attempt to starve and slaughter all the Armenians at the beginning of the century—which added the word "genocide" to the languages of the world—through World War I's trench warfare and poison gas and continuing into World War II's enormous incendiary bombing of civilian cities, incredibly efficient death camps, the Stalin purges and murders of 100 million people, the instant death and lingering effects of the atomic bomb down to the carnage in Vietnam, the slaughter on the Highway of Death in the Gulf War, the ethnic cleansing in what used to be Yugoslavia, or the atrocities of ISIS. Sadly, such violence and destruction, although an old story in human history, display the characteristic mark of the twentieth- and now the twenty-first century of exponentially increased size.[19]

Besides the increasing scope and efficiency of destruction, the twentieth century also witnessed increasingly widespread state-sponsored torture that aims "to coerce the personality of the individual into submission, to destroy self-worth" (William James qtd. in Gifford, *Farther Shore* 202).[20] Don Gifford in *The Farther Shore* (1990) epitomizes "the purpose of state

---

19. Contrast, for example, the Somme battlefield, which measured five by twenty-five miles within a four-hundred-and-eighty-five-mile line of siege with the currently projected six-hundred-mile-deep killing zone of a battlefield on which were to be deployed "battlefield nuclear weapons" (defined by the superpowers as those weapons with a maximum range of three hundred miles; see Gifford, *Farther Shore* 241-42 for further details.) In addition, for most of the twentieth and all of the twenty-first century people have had to coexist with weapons of mass destruction in the form of the atom, hydrogen, and more recently the neutron bomb. Vonnegut himself survived one of the more famous examples of massive modern mechanized destruction when as a Prisoner of War in Dresden he escaped immolation while that city was being destroyed. In his novels through *Slaughterhouse-Five*, he explores the survivor's psychological state perhaps best summed up in the question: why, when so many died, was I allowed to survive? His answer differs from novel to novel. Malachi Constant in Vonnegut's *Sirens of Titan* (1959), for instance, discovers: "I was a victim of a series of accidents, as are we all" (229), while the Tralfamadoreans in *Slaughterhouse-Five* inform Billy Pilgrim that they have traversed the universe from one end to the other and only on one planet, Earth, is there any belief in free will. If everything is determined, then no one is responsible for what may or may not happen. "The rain falls on the just and the unjust"—some good survive, some die—from the human point of view, there is no reason for anything: it simply is. For an extended discussion, see Morse, *Imagining* 22-30, 35-56.

20. Compare with Harold Pinter's plays *Mountain Language* (1988) and *One for the Road* (1984) or Csaba Lászlóffy's *The Heretic*; see also Morse, "Ditches."

terrorism" as that which "undermine[s] the personal worth
and self-esteem of entire populations" (202). Under the Nazis
this purpose of "mass dehumanization" was carried out with
inconceivable efficiency using all the resources available to the
modern highly industrialized state, yet with the chilling
anonymity of the equally efficient modern bureaucracy. "The
death camps were designed as great machines" whose object
was to reduce the inmates "to beasts" (202). Gifford quotes
Auschwitz survivor Primo Levi: "The SS Command showed
itself . . . to possess satanic knowledge of human beings"
(*Survival in Auschwitz* [1959] 81; qtd. in Gifford 202). At the
heart of this method was what Levi calls "the sole usefulness of
useless violence" that "before dying the victim must be
degraded so that the murderer will be less burdened by guilt"
(Levi 101).[21] Moreover, as David H. Hirsch maintains in *The
Deconstruction of Literature: Criticism after Auschwitz* (1991),

> The inescapable essence of Nazism lies . . . in its racist
> ideology, which led all too many of the German people to
> believe they were a superrace and the SS to believe they were
> gods . . . who not only enjoy the power to decide who will live
> and who will die, but who can also enjoy toying with their
> victims. (152-53)[22]

It is this set of inhuman values that Amis mirrors when he
uses the Nazi SS as his model for the traditional ruler of
Hell. Customarily, the devil meets people in their own image of
him, like when Young Goodman Brown in Nathaniel

21. The useless violence had the added benefit that should an inmate effect
an unlikely escape any description of such a macabre, perverse
institution would be self-discrediting.

22. The elite SS divisions were famous for their gratuitous violence—the
committing of atrocities—on the battlefield as well as in the death
camps. Nor should it be thought that the SS was made up of ignorant

Hawthorne's well-known story of the same name ventures into the woods around Salem to keep his appointment with the devil and the latter appears to him in a guise resembling his father, or earlier when Faust the novice makes his pact with a monkish Mephistopheles. In *Time's Arrow*, the towering nightmare figure who presides over hell proves a distorted image of Odilo himself clothed in a doctor's "white coat (a medic's stark white smock)," the black jackboots of the SS, "and a certain kind of smile." He "was . . . a male shape, with an entirely unimaginable aura, containing such things as beauty, terror, love, filth, and above all power" (12). Clearly this personage enjoys exercising power, smiles while torturing victims, and is in every way a monstrous perversion of the image of the helpful healer.

For the doctors of the death camps, such as Odilo, human beings were so much garbage to be disposed of during and after diabolical experiments in the ironically named camp "hospitals."[23] It is, therefore, doubly fitting in his time-reversed hellish afterlife that the narrator describes him and his fellow humans as "kings of crap and trash" (51); first, because the traditional image of Hell is a place of fire and brimstone but also filled with excrement—Dante, for example, pictures Hell's

louts. Elie Wiesel in his well-known essay on the death of the Jewish historian Shimon Dubnow, killed by his former student now an SS officer, "discovered that most of the killers of the four Einsatzkommando (killing squads) had college degrees. They had Ph.D. degrees in philosophy and literature, in the sciences. They were doctors. There were two opera singers, and one of them, may God save us all, had a . . . Ph.D. in Divinity" (105). Amis has Odilo in *Time's Arrow* represent those educated doctors who through the use of torture and intimidation became in their own eyes and—all too often—in the eyes of their victims like gods.

23. Dr. Johann Paul Kremer, one of the doctors of the death camps, notes in the diary which he kept during his three-month service at Auschwitz that on 3 October 1942 "I got quite living-fresh material of human liver,

inhabitants as not only existing in utter darkness but as themselves being only so much cosmic waste or garbage—and second, the death camps, as described by most commentators, were "deliberately organized to become monuments to filth and excrement" (Hirsch 152).[24]

Amis confronts this horror of the a-human in *Time's Arrow* through his reversed-time world perspective that also yields irony and bitter comedy:

> [People] say hello when they mean goodbye. Lords of lies and trash—all kings of crap and trash. Signs say No Littering—but who to? . . . Government does that, at night, with trucks; or uniformed men come sadly at morning with their trolleys, dispensing our rubbish, and shit for the dogs. (51)[25]

---

spleen, and pancreas . . . ." which came, of course, from newly executed prisoners injected with phenol (qtd. in Hirsch 159). He makes no comment on the human beings which supplied his "living-fresh material" at the cost of their lives. Similarly, on 23 September 1942, he witnessed the gassing of two transports full of prisoners, then went on to describe "the evening supper . . . a truly festive meal. We had baked pike, as much of it as we wanted, real coffee, excellent beer and sandwiches" (Hirsch 148-49). One might imagine he had spent the afternoon at a sporting event or in the theatre rather than witnessing the deaths of hundreds of his fellow human beings.

24. Hirsch cites as his source Terrence Des Pres's brilliant chapter "The Excremental Assault" in *The Survivor: An Anatomy of Life in the Death Camps* (New York: Oxford University Press, 1976).

25. "Lords of lies and trash" is a variant on the traditional title and picture of Satan as "Lord of Lies," whom Dante pictures as trapped at the bottom of Hell in the frozen cesspool formed by all the rivers of the world dumping their sewage (that is, their excrement and trash) down into Hell.

That telling detail of "shit for the dogs" convinces the reader of the verisimilitude of Amis's fictional reality much as the incident in which

Everything of worth in Odilo's world, "[a]ll sustenance, all meaning (and a good deal of money) issues [most appropriately] from a single household appliance: the toilet handle" (18). He asks rhetorically: "Where would Tod [one of Odilo's several false identities] and I be without the toilet? Where would we be without trash?" (40). The fullest irony is, however, reserved for the worst events, now seen reversed in time, such as the "new smell in the air. The sweet smell [of the crematoria]" (127). After observing "the evening sky, hellish red with the gathering souls" (128), Odilo then begins the proud process of creation:

> It was I, Odilo Unverdorben, who personally removed the pellets of Zyklon B and entrusted them to the pharmacist in his white coat. . . . Entirely intelligibly, though, to prevent needless suffering, the dental work was usually completed while the patients were not yet alive. (129)

So proud of his good work Odilo stresses his pure, even disinterested, motivation: "I am not 'in it' for gratitude. No. I am 'in it' . . . because I love the human body and all living things." This is his "war on death that now comes in many forms" (144). His acts in combating death take many substantial forms: "I now extract benzene, gasoline, kerosene and air. . . . Twenty cubic centimetres of air . . . with a hypodermic almost the size of a trombone and my right foot firmly stamped on the patient's chest, I continue to prosecute the war against nothing and air" (145). His is truly, if ironically, "creation" ex nihilo: out of the nothing but trash, excrement, and ashes.

Bereft of choice, a king of crap flung backwards through time, Odilo himself in his torment will experience the

Daniel Defoe's Robinson Crusoe, walking on the deserted beach after the storm that shipwrecked him, finds "two shoes that were not fellows," a detail that instantly establishes the reliability of Crusoe's world.

privative nature of evil as he arrives at his early months where he will enter the infant's world where before-and-after relations have no meaning. Samuel Beckett in *Act Without Words I* (1957) portrays humanity flung backwards almost at random into chaotic experience from which no reflection will yield knowledge reliable enough to become a basis for action (see chapter 4). Yet underlying even Beckett's graphic picture of human frustration at trying to make some order out of seemingly arbitrary random events is the minimal assumption of "before-and-after" in time without which neither knowledge nor freedom becomes possible. But as Odilo moves literally and physically from "after" to "before," his knowledge together with his memories are erased serially along with that much consciousness—exactly the reverse process of Younger in O'Faolain's *And Again?*

Deprived of any future time during his hellish trip to nonexistence Odilo exhibits neither understanding nor awareness of possibility. The soul's futile attempts to make sense out of this experience fail because without the crucial knowledge that time is running in reverse all of its theories, as is also true of all of its perceptions, prove incorrect except the final one achieved in the very last painful moment of existence:

> Look! Beyond, before the slope of pine, the lady archers are gathering with their targets and bows. Above, a failing-vision kind of light, with the sky fighting down its nausea. Its many nuances of nausea. When Odilo closes his eyes I see an arrow fly—but wrongly. Point-first. (173)

Intuitively, the soul realizes the implications of this wrong-headed arrow—the arrow of time of the book's title: "Oh no," he says, "but then . . ." (173). And the unfinished sentence says it all: Odilo's closed eyes and contentless dreams indicate how close he is to obliteration.[26] This final revelation is specific about the direction of time's arrow, but it is not the first or only revelation. In the final weeks of Odilo's life, the narrator attempts to understand what happened but finds only many unanswered questions "of time: certain durations" (172). The narrator—this "passenger or parasite" (16), this conscience or soul, this spirit or essence, this "I within" (173)—realizes at last the awful truth: "I within, who came at the wrong time—either too soon [if life is lived backwards], or after it was all too late [if life is lived forwards]" (173). Thus at the end of the novel all illusions of benevolent good will shatter violently upon the soul's apprehension of the true direction of time's arrow. The truth about the direction of time and time's truth about Odilo's life also dissolve the dramatic tension between the soul—which Odilo long ago jettisoned—and its longing for redemption and the person actively choosing moral ruin.

Novelist Stephen Donaldson contends that "it is the responsibility of every human being to create the meaning of his/her life," and the action of *Time's Arrow* implies that the large choices for such meaning will be either "redemptive [or] . . . ruinous." The parasitic soul might still wish for redemption, but Odilo chose ruin for them both. Like virtually all of the Nazi death camp doctors and guards Odilo was as impotent morally and spiritually as he was impotent sexually.[27] He traded

---

26. There were also hints earlier in paintings he observed in the Metropolitan Museum of Art in New York (Amis, *Time's Arrow* 95).

27. Amis drew heavily upon Robert Jay Lifton's *The Nazi Doctors: Medical Killing and the Psychology of Genocide* (1986): "My novel would not and could not have been written without it. Probably the same applies to the works of Primo Levi . . ." (Amis, *Time's Arrow* 175). The subtitle of *Time's Arrow*—"or The Nature of the Offense"—acknowledges the debt to Levi, who titles the second chapter of *The Drowned and the Saved* "The Memory of the Offense" (11).

his personal potency for omnipotence over others—"I am omnipotent. Also impotent. I am powerful and powerless," he boasts and laments in the same breath (148). Rather than inviting his soul to travel the road with him, he discarded it. Only at death did the forgotten soul appear flung back out of "the blackest sleep," forced to re-enter the corpse, to re-animate it until both could be safely dissolved into sperm and egg. Snapped backwards through his own life Odilo must undo each horrible act reaching at last the moment everything ends, for when he arrives at his beginning (conception) that proves to be his dissolution (extinction).

Amis says he borrowed this reverse movement for his plot from the incident in *Slaughterhouse-Five*, where Billy Pilgrim watches films backwards of World War II bombing raids over Germany (175). Each film ends happily with all the fire and destruction safely packed up into the bombs which then disappear into the bellies of planes and are subsequently returned first to factories to be taken apart and their components then disposed of harmlessly in the earth (Vonnegut, *Slaughterhouse-Five* 54-55). In his short story "Bujak and the Strong Force" (*Einstein's Monsters* 1987), Amis first employed a narrator who speculated, in ways predictive of the narration in *Time's Arrow*, on what it might be like to experience time backwards:

> Bujak was an Oscillationist, claiming that the Big Bang will forever alternate with the Big Crunch, that the universe would expand only until unanimous gravity called it back to start again. At that moment, with the cosmos turning on its hinges, light would begin to travel backward, received by the stars and pouring from our human eyes. If . . . time would also be reversed, as Bujak maintained (will we move

backward too? Will we have any say in things?) . . . ("Bujak" 58-59)

The story ends with a vision of the character going backwards in time until "big Bujak shrinks, becoming the weakest thing there is, helpless, indefensible, naked, weeping, blind and tiny, and folding into Roza [his mother]" (59). These striking images of characters backing their way through time and the hero progressively shrinking as he becomes once more a child until absorbed into his mother all reappear in *Time's Arrow*.

Unlike Vonnegut in *Slaughterhouse-Five*, Amis directs the focus of his novel not upon the innocence of those who suffer, but upon the diabolical psychology of those sworn to heal who volunteer as SS to torture and destroy systematically in clear violation of their Hippocratic oath,[28] their common humanity—which they then will forfeit—and any least dedication to the healing arts. The atrocities committed by these Nazi doctors of the death camps of which Odilo is the example are so mind-numbing, so brutally inhuman, as to appear almost beyond the reach of imaginative representation "in either consciousness or discourse" (White 57). As Hirsch summarizes:

---

28. "I swear by Apollo Physician, by Health, by Panacea, . . . I will keep pure and holy both my life and my art. In whatsoever houses I enter, I will enter to help the sick, and I will abstain from all intentional wrongdoing and harm . . ." (qtd. in Amis 32). For whatever reason Amis does not quote an equally if not more relevant section of the oath: "The regimen I adopt shall be for the benefit of my patients, according to my ability and judgment, and not for their hurt or for any wrong. I will give no deadly drug to any, though it be asked of me, nor will I counsel such" (qtd. in Vonnegut, *Fates Worse than Death* 120). Vonnegut speculating on the doctors of the death camp asks: "And why has the late Josef Mengele become the most monstrous of all the Nazis, in the opinion of most of us? He was a doctor, and he gleefully violated his Hippocratic Oath" (119-20).

The futility of all attempts at [such] representation was encapsulated in Theodor Adorno's famous dictum (which he later recanted), that it is not possible to write poetry after Auschwitz. Basically, Adorno raises the issue that any literary representation of Nazi atrocities would aestheticize, and thus make acceptable, the horrors and cruelty. (158)[29]

Amis's solution to this problem lies in following Vonnegut's model of the "harmless" bombs which suck up fire and so by inventing a fictional life lived in reversed time he creates in turn the almost diabolical illusion of a death camp doctor accomplishing good works. Odilo, for example, removes gas pellets from the death camp showers rendering them harmless before returning them to the camp pharmacy. His culminating act is when he "knock[s] together a human being out of the unlikeliest odds and ends" (142), or most spectacular of all he "make[s] a people from the weather. From thunder and from lightning. With gas, with electricity, with shit, with fire" (128). Readers encountering such images but knowing however dimly or in whatever repressed fashion something of the historical truth, must then actively and painfully reverse them. By so involving the reader Amis insures that far from anesthetizing such atrocities or providing aesthetic pleasure from the misery

29. Adorno actually spoke of lyric poetry rather than poetry in general. Later he added:

> I have no wish to soften the saying that to write lyric poetry after Auschwitz is barbaric; it expresses in negative form the impulse which inspires committed literature. The questions asked by a character in Sartre's play *Morts Sans Sépulture*, "Is there any meaning in life when men exist who beat people until the bones break in their bodies?" is also the question whether any art now has a right to exist; whether intellectual regression is not inherent in the concept of committed literature because of the regression of society . . . . (95)

and pain of the victims as Adorno feared,[30] this process renders them part of the reader's immediate experience in their time-present since in re-reversing time as read a reader must impel time forward towards the full banality of its horror, since of all the potentialities which become possibilities only one will be actualized. Thus a horrific post-historical reality is brought back to consciousness in time-present through imagination.

Amis achieves in *Time's Arrow* exactly what Adorno despaired of poetry or any imaginative literature accomplishing, for as the reader goes through the novel, inevitably, inexorably, the full awful truth of this evil with its attendant horrors and cruelty strikes home. Far from being "the native medium of evil . . . [which] obscures things" (Grudin 82), time in Amis's novel serves to unmask evil.[31] The reader is left confronting the debris of the past in the mud mixed with the ashes of the dead. One of the most moving moments in television history occurred when decades after the discovery of the death camps Jacob Bronowski waded into the shallow waters around Auschwitz, scooped up handfuls of mud and water from the ash-clogged swamp, and holding them

---

30. Adorno rightly objected to

> victims [being]. . . used to create something, works of art, that are thrown to the consumption of a world which destroyed them. The so-called artistic representation of the sheer physical pain of people beaten to the ground by rifle-butts contains, however remotely, the power to elicit enjoyment out of it. The moral of this art, not to forget for a single instant, slithers into the abyss of the opposite. (96)

Diving head-long into that abyss, however, is an advertised discussion "Humor and the Holocaust" at an international scholarly conference held in the late twentieth century.

31. "The fourth dimension is the native medium of evil. Villains traditionally love the night because it obscures their deeds; but no darkness obscures things as effectively as time" (Grudin 82).

dripping before the camera exclaimed that here are all that remains of thousands of victims of this death camp. (Odilo reverses this image creating humans out of these ashes.) The ashes themselves serve not only as a reminder of the atrocities, but also become symbolic of the huge technological problem facing the Nazis of how to make those the Third Reich considered defective or alien disappear completely leaving behind no trace whatsoever. All that advanced technology, industry, and thought lies defeated in this image of a small barefoot man with his pants rolled up to his knees scooping handfuls of ashes and mud and water to show on camera, thereby forcing the memory of the victims onto center stage in the world of the present and thus bringing about exactly the opposite of what the Nazis hoped to accomplish (Gifford, Conversation 6 Oct. 1992; Debrecen, Hungary). This ironical situation might well be embodied in Walter Benjamin's startling image of the angel of history, whose

> face is turned toward the past. Where we perceive a chain of events, he sees one single catastrophe which keeps piling wreckage upon wreckage and hurls it in front of his feet. The angel would like to stay, awaken the dead, and make whole what has been smashed. But a storm is blowing from Paradise; it has got caught in his wings with such violence that the angel can no longer close them. This storm irresistibly propels him into the future to which his back is turned, while the pile of debris before him grows skyward. (258)

As this angel of history hurtles into the unknown, the pile of debris rising ever higher, Odilo himself hurtles toward oblivion.

Each of these works of imaginative literature from Ford, Twain, and Stoker through Wilder and O'Faolain to Vonnegut and Amis reflects the deeply felt human wish to overcome time, to do the impossible and step into the same river twice, to come unstuck from the lifetime-line, to revisit the past, to relive life all over again—"be again . . . All that old misery" (Beckett, *Krapp's Last Tape* 223)—in short: to "re-commence" for some time in some way. They also contain a warning against the fulfillment of this wish, for as Robert Younger finds initially to his sorrow in *And Again?*, Emily learns to her mild regret in *Our Town*, and the parasite with Odilo discovers to his horror in *Time's Arrow*, "Nobody can live the same life all over again unless the same world lives it with him" (O'Faolain 34).

But people do try. Ralph Waldo Emerson, for example, thought that he could store up memories against a future time when his inspiration might dry up. Yet, years later when he attempted to draw upon those memories, nothing happened. Late in life Emerson replicated the conditions as exactly as he could of the event that changed his life forever: the moment of his great inspiration and insight that led to his writing what many scholars assess as the greatest American essay, "On Nature." (1836) But instead of acquiring new power and inspiration, he discovered only Jay Gatsby's truism, "you can't repeat the past" (Fitzgerald 106).

Besides confirming the irreparability of time-past, each of these works of literature also testifies to the importance of keeping that past in the present through memory. Heraclitus himself, after asserting that "you cannot enter the same river twice,"[32] went on to declare that "the way up and the way down

---

32. Jorge Luis Borges notes the complexity of Heraclitus's metaphor: "every time I remember the ninety-first fragment of Heraclitus 'You shall not go down twice to the same river,' I admire its dialectical dexterity, because the ease with which we accept the first meaning ('The river is different') clandestinely imposes upon us the second ('I am different') and grants us the illusion of having invented it . . ." ("A New Refutation of Time" 259).

are one and the same." Memory, like events, always exists in the present tense, which leads Hayden White, as already mentioned, rightly to conclude that both in consciousness and in discourse humans must represent the past "in an 'imaginary' way." Prevented by the gods from remembering his past, Robert Younger sets out whether knowingly or not to reacquire his boyhood, childhood, and infant memories, while Odilo, who escaped punishment by denying and hiding his Nazi past, appropriately loses all his memories as his very lifeline in time itself is erased. In contrast, Emerson could begin his famous oration "The American Scholar" (1837) by greeting his Harvard audience "on the re-commencement of our literary year" precisely because he and they in the very moment of welcoming the beginning of a new academic year remembered and re-remembered the commencements of past years, thus bringing those memories into time-present (53). In other words: they made the past part of their present by presenting past "commencement[s] of . . . [their] literary year"; that is, by bringing them into the present. As St. Augustine so wisely observed, "the present of things past is in memory." While it is true that neither in fiction nor in history—much less in life or in memory—can we step into the same river twice, yet literature and history enable us to travel down that river of time as we recall "events, processes, structures . . . considered no longer perceivable" and thus bring them into the present "either in consciousness or discourse . . . in an 'imaginary' way" (Hayden White 57). This making the past present through memory becomes a quintessential human activity as will be explored in more depth in chapter 5, "Time, Memory, and Dementia."

Chapter 3
Two Time Fallacies:
Apocalypse Now and Progressing in Time

Is the End near?
——Brian Greene

Children on a family trip very often ask their parents, "Are we there yet?" Another more general yet related question that they and many of us also ask frequently, "Will we ever come to the end of time?" Or, "does time have an end?" "How and when will time end?" Questions few of us are prepared to answer. Such questions also puzzle the majority of time scholars, such as J. T. Fraser, who during a productive lifetime spent studying and thinking about time concluded that "[t]he riddle of time is as much a riddle of its ending as it is one of its beginning" (*Time, Passion, and Knowledge* 170). Yet many Americans believe they have solved the riddle of time and tell us that everything including all time will end on or before the year 2050. Such beliefs are not new but are a staple in the United States.

Back in the seventeenth century Michael Wigglesworth wrote America's first "best seller," an account of the last days of Earth called *The Day of Doom* (1662). A Pew Research Center national poll from 2010 found this notion of a Dooms Day bringing an end to all time remains popular with about 41% of Americans generally and 58% of white evangelical Christians specifically, who say they believe that Jesus will reappear by the year 2050 bringing with him an end to all time (Torres). Such large numbers may very well increase in the decades ahead as that assumed end time of 2050 approaches as has happened in the past with other similar predictions, such as 2000 as well as 2001. Such beliefs on the end of time helped propel various individual books of the "Left Behind" series of sixteen apocalyptic novels published between 1995 and 2007 onto the *New York Times, USA Today*, and *Publishers Weekly*'s Best Seller lists where one or another of them stayed for well over a decade, resulting in more than seventy million copies in print. Written by Jerry B. Jenkins and Tim LaHaye—one of the most successful popular writing teams of modern times— the novels are based upon a non-biblical, but in the United States widely-held, belief in the apocalyptic notion that we are living in the "Last Days" when time will come to an end and the saved will be taken up into heaven in "The Rapture."[1] This notion of "The Rapture" was brought originally to the United States by an Irishman, John Nelson Darby, in the early nineteenth century and quickly spread "through the ministry of Dwight Moody and the efficient distribution network created by the Moody Bible Institute" (Taylor 275). Based on this belief the "Left Behind" series introduces the reader in the first novel to the sudden end of the world as we know it and with it the abrupt end of time as we know it. At that "time" at the End of Time, when the saved are suddenly taken up into heaven, those unfortunates "left behind" undergo a thousand years of Tribulation becoming, in novel after novel, characters who play out Jenkins and LaHaye's literal reading of the biblical books of Revelation, Daniel, Isaiah, and Ezekiel.

---

1. "A nation whose quasi-official high priest is the reverend Billy Graham, author of *Approaching Hoofbeats: The Four Horsemen of the Apocalypse*, is rather clearly more likely than most other countries to have strong intimations of the Millennium" (Bloom, *Omens* 13). I have not studied the whole series of the "Left Behind" novels in any great detail, but the triumphal tone of the volumes I did peruse appeared directed against scientists in particular and all those others who refused to take the Rapture seriously and, therefore, could not imagine all the fantastic things that would happen—that is, become consensus reality (see note 3)—when the world and time ended with the Second Coming.

Besides reflecting this American belief in the Apocalypse,[2] the series also plays to the enjoyment many Americans derive from reading about or watching vivid scenes of mass destruction and extensive bloody battles as everyone left behind after the Rapture is doomed to die and usually doomed to die a violent death.

The belief in an immediate End of Time, that is, Apocalypse as an impending reality—rather than as the subject of religious fantasy novels—has more than once defined consensus reality in the United States.[3] Throughout the early nineteenth century, for instance, "reality" in the popular imagination became for many a joining of the widespread belief in Apocalypse with an increasing belief generally in human progress. Progress appeared obvious given that century's unprecedented fast-paced technological innovation and change that occurred in the wake of the eighteenth century's more fundamental changes.[4] In the nineteenth century, sitting in the British Museum Karl Marx formulated his Christian heresy of unlimited progress for the masses, while in Paris, historian, statesman, and politician François Gizot "drew vast audiences to his masterly lectures on the

---

2. *Apocalypse*, a Greek word for revelation or unveiling, derives from the Book of Revelation (the last book in the Christian biblical canon).

3. There are many definitions of the fantastic, but most rely on a contrast between our notions of how and where reality relates to the fantastic. Kathryn Hume, for instance, describes the fantastic as "the deliberate departure from the limits of what is usually accepted as real and normal" (xii) and goes on to define fantasy as "*any departure from consensus reality*" (21).

4. These fundamental changes included the disquieting scientific discoveries of "deep time" and natural selection that altered forever humanity's view of time, this world, and humanity's place in both. (Discussed at length later in this chapter.)

history of Europe in which he argued that the fundamental idea embedded in the word 'civilization' is progress" (Whitrow 177). The books and lectures of nineteenth-century British historians in general, from Edward Gibbon at the beginning of the century to the Edwardians, such as William Gordon Holmes, at the end, reflected their passionate commitment to recording human progress, English supremacy, and the positive goodness of science.[5] E. B. Taylor, the Oxford anthropologist, argued in 1871 "that the history of man, as revealed by a study of the implements he has used, is indubitably 'the history of an upward development'" (qtd. in Whitrow 178).

The nineteenth-century missionary movement sent out men and women from England and the United States to save the souls of those dwelling in the dark of Africa, South America, and Asia. A member of one of the less fortunate races would, thanks to their efforts, be able to eat with knife and fork and "sit one day, his hair cut, washed, smoothed with macassar oil, in a huge armchair reading a paper" (Wertenbaker 30). Herbert Spencer summed up much of the current thinking in his highly influential, timely essay "Universal Progress, Its Laws and Cause."[6] But it was Alfred Lord Tennyson, the poet

---

5. "This uniquely and distinctively Lamarckian style of human cultural inheritance gives our technological history a directional and cumulative character that no natural Darwinian evolution can possess" (Gould, *Full House* 222). Holmes's linear model of history supported his belief in "the ultimate culmination of Greece and Rome in resistance to the barbarian hordes from the East, and the birth of the British Empire" (Hart 21).

6. "Spencer arrived at his concept of evolution as the trend towards increasing differentiation coupled with integration by giving greatest generality to the idea of progress as the product of advancing division of labor . . ." (Andreski 8n1). But Spencer's definition of the evolutionary process appears more applicable to human society than it does to the flora and fauna of nature.

laureate, who best caught the temper of the times in his popular poem "Locksley Hall" (1835):

> Not in vain the distance beacons. Forward, forward let
> us range.
> Let the great world spin for ever down the ringing
> grooves of change.
> Thro' the shadow of the globe we sweep into the
> younger day;
> Better fifty years of Europe than a cycle of Cathay.
> (181-84)

In contrast, Henry David Thoreau, Ralph Waldo Emerson, and Emily Dickinson, among others, distrusted this adulation of progress believing that at its best it was a mere will of the wisp. "Society never advances," pronounced Emerson in "Self-Reliance" (279), and Thoreau agreed (see the latter part of this chapter). Emily Dickinson also vigorously dissented from the proposition that humanity was enjoying a "younger day." In her vision of the world, God approves of the death and destruction that she saw all around her from the cemetery behind the house where she lived to the robin eating the worm on the front walk and the frost killing the early spring flowers:

> A Bird came down the Walk—
> He did not know I saw—
> He bit an Angleworm in halves
> And ate the fellow, raw . . . (328)

> Apparently with no Surprise
> To any happy Flower
> The Frost beheads it at its play—
> In accidental power—
> The blonde Assassin passes on—

> The Sun proceeds unmoved
> To measure off another Day
> For an Approving God— (1624)[7]

But rather than sharing Dickinson's vision of omnipresent death, American millenarians saw the then-current technological progress as evidence that time's arrow—along with all the humans perched on it—was heading straight for the Heavenly City. And, even more important, they believed that time's arrow in following such a progressive, essentially straight line upward also meant that that line could and must have a stop in apocalypse. As the historian of time G. J. Whitrow observes: "Time for Christians began with the Creation and would end with Christ's Second Coming. World history was bounded by these two events. . . . our modern concept of history, however rationalized and secularized it may be, still rests on the concept of historical time which [he claims] was inaugurated by Christianity" (65). Many historians of religion and many contemporary theologians would disagree with Whitrow, however, noting that the idea of historical time begins not with the advent of Christianity but with Judaism's far older belief in "saving history" (see chapter 4, "The Fullness of Time"), to which Christianity added a center point with the birth of Jesus. Nevertheless Whitrow's contention (as modified) is correct that "our modern concept of history . . . rests on the concept of historical time . . . [taken over from Judaism] by Christianity" (65).

---

7. Robert Frost continues this attack on cosmic order in "Design"—a poem very much in the spirit of Dickinson's "Apparently with No Surprise" discussed later on.

Apocalypse as an End of Time

Apocalypse or the End of Time requires, by definition, that time be viewed as finite, linear, and directional. If time were to continue into infinity as contemporary physics has uncovered evidence that it well might (see the introduction)— then there could be no Last Things, no Last Judgment, obviously, no End of the World, and certainly no "Rapture." To be credible, therefore, Apocalypse depends first, upon time being finite and second, upon time being linear rather than an unending circle, spiral, or whatever.[8] Time's arrow thus becomes a string of unique events between two fixed points of creation as the beginning and *eschaton* (from the Greek, *askhaton*, "the final event") as the termination or, in Jenkins and LaHaye's formulation, the thousand-year post-historic era before the Last Judgment. However defined time must finally proceed in the direction of this Final Judgment.

This last requirement of directionality derives from the belief that the Other World or the After Life will occur only with the *eschaton* rather than being always present. There is, therefore, a necessary and important difference between a pre- or non-apocalyptic notion of the Other World as a *place* with time as continuous and the apocalyptic notion of the Other World not as a place but as a *time to come*; that is, a time that comes into existence only at the end-stopped line of current time. Contrast, for example, the non-apocalyptic Other World

---

8. Once an End to Time is granted, once a Last Day is accepted, Apocalypse becomes possible. And once Apocalypse becomes possible, it is but a short step to predicting when it will occur and from there but another short step to the rise of millenarianism. A striking exception to the linearity of most apocalyptic thinking is Bishop Thomas Burnett, who postulated time as circular beginning with the Creation and returning via the Eschaton. See *Sacred Theory of the Earth* (1680), the frontispiece of which Gould analyses in some detail in *Time's Arrow* (see especially 20-59).

as seen in Dante's *Commedia* (ca. 1308) with the apocalyptic one pictured in Michelangelo's Sistine Chapel: In Dante's vision, as people die, they enter serially the Inferno (Hell), Purgatory or Paradise, much as they entered the Underworld as soon as they died in Greek and Egyptian mythology. There is no waiting. For Dante in his vision, Apocalypse becomes impossible—let alone predictable—since although the dead are judged in the Other World, that judgment is rendered continuously in time. Since individuals enter one-by-one when they die, the Other World is simply a place.[9] In Michelangelo's fresco, on the other hand, all the dead from all of time are summoned to appear before the throne of God on one future Day of Judgment and then *and only then* does time come to an end. This Last Judgment thus makes the Other World a *time*, an era, which all individuals experience simultaneously, a "Divine Event to which all Nature moves." The doctrine of the Last Judgment is, therefore, the doctrine of Apocalypse (see Burkitt 2).

Reinhold Niebuhr in *The Nature and Destiny of Man* (1964) discusses the differences between those cultures and societies that expect a Messiah and those that do not (see especially volume 1). A similar distinction might be drawn between those apocalyptic societies and cultures that expect a Last Judgment—often within the believer's lifetime—and those non-apocalyptic societies that do not. Irish culture, for example, does not expect a Last Judgment being firmly rooted in a view of the Other World as a place similar to Dante's that everyone

---

9. The continuous movement of the dead to the Other World provides a staple of literature from Homer to the present. See, for example, Tom Stoppard, *The Invention of Love* (1998) and Michael Frayne, *Copenhagen* (1998). The latter is discussed in detail by Nicholas Ruddick in "The Search for Quantum Ethics: Michael Frayne's *Copenhagen* and Other Recent British Science Plays," *Hungarian Journal of English and American Studies* (2001); see especially 120-21, 129-32.

enters serially upon death. But, that sizable portion of the United States that shares the apocalyptic belief in the Other World as occurring only at the End of Time clearly does expect such a Last Day of Judgment.

Believers in the coming reality of Apocalypse, whenever it is predicted to occur, exhibit total devotion to this idea. "The emotional effect of apocalyptic writing is that everything is subordinated to the announcement of the End. Everything leads up to the Judgment and to the New Age that follows it" (Burkitt 47). From this belief, it is but a short yet necessary step to proselytizing: "the Apocalyptist's part is to stimulate his comrades by sketches of the future" (Burkitt 48). Beginning in the early nineteenth century and continuing today in the twenty-first century the United States has echoed and re-echoed with exhortations from one or another apocalyptic or millennial group to their fellow citizens to turn and follow their leader before it is too late. (See, for example, the green bus that circulated throughout New York City in 2011 warning people by way of its large signs painted on both its sides proclaiming "Judgment Day, May 21, 2011.") Historically, as Harold Bloom notes, "[a] radical alternation of American religion commenced with the start of the nineteenth century . . . . Enormous frontier revivals surged on into the cities, and premillennialism accompanied the revivals" (*Omens* 223). One of the most famous of the nineteenth-century millennial movements, the one that had the longest-lasting consequences, occurred immediately before the Civil War. The apocalyptic preaching of William Miller of New York state became the basis for a widespread, popular nineteenth-century religious revival movement throughout the Northeastern United States and the Midwest, which later also swept through part of England. "The estimated number of Millerites has varied from

10,000 to over one million. . . . Millerism was a mass movement" (Rowe 2). Miller, a devoted student of the bible, himself concluded that the world would end "on or about" 1843. He based his predictions on carefully worked out, mathematically exact charts. Equating the Earth with the universe and reading the myths and stories in Genesis as literally true, Miller then added a symbolic reading of what he termed the "prophetic" biblical books. A day mentioned in one of the "prophetic" books, for example, was read as a year of current Earth time.

In making such elaborate calculations, Miller was following the well-tried method of several prophetic predecessors. The most famous, Dublin-born James Ussher, who became Archbishop of Armagh in the Church of Ireland, had gone through much the same process in Ireland in the seventeenth century.[10] Ussher's predictions were destined to become almost synonymous with Apocalypse and millennialism well into the twenty-first century. He described his method employed in arriving at his conclusions in *Annals of the Old Testament* (1650) as "translating the myth/metaphor of the creation into the literal realm of calendar and clock time" (Gifford, *Farther Shore* 72). In 1611 Ussher calculated that creation occurred "on the beginning of the night which preceded the 23rd day of October, in the year 4004 B.C." and that the end of the world would occur exactly six thousand years later precisely at noon on a Thursday in October 1997— most probably on 23 October 1997 (Davies, *About Time* 126).[11]

---

10. The Church of Ireland was the surrogate for the Church of England in Ireland.

11. In 1925 at the famous "Monkey Trial" in Dalton, Tennessee when "Bishop Ussher was quoted placing creation, with lunatic precision, at '9 a.m., on October 23, 4004 B.C.' some audience wag . . . shouted out,

Although Ussher's was only one among many such calculations, it became the most famous and one of the most
notorious because, like Miller's, it was also one of the most
exact. In giving a definite date—though one far in the future—
Ussher, like Miller two centuries later, left himself open to
ridicule by those who did not sympathize with his dire
warnings. Since Ussher's end date lay almost three and a half
centuries in the future, it had all of the advantages but none of
the disadvantages of being precise. It was obviously neither
demonstrable nor provable. In contrast, Miller's date for the
end of the world in 1843 lay well within his life expectancy and
that of most of his followers. "I found," he wrote later in his
three-volume *Works*, "in going through the Bible, the end of all
things was clearly and emphatically predicted, both as to time
and manner. I believed; and immediately the duty to publish
this doctrine . . . was impressed upon my mind" (1.12 qtd. in
Rowe 21). So he began to preach that the world would end "on
or before" 1843. But even that prediction was not specific
enough for his audiences. Only when an exact date was agreed
upon did Miller gain an extensive following and only then did
his movement acquire real authority.

As several historians of Millerism have noted, "the power
of the Millerite message increased in tandem with its
immediacy. The promise and threat of meeting the Lord at any
moment brought audiences to a pitch of excitement. . . . The
result was the astounding impact of his preaching that has led
historians to consider the great revival of 1843-1844 as

'eastern standard time!'" (O'Malley 305). (This end time of 23 October
takes into account all of the many calendar changes through the
centuries and several other problems helpfully outlined by Stephen Jay
Gould in "Today is the Day" published in the *New York Times* precisely
on that Last Day, 23 October 1997.)

essentially inspired by Millerism" (Doan 122). Cries of "1843! 1843!" echoed from Miller's great revival tent. "For most Millerites, mention of 1843 served as a reminder of a supernatural order so real as to be almost palpably, physically present" (Doan 123). Some well-to-do farmers sold or gave away their farms, their clothes, and other possessions; others did not plant crops because the end was so immediately at hand. But 1843 came and went without incident. The faithful had once again to endure yet another disappointment. In a state of shock, they returned to their homes and communities and painfully re-began their lives. They had expected the Second Coming in 1844 but would receive instead the American Civil War.

Ironically, the widespread acceptance of Miller's prophecy of the end of all time coincided with two of the most extraordinary scientific discoveries about the extent and nature of time. Both would undermine completely the very possibility of Apocalypse—except for fantastic fiction and popular belief. James Hutton and Charles Darwin discovered that time, far from being a finite arrow pointing towards The End, was potentially infinite and virtually without direction pointing towards nothing but an indefinite future. The geologist's discovery of "deep time" extended the life of the universe from thousands past millions into billions of years.

> Time which measures everything in our idea [wrote Hutton], and is often deficient to our schemes, is to nature endless and as nothing; it cannot limit that by which alone it had existence; and as the natural course of time, which to us seems infinite, cannot be bounded by any operation that may have an end. (Hutton, *Theory of the Earth*, vol. 1, 15; qtd. in Mitchison 9)

Charles Lyell in his highly influential *Principles of Geology* (1830) linked Hutton's discovery at the end of the eighteenth century to Newton's discovery decades earlier of the immensity of space: "Worlds are seen beyond worlds immeasurably distant from each other and beyond them all innumerable other systems are faintly traced on the confines of the visible universe" (qtd. in Gould, *Arrow* 2). Together Lyell and Hutton forced a confrontation with the concept of deep time. A concept so alien to human experience that it was not until well into the nineteenth century that it became generally accepted in the scientific community. Moreover, most people even today appear unable to comprehend this concept except through metaphor. Stephen Jay Gould suggests that "John McPhee has provided the most striking metaphor of all (in *Basin and Range* [1980]): Consider the earth's history as the old measure of the English yard, the distance from the king's nose to the tip of his outstretched hand. One stroke of a nail file on his middle finger erases human history" (*Arrow* 3).

A second ontological shock occurred with Darwin's discovery and publication of the principle of natural selection. Darwin's idea that local adaptation could, over time, lead to the creation of an entirely new species came into conflict with received wisdom, which often meant simple biblical literalism. All species were accounted for in Noah's Ark, according to the literalists. God had not created anything new since the time described in Genesis.[12] Darwin's local adaptation—he studiously avoided using the word "evolution" until forced to do so by Herbert Spencer's popularization—vastly increased the world's time by postulating continuous creation over eons.

---

12. The most dramatic challenge to this belief probably occurred with the mid-nineteenth-century discovery of dinosaur fossils, since these giant creatures were far larger than any ark.

These seismic shocks to popular, received wisdom and belief proved exhilarating to the scientific community. Gould reflects on the unique importance and excitement of Darwin's discovery, for example, when he poignantly exclaims, "no one will ever again experience the ultimate intellectual high of reconstructing all nature with the passkey of evolution—a privilege accorded to Charles Darwin, and now closed to us" (*Full House* 224-25).

But not everyone so reveled in these discoveries. Barely had the nineteenth century ended and a new century dawned when George McCready Price, refusing to accept either the concept of deep time or the concept of natural selection over time, originated "the pseudoscience known to its adherents by the oxymoron 'scientific creationism.' . . . Price wished to affirm biblical literalism by an inductive approach based strictly on fieldwork" (Gould, *Arrow* 23). His book, *The New Geology* (1923), remains a forceful reaction against this new knowledge of endless time with its clear implication that humans were no longer at the pinnacle of creation but were instead a local response to local conditions—conditions created over billions and billions of years. Still in print today, Price's book is regularly cited during debates in state legislatures of the United States. More shamefully still, some of those states have mandated the study of oxymoronic "scientific creationism." Recently creationism became embodied in that most American of all ephemera, the theme park, but this one devoted to "Darwin-free" entertainment presided over by Dr. Dino—a charlatan if ever there was one. Perhaps this park is, however, only appropriate for the most millenarian of nations, where large numbers of people at the beginning of the twenty-first century still deny the truth of the revelations of geologic time and natural selection over time. Many imitate those who, at the end of the nineteenth century, fled to the safety of millenarianism or to Price's ironically titled "new geology." Despite the seismic shocks of the Copernican, Newtonian, and Galilean revolutions, despite the discovery of "deep time" and Darwin's discovery that local adaptation to change produces new species, the popular view of time held by many in the United States remains that of a record of human progress that will lead to Apocalypse.

Separating fantasy from reality, however, can often prove difficult.[13] Looking back to the nineteenth-century Millerite movement from a twenty-first century vantage point, for instance, two observations appear crucial, although perhaps surprising to twenty-first-century eyes. First is the means Miller used to deliver and spread his message, which was the large tent revival. Such revivals were "among the earliest forms of mass entertainment. Deploying theatrical techniques developed in carnivals, circuses, and traveling road shows, preachers learned to pitch their message like carnies on the midway. . . . these revivals became the prototype for political rallies [compare Donald Trump's massive rallies]," as the contemporary theologian and historian of religion Mark

---

13. It might be well to recall that there are Flat Earth Societies in the United States, Canada, and Great Britain that maintain in all seriousness that the rotundity of the earth is but an illusion. The first Flat Earth convention in the United Kingdom held in Birmingham in May 2018 drew some 200 attendees.

Perhaps the most famous or more likely the most notorious flat-Earther was Mike Hughes, better known as "Mad Mike" because of his daredevil stunts. Hughes built a homemade rocket with which he hoped "to reach the Kármán Line, where Earth's atmosphere and outer space meet, 62 miles above the ground. From there Hughes claimed he'd be able to tell whether the Earth is a flat disk (as he suspected) or a sphere. He climbed in his rocket and fired it up, but unfortunately it malfunctioned and pancaked into the desert killing Hughes on 22 February 2020 (see Leman).

Taylor observes (287). Second, the outstanding characteristic of the participants appears to be their religious commitment, rather than their foolishness. Although speaking of a vastly different experience, Thoreau describes exactly the Millerites' position that morning after the failed apocalypse when he declared: "Every man has to learn the points of compass again as often as he awakes, whether from sleep or any abstraction" (118). In time, many Millerites came to acknowledge that they were still in the world of reality and not of the fantastic and so reached an accommodation with what had failed to occur. The physical non-event became known among them as the "Great Disappointment" as it became slowly, painfully transformed into an event of deep metaphysical significance. Ellen White, the Adventist visionary, for instance, "linked the delay of the Advent to the need for morally improving God's people" (Butler 201). Jonathan Butler describes how

> these Adventists believed that on the fateful tenth day of the seventh month Christ . . . had come not to earth but had moved from the holy to the most holy place in a heavenly sanctuary. The "cleansing of the sanctuary" [a typical Millerite millennial belief] had not referred to Christ's Second Coming but rather to the investigation of the sins of God's people in preparation for the end of the world. (200)

White's disciples—those Adventists who were formerly Millerites—followed a well-established pattern in moving from Apocalypse to Gnosis or from looking without to looking within. "Prophetic religion becomes apocalyptic when prophecy fails, and apocalyptic religion becomes Gnosticism when apocalypse fails, as fortunately it always has and, as we must hope, will fail again" (Bloom 30). The Millerites began with prophecy, continued with apocalypse, and when apocalypse failed in the Great Disappointment, they looked within themselves. That inner faith became, in turn, the basis for the establishment of a new religion. Kenelm Burridge, a sympathetic observer of millenarian movements, describes the value of such experience: "Whether as fool, fraud, saint, respectable bourgeois, farmer or tycoon, the pain of the millennium belongs only to man. It is why he is man, why, when the time comes, he has to make a new man" (qtd. in Numbers and Butler xx). Of those Millerites who stayed in the advent movement, who went beyond the pain and disappointment, some found new dedication and did experience a religious awakening that resulted in a dramatic renewal of Shakerism, the establishment of the Church of the Seventh Day Adventists, and, later, the beginning of the Jehovah's Witnesses. As the Advent historian Jonathan M. Butler contends, "[l]ike every other millenarian movement, Millerism met with obvious failure, and yet out of this failure eventually emerged another of the American sectarian success stories . . . [in t]he durable, complex, and established Adventist sect . . ." (190). Rather than a belief in either Progress or Apocalypse, the lesson of Millerism appears to lie closer to those to be derived from a reading of Emerson's essays or Dickinson's poetry or, especially, of Thoreau's *Walden.* "Not till we are lost . . . do we begin to find ourselves, and realize where we are and the infinite extent of our relations," remarked Thoreau, and he might have been speaking of the failed Millerite movement (118).

The Millerites believed in the reality of Apocalypse enough to make it the center of their lives and they were willing to risk all for their belief. Ironically, in their own way, and out of their Great Disappointment, they, too, like Thoreau, Dickinson, and Emerson, had to "front . . . the essential facts of life" (Thoreau 62). The central, essential fact was time's continuation rather than the End of Time and therefore the failure of their millennial beliefs. The world was no different on 23 October 1844 than it had been on 22 October except for their Great Disappointment. The Earth and the humans on it remained the product of billions of years of evolutionary activity. There would be no progress, no following time's arrow to the very End of Time, to the Day of Judgment, to the Parousia. Turning away from failed prophecy to gnosis, many Millerites followed a pattern of self-knowledge and self-reliance expostulated by Emerson, and embodied in the lives and works of Emerson, Dickinson, and Thoreau. Emerson advocated self-reliance, being "empowered by eloquence and vision" (Bloom, *Omens* 16) rather than being distracted by what he called the "popgun" of Apocalypse that sounds like "the crack of doom" ("The American Scholar" 64).

At the end of the twentieth century and well into the twenty-first, as at the end of the nineteenth, a significant number of Americans still expected a new Age to dawn, and many believed the New Age would coincide with the new century and the new millennium. The current Age of Agony would then be over "by God's victorious intervention on behalf of His saints, when He comes, or sends His Representative to come, to set things right" (Burkitt 7).[14] The early "Christians

---

14. Bloom reports:

> Pollsters estimate that there are about 10 million American premillennialists, that is, people who expect Jesus to return, in his resurrected body, before he then inaugurates a thousand-year kingdom on Earth, over which he will rule. Yet the premillennialists are only a small fraction of believers; rather more than 100 million American adults who expect a Second Coming of Jesus, even if they do not necessarily believe that he will found the Kingdom of God in this world. (219-20).

expected the visible return of their lord to judge the nations: they received instead the Roman Empire itself" (Burkitt 13).[15] Other, more current expectations such as the "Rapture" depicted in Jenkins and LaHaye's novels have also been thwarted. Those who, at the end of the nineteenth century, expected Apocalypse to coincide with the arrival of the new century received instead World War I and the twentieth century of wars. What do the current millenarians, their number estimated at over ten million Americans, expect? Some of their stated expectations were punctured by a ten-year-old girl who, perhaps wise beyond her years, observed that "hundreds of American adults long for eternity do not know what to do with themselves on a rainy day." And then there are the answers given by popular culture, popular religion, popular cults, and the morning newspaper: besides The Rapture, there is also Childhood's End, The Age of Aquarius, Jonesville, Waco, the pandemic and/or children slaughtering other children with automatic weapons on school playgrounds.

Emerson had great respect for science, especially the work of contemporary astronomers and science was, indeed, central to his thought.[16] Thoreau, one of America's great naturalists, collected specimens for Harvard's famous naturalist Louis

---

A dominant faction within this group is the dispensationalists with their distinguishing "preoccupation with the end of history . . . . dispensationalists view history as a story of decline from which the elect must be redeemed by God's apocalyptic intervention. . . . we are now living through the Last Days, or End Times, which lead to the Rapture. . . . In recent years, the two most influential dispensationalists have been [Hal] Lindsey and LaHaye" (Taylor 275, 276).

15. So certain were many of the early Christians of Christ's eminent return that they, like Paul, never bothered to date their letters.

16. For an extensive discussion of science in Emerson's thought, see Laura Dassow Walls.

Agassiz and had such an enviable reputation for scientific accuracy in his work that his fellow townsmen in Concord hired him to be their official surveyor of the town's boundaries! Emily Dickinson acquired first-hand knowledge of nineteenth-century microscopes and telescopes through her attendance at Mt. Holyoke Seminary. All three advocated in varying degrees for what Emerson proclaimed as America's true religion of self-reliance. American science and scientific speculation grows out of and is nurtured by this vibrant tradition.

Rather than simplistic literalism, Dickinson endorsed telling "all the Truth but tell it slant— / Success in Circuit lies . . . The Truth must dazzle gradually / Or every man be blind—" (1129). Thoreau juxtaposed to a belief in the End of Time, a belief in being "anxious to improve the nick of time. . . . to stand on the meeting of two eternities, the past and the future, which is precisely the present moment" (10). If those "ladies of the land weaving toilet cushions against the last day" were "injuring eternity" (4), then the best remedy was not to believe that eternity would arrive next week or next month or next year with the Second Coming, for that was a fantasy, but to fill every minute of today so that one would acquire a sense of life and having lived—that would indeed be reality. "I went to the woods," Thoreau confessed, "because I wished to live deliberately, to front only the essential facts of life, and see if I could not learn what it had to teach, and not, when I came to die, discover that I had not lived" (62). To do so he went fishing in the stream of time rather than progressing along the arrow of time to the apocalyptic End of Time. Against this nineteenth-century backdrop of unrealized apocalypse and opposed to views of time as either apocalypse or a "knife-edge present," Emerson looked with confidence to the future refusing to be distracted by that "popgun" of Apocalypse.

Jenkins and LaHaye's multi-volume twentieth- and twenty-first-century sequential novel would appear even more fantastic were it not for the authors' obvious, if unstated, commitment to an imminent apocalyptic moment. Missing from their work, however, is a date similar to Miller's "1843" or Ussher's 23 October 1997—a definite time-certain for the End of Time. Had any such similar date appeared in these sixteen novels, then the whole series would have aligned itself not with the literature of the fantastic but with the consensus reality of their millennial community of true believers and readers. But such a departure from the fantastic has its dangers, for that consensus reality would, in turn, have had to assimilate the inevitable disappointment "when apocalypse fails, as fortunately it always has . . ." (Bloom, *Omens* 30), or, as Gould summarizes: "The only true pattern of the ages—the failure of apocalyptic prediction" as time flows ever on ("Today Is the Day").

Possible Futures in Time

Emerson once famously quipped that humans had their "eyes in the forehead not in the back of the head" for a purpose. Yet to speculate about the future is to investigate what happened in the past, for surely in many important ways the deep future does mirror the deep past. For instance, in the deep past we have abundant evidence of mass extinctions caused by collisions between the Earth and passing cosmic debris—the last occurred only some sixty-five million years ago—a mere blink of the eye as evolutionary or geologic time is measured. "Cometary or asteroid impacts of this [significant] magnitude occur, on average, every few million years," observes Paul Davies (*The Last Three Minutes* 3). Only a few years ago in 1993, comet Swift-Tuttle swept by the Earth and "early calculations suggested that a collision in 2126 was a distinct possibility" which would result in global devastation. "Since then, revised calculations indicate that the comet will in fact miss Earth by two weeks . . . . However, the danger won't go away entirely. Sooner or later Swift-Tuttle, or an object like it, *will* hit the Earth" (Davies 3). The serious effects of such an encounter would mean the mass extinction of humanity and the fulfillment of at least some of those predictions of Apocalypse. Mass extinction has occurred several times in the past: around 440 million years ago, 360 million years ago, twice between 240 and 200 million years ago, and most famously only 65 million years ago. Such extinctions will occur again. If the past is any guide, after a future mass extinction new forms of life will again evolve. "The Future is Wild"—like a wild card in a card game—anything may be possible in the future within certain constraints.[17]

The end for humanity will not, however, necessarily mean the end of planet Earth. What then? Will humanity by then have colonized other words spinning around other suns? James Gunn may have been reflecting the optimism of the early 1970s when he declared that "the farther into space one travels the less significant become the passions and agonies of man, and the only matter of importance in the long morning of man's struggle to survive is his survival so that his sons could be seeded among the stars" ("Science Fiction" 199). Yet that morning appears to have barely dawned. Some contemporary scientists sounding more like science-fiction writers than objective scientists enthusiastically postulate

---

17. Dougal Dixon and John Adams's *The Future Is Wild: A Natural History of the Future* remains one of the most vividly concrete renderings of possible futures after the extinction of humanity.

that technology will continue to rise exponentially over billions of years, constantly accelerating in proportion to existing technology. The more star systems that intelligent beings have colonized, the more star systems they can colonize. . . . [O]ver several billion years, intelligent beings will have completely colonized vast portions of the visible universe. (Kaku 308, summarizing Barrow and Tipler, *The Anthropic Cosmological Principle*)

This grand sweeping vision of future time when humanity will populate dozens if not hundreds of Earth-like planets is equally fantastic yet almost the opposite of the vision given in Jenkins and LaHaye's sixteen Left Behind novels—based as they are on the assumption of humanity's end in "The Rapture." But like Archbishop Ussher's predictions for the twentieth century and William Miller's for the nineteenth, Jenkins and LaHaye's for the twenty-first century needs to be tested by the passing of time and thus far all past time and all history suggest that like their predecessors their hoped-for End of Time will not take place, leaving almost half the United States' population facing yet another potential Great Disappointment. Whether the contemporary scientists' equally fantastic vision of the far-distant future of humanity spread across the galaxy populating other hospitable exoplanets fares any better thanks to various technological breakthroughs only eons of time will tell.

Kurt Vonnegut, Time, and the Notion of Progress

> *We went to the World's Fair and saw what the past had been like, . . . saw what the future would be like.*
>
> *And I asked myself about the present: how wide it was, how deep it was, and how much was mine to keep.*
>
> ——*Kurt Vonnegut,* Slaughterhouse-Five

> *We worship at the altar of progress without adequately acknowledging its limits.*
> ——*Robert Samuelson*

Time and the notion of progress are so conjoined for those living in the United States and Great Britain that it becomes almost impossible to untangle one from the other. The assumption that as time goes on life gets better is hard to resist if you grow up privileged and living in one of the world's richest countries. Such people enjoy many of the products of the several technological revolutions such as cars, planes, washing machines, refrigerators, central heating and/or air conditioning, and the ubiquitous internet, along with a greatly increased availability of education, modern medicine, clean water, fresh produce, and the list goes on and on. Under such conditions life is clearly better in so many ways than it was a hundred and fifty years ago. Moreover, with the reduction in infant mortality and the conquest of many diseases we rightfully expect our lives to be longer than those of our great-grandparents. All of which led in the popular imagination to a vision of continuous progress from the twentieth century into the twenty-first until the advent of the Coronavirus pandemic called all such assumptions into question and forced many of us to acknowledge that even progress has "its limits" (Samuelson). Progress before the pandemic appeared obvious for reasons given earlier in this chapter and a person would have to be a curmudgeon—a grumpy old man or woman—not to hail such dramatic improvements as evidence that humans over time are ever advancing onward and upward.

A strong dissenting voice to this assumption was American novelist Kurt Vonnegut, who in all of his novels and short stories sounds several clear warnings against the uncritical acceptance of such a belief. Like Darwin or Hutton, he remained skeptical about the notion of humans progressing over time rejecting any idea of humanity's emerging from a dark past into the bright present and moving on into an ever-brighter future. To all such speculation Vonnegut responds with a resounding "No!" Taking a long view of human prospects he declares in spite of all the myriad of improvements in living "[t]hat Humanity is going somewhere really nice was a myth for children under 6 years old, like the Tooth Fairy[,] . . . the Easter Bunny and Santa Claus" (*Hocus Pocus* 206). Like Darwin, who championed evolution, and Hutton, who discovered "deep time" (previously discussed in this chapter), Vonnegut saw no evidence for any social upward thrust that would justify concluding that humanity over time has continually improved, nor did he discern any desire and/or ability of his fellow humans to confront, much less overcome, many serious and life-threatening contemporary challenges. Rather than accept his former employer General Electric's slogan, "Progress is our most important product," Vonnegut said more than once, "I don't have the feeling that we are going anywhere." Moreover, he rejected the facile optimistic view of many of his contemporaries that through the wise use of technology combined with humanity's ever-expanding knowledge in general any crisis now or in the future could be averted, any challenge could be met. He had no use for the kind of speculation cited earlier in this chapter "that technology will continue to rise exponentially [until] . . . [o]ver several billion years, intelligent beings will have completely colonized vast portions of the visible universe" (Kaku 308). While there may be no absolute barrier to what humans could accomplish over time through technology, there remains an absolute barrier to what they can do physically in addition to the seemingly insuperable barrier to what they may become morally. Progress in technology or in science, as important as it is, appears not to equate with humanity's social or moral progress despite a vague popular notion linking them. What Thoreau observed of his nineteenth-century neighbors still holds true today: "While civilization has been improving our houses, it has not equally improved the men who are to inhabit them" (23).

For Vonnegut true progress over time cannot be equated with motion, no matter how fast or how extensive. In *The Sirens of Titan* (1959), Malachi Constant rockets around the solar system like a high-speed yo-yo going nowhere—from getting rich to becoming poor, ricocheting off one planet to another, from being kidnapped on Earth to arriving eventually on Titan, one of Saturn's moons, then being shipped back to Earth to die; yet, despite all of this movement, he never really goes anywhere. His non-arrival becomes doubly ironic in light of his dubious lifetime wish to become a modern-day Mercury carrying a really significant message "sufficiently dignified and important to merit his carrying it humbly between two points" (17). His prayer goes unanswered for he does not get to carry such a message. Instead, it is Salo from the planet Tralfamador who is an actual messenger and has been for many eons. The message Salo carries, which lies at the heart of the novel, while truly important, given its source is simply trivial in its contents and is certainly not "dignified," nor is it really his since it means nothing to him. Rather than either he or Salo becoming a Mercury, the messenger of the gods, Malachi becomes a poster boy for Rumford's Church of the Utterly Indifferent while Salo becomes a mere errand boy sent off on a fool's task. Perhaps the best comment in *The Sirens of Titan* on the foolishness of believing that progress over time equates with speed or distance covered comes from Ransom K. Ferm, who supplies the novel's fatuous epigraph:

> Every passing hour brings the Solar System forty-three thousand miles closer to Globular Cluster M13 in Hercules—and still there are some misfits who insist that there is no such thing as progress. (50)

If progressing in time by itself becomes measured in motion or in speed, then, of course, Ferm is right, but if instead progress is measured in purposeful movement in time and in a carefully chosen direction, then his words become bitterly ironic—much like the message Salo is carrying.

Charging ahead on a course not chosen but randomly taken at an unregulated speed creates only the illusion of progress in time no matter how swift the movement. In *Galápagos* (1985), Vonnegut suggests that such illusionary progress is a good example of humanity's penchant for driving at high speed on a superhighway that will end abruptly at the cliff edge of ecological or nuclear suicide. Once again, humanity has conflated the means (high-speed driving) with the end (survival of the species). One way out of this dilemma would be to extirpate the great big brain humans have or, at least, let it evolve over time into something smaller and hence less harmful to humans, other creatures, and life on the planet. In *Galápagos*, therefore, Vonnegut sends humanity back to the sea to fish equipped with fins but with a much more modest-sized brain.

Vonnegut in *Galápagos* thus reverses the clichéd misreading of evolutionary history as evidence for humanity marching ever onward and upward from ape to Neanderthal to upright human. Such popular views of humanity's increasing complexity as the result of progress over eons of time are simply false; that is, that life ever advances from bacteria to insects to fish to animals to humans. This simplified evolutionary belief comes about in part through misconstruing Darwin's observation that local adaptability to changed or changing conditions leads to the establishment of new species.

> Everybody knows that organisms get better as they evolve. They get more advanced, more modern, and less primitive. And everybody knows . . . that organisms get more complex as they evolve. From the first cell that coalesced in the primordial soup to the magnificent intricacies of *Homo sapiens*, the evolution of life—as everybody knows—has been one long drive toward greater complexity. The only trouble with what everybody knows . . . is that there is no evidence it's true. (Lori Oliwenstein qtd. in Gould, *Full House* 212; ellipsis in the original)

Such fallacious reasoning often culminates with the placing of human beings at the pinnacle of evolution, where they do not belong, as they were once similarly placed at the pinnacle of creation. But substituting evolution for creation still leaves unresolved the problem of the absence of evidence for assuming that humans are indeed the "goal" of evolution over time rather than an adaptation to local conditions. As the evolutionary biologist/paleontologist Stephen Jay Gould contends, "We are glorious accidents of an unpredictable process with no drive to complexity, nor the expected results of evolutionary principles that yearn to produce a creature capable of understanding the mode of its own necessary construction" (*Full House* 216).

Darwin's best examples of evolution occurred on the Galápagos islands, where he encountered isolated animals— like the humans in Vonnegut's novel—that had evolved into new species. Over time in isolation neither the strongest nor the most complex survived, but the fastest and best at adaptation. Rather than viewing species as superior or inferior, Darwin emphasized their differences, especially those that enabled certain species to survive changing conditions. The wooly mammoth, which evolved over a lengthy period of time into the elephant, did so to survive changing climatic conditions as its habitant warmed. To say that the elephant is somehow superior to its ancestor, the wooly mammoth, establishes an indefensible scale of value. Similarly, the animals of Australia evolved to live under incredibly difficult conditions of small erratic rainfalls, scarce food, and intense heat. The kangaroo, for instance, leaps rather than runs because leaping over long distances uses only a fraction of the energy that running does. The wombat and the sheep have about equal body mass, but the native-to-Australia wombat being perfectly adapted to scarcity requires only a small fraction of the non-native sheep's daily intake of food to survive.

Vonnegut's *Galápagos* describes a world in which only a tiny remnant of humanity survives into the future. This happens because of a worldwide biological crisis reminiscent of pandemics and not because a nervous finger on the nuclear trigger led to a worldwide conflagration; hence mutation as

happened in *Cat's Cradle* (1963) the Vonnegut novel that
metaphorically described a world in the grip of nuclear winter
before the term became popular. In *Galápagos*, the majority of
humanity mysteriously becomes sterile and therefore fails to
reproduce. Initially, such conditions may appear more benign
than, say, a world subjected to radioactive fallout, but in the end
they prove equally as effective in eliminating the human menace
as those the Bomb would create. This scenario, derided as too
improbable by some critics, appears now, in the early decades of
the twenty-first century, as all too possible. There is, for
instance, a large area in Siberia where the human and animal
populations are under threat of extinction because of
becoming increasingly sterile from the large amounts of
leaking nuclear waste deposits. For decades the atmosphere
there has been polluted with radiation. Should that waste leach
into the Arctic Sea, as appears now possible or even probable,
then the poisoning of all the globe's northern latitudes could
become a distinct possibility (Hays). The much-vaunted human
technology rather than rescuing humans could yet aid in
destroying all humanity. Gould warns that

> Accumulating technological progress need not lead to
> cultural improvement in a visceral or moral sense—and may
> just as well end in destruction, if not extinction, as various
> plausible scenarios, from nuclear holocaust to environmental
> poisoning suggest. I have long been impressed by a potential
> solution . . . to that problem of why we haven't been
> contacted by the plethora of advanced civilizations that
> ought to inhabit other solar systems in our universe. Perhaps
> any society that could build a technology for such interplan-
> etary, if not intergalactic, travel must first pass through a
> period of potential destruction where technological capacity
> outstrips social or moral restraint. And perhaps no, or very

few, societies can ever emerge intact from such a crucial episode. (*Full House* 223)

Vonnegut agrees with Gould's premise that there can be no genuine progress in whatever time frame as long as we live in a society "where technological capacity outstrips social or moral restraint," hence his solution of sending humans back to the sea to fish.

Vonnegut continues exploring this issue of technological progress undercut by its misapplication or its abuse in *Deadeye Dick* (1982). As in most of his novels, a belief in benign or beneficent progress over time crashes into a barrier perhaps best described by C. P. Snow in his witty reformulation of the three laws of thermodynamics:

1. *You cannot win* (that is, you cannot get something for nothing because matter and energy are conserved).
2. *You cannot break even* (you cannot return to the same energy state, because there is always an increase in disorder, entropy always increases).
3. *You cannot get out of the game* (because absolute zero is unattainable). (qtd. in Kaku 304)

This barrier to human progress in time—a leitmotiv of so many Vonnegut novels—in *Deadeye Dick* becomes entangled with the understandable wish for a better world after the horrors of World War II. During a luncheon with Rudy Waltz's family, Mrs. Eleanor Roosevelt shared her belief with the Waltzes that

there would be a wonderful new world when the war was won. Everybody who needed food or medicine would get it, and people could say anything they wanted, and could choose any religion that appealed to them. Leaders wouldn't dare to

be unjust anymore, since all the other countries would gang
up on them. For this reason, there could never be another
Hitler. He would be squashed like a bug before he got very
far. (*Deadeye Dick* 59)

But these brave and hopeful words collide with subsequent
events in world history as well as events in the world of the
novel. Immediately after Mrs. Roosevelt's visit, Rudy goes
upstairs to the gun room and fires the shot heard round
Midland City that kills the pregnant Mrs. Eloise Metzger.
Rather than that brave new postwar world, Rudy enters a
world where his random unthinking event exercises control—
an absolute control—over the rest of his life. His time is
effectively over. As he painfully learns—*You cannot win, You
cannot break even* and *You cannot get out of the game.*

In contrast, the aptly named John Fortune Farm in
Deadeye Dick becomes symbolic of the kind of progress seen in
the United States during the twentieth century. First, in the
1920s the farm thrived, was self-sustaining and productive.
During the Great American Depression, however, it became
economically unviable, whereupon the owner, John Fortune, set
off on a fruitless search for Shangri-La, that imaginary
paradise on Earth rumored to be somewhere in the Himalayas.
In the 1940s the farm shifted from being productive to being
destructive as the United States armed forces fighting in World
War II used it for a tank proving ground. In the 1960s the farm
transformed once more and became "Avondale," an archetype
of suburban tract housing made up of the "little shitboxes," as
Rudy describes them (59). Abruptly in the 1980s the farm
disappeared from the map altogether when it, along with all of
Midland City, became a test area for the neutron bomb. (There's
even speculation that the bomb was dropped under orders of

the United States government, since Midland City was classified as clearly expendable being the least objectionable place on which one could test such a weapon [234]). "What I showed happening to Midland City [over a period of about fifty years] is the indifference of our government to the closing down of these towns," comments Vonnegut and goes on to give as an example of such destroyed towns or cities Terra Haute, Indiana.

> The last business just closed down there [Terra Haute, Indiana]—Columbia Records closed down its plant . . . permanently . . . [T]his place has got twenty-seven churches, . . . a railroad yard, it's got all this, and it might as well have been neutron bombed, and so there was that analogy. . . . If a neutron bomb did go off accidentally in Terra Haute, it would be on the news for about three days because the feeling is that these people weren't really of any importance. (qtd. in Reed 9)

Like Vonnegut's Midland City, Terra Haute, a once viable Indiana town with a livable environment, becomes consigned piece by piece over time to the scrap heap of American progress—a huge mistake in Vonnegut's eyes, but like so many mistakes this one has no one single cause and no clear force or person to blame. Like so much that is radically changing the face of America, Terra Haute's fate was decided in corporate boardrooms far removed from the actual city itself. The neutron bomb becomes an apt symbol for this kind of negative progress measured by corporate bottom lines.

The destruction of viable human environments, such as Terra Haute or Midland City, is an old story in the United States—almost as old as the country itself. In 1620 the Pilgrims, upon first viewing the shore of the New World, saw not a green and pleasant land, but only wilderness and savages. They quickly set about destroying both by utilizing their vastly superior technology replacing them with more familiar "civilization." In *Slapstick* (1976), Vonnegut reverses time by reversing that movement from nature to city, from savage to civilized in creating an Eden in the wilderness—or in as much wilderness as modern Vermont allows—and peopling it with a primitive-appearing, simian-like, monstrously tall Adam and Eve. In the same instance he also appears to be reversing another popular evolutionary stereotype of the superior humans over time progressing up and away from the primitive apes. Armed only with astronomical intelligence quotients (IQs), the zygotes thrive in their idyllic setting and, when together, make up one suprahuman person. When together, they write a book critical of Darwin's theory of evolution and a "precocious critique of the Constitution of the United States" (52), learn ancient and modern languages, and master the calculus. Apart, each becomes "stupid and insecure" as each feels as though his or her "head were turning to wood" (87). "Progress" in the person of an embittered psychologist, who plays the role of a modern snake in this paradisal garden, condemns each to separation and exile, and so they are expelled forever from paradise. Worse, they are separated.[18] Thus *Slapstick* suggests that if a genius should appear, humanity would treat her or him not as a potential means to genuine social, political, or cultural progress, but as a pariah. Collective wisdom would conspire to throw him or her out, not just out of Eden, but out of the human community by confining her or him to a mental ward.

18. Oliver Sacks reports a similar kind of expulsion of similarly gifted twins from their idyllic serene world of numbers into the mundane world of bus transportation and menial tasks. See "The Twins," *The Man Who Mistook His Wife for a Hat*, 204–24.

Vonnegut is equally pessimistic about humanity and its ability to progress even in a new millennium. Since people continue and will continue to follow "the complicated futility of ignorance" (*Hocus Pocus* 14), events and humans in the twenty-first century, in the new millennium, continue much as they had in the previous century. The result will not be progress toward enlightenment or toward a new heavenly city or even toward a better life, but a movement toward disaster. In Vonnegut's universe, help is not on the way to Earth and, therefore, humans, if they are to survive, if they are in some sense going to "progress," must realize they are alone and, therefore, must of necessity become their own best resource. Unlike in Arthur C. Clarke's and Stanley Kubrick's *2001*, in *Hocus Pocus*, Vonnegut's own millennial novel, humans will not travel to other parts of the universe in the new century, nor will they receive help from some mysterious source outside themselves, this planet, or this solar system.

The name of the "author" of *Hocus Pocus*, Eugene Debs Hartke, is itself ironic in that it combines the names of Eugene Victor Debs, the great late-nineteenth-century early-twentieth-century social reformer, with that of Vance Hartke, the Indiana Senator who in 1968 narrowly won reelection having bravely campaigned against the Vietnam War—one of the very few congressmen who dared to do so. Eugene Victor Debs (1855-1926), four-time candidate for president of the United States, received almost a million votes as a third-party candidate in 1920. In 1922 Debs chose as his epitaph "While there is a lower class I am in it. While there is a criminal element I am of it. While there is a soul in prison I am not free" (qtd. in *Hocus Pocus* 2). Against this moral yardstick Vonnegut measures the United States in the year 2001. If Eugene Debs at the beginning of the twentieth century was an exponent of the Sermon on the Mount, Eugene Debs Hartke at the end of that century is an exponent of getting along by going along— a man not tormented by his conscience, though he has killed eighty-five people. If Eugene Debs identified with the outcast, the down and out, the lower classes, the jailed, Hartke does not. "I have no reforms to propose" (242), he reiterates. Furthermore, if Debs went to jail voluntarily because of sympathy toward those already incarcerated, Hartke goes involuntarily because of the white racism of those in authority. In his defense, he makes lists of those he has killed and of those to whom he has made adulterous love: "Quantification becomes the latest escape valve discovered by a Vonnegut narrator from a condition too troublesome for him to confront" (Mistichelli 322).

Like Howard Campbell in *Mother Night* (1962) and Walter Starbuck in *Jailbird* (1979)—and not unlike Miguel Cervantes—Hartke writes his book in prison, the very place where the novel was born. Like so many prison writers, he must use whatever scraps of paper come to hand.[19] It was on just such scraps of paper in 1963—actually on the blank edges of *The New York Times*—that Martin Luther King, Jr. wrote his "Letter from Birmingham Jail," his prophetic call to resist and end racism in America. *Hocus Pocus* itself becomes a ringing denunciation of American racism as well as a firm condemnation of the Vietnam debacle. Another of Vonnegut's single-book authors, Hartke questions the sanity of his time. Were not those in charge of prosecuting the war in Vietnam,

---

19. One critic ridiculed Vonnegut for presenting these scraps literally by dividing his novel's pages into sections: "The narrator did not have access to uniform writing paper, see? The writer, locked up in a library and facing trial, was desperate [sic] to express himself .... The snippet-technique soon begins to wear" (Phillips 135). Yet those dividing lines do serve to remind readers that this book is being written in jail.

for instance, a little like the governor and his wife in the second part of *Don Quixote*—that is, people so caught up in their delusions derived from fiction that they produced fake events for real people to participate in, rather than for actors on stage or in television to act out or for characters in a novel to follow? Hartke, like the Knight of the Woeful Countenance, became the victim of someone else's script, speaking someone else's lines, himself offering encouragement in a futile enterprise: "I was a genius of lethal hocus pocus!" he exclaims (154). If Billy Pilgrim in *Slaughterhouse-Five* symbolizes the innocent child playing at war, Vonnegut's characterization of soldiers in World War II, then Eugene Debs Hartke symbolizes the disgraced adolescent playing at saving nations from themselves, Vonnegut's characterization of American policymakers in Vietnam. The last American to leave Saigon when it fell, Hartke had the unenviable, if highly symbolic, job of keeping "Vietnamese who had been on our side from getting into helicopters that were ferrying Americans only . . . to our Navy ships offshore" (52). Few sights better illustrate the United State's ignominious defeat than its utter failure to protect the Vietnamese it alleged it was saving when it entered the war. A hypocritical talk show host in *Hocus Pocus* observes that stories of defeat are not good for morale (126-27). True enough, but they do serve the far more important function of roughing up human pride, chastening mindless patriotism, and giving poor mortals a realistic perspective on themselves as individuals, on the human race in general, and on the planet they inhabit.

In *Galápagos*, it was the great big human brains that were to blame not just for the lack of progressing in time but also for the pending destruction of the planet, while in *Hocus Pocus*, Vonnegut identifies the enemy more narrowly as human indifference as seen in his parable of the stranded elevator.

Humanity's representative, six-year-old Bruce Bergeron, stands trapped in an elevator stuck between floors in a large department store. Bruce mistakenly believes he must be "at the center of a major event in American history" (165)—as most six-year-olds will do. When at last the elevator becomes freed, it moves on to the next floor and deposits its passengers safely. Little Bruce, who "survived" the ordeal, discovers to his shock that no one else is remotely interested in his or his fellow passengers' predicament, as the rest of humanity either impatiently waits for the next elevator or madly participates in the department store's white sale. "There wasn't even somebody from the management of the store to offer an anxious apology, to make certain everybody was all right" (166). Everyone—whether inside or outside the elevator—is so completely wrapped up in his or her own plight, activities, or desires that no one has any emotional room left to sympathize with anyone else—much less any vision of the needs of society as a whole. Discussing *Hocus Pocus* Vonnegut once quipped, "everybody wanted to build and nobody wanted to do maintenance. So there goes the ball game. Meanwhile, truth, jokes, and music help at least a little bit" (*Fates Worse than Death* 201). But truth, jokes, and music, which may indeed offer some solace, do not and cannot replace Eugene Debs's now abandoned compassionate ideal as all too often Americans content themselves with ignorance, sentimentality, and noise.

"The biggest character in *Hocus Pocus*," Vonnegut says, "is imperialism, the capture of other societies' lands and people and treasure by means of state-of-the-art wounding and killing machines, which is to say armies and navies" (*Fates Worse than Death* 130). Against the view of the twentieth century as "The American Century" when the United States "sustained Western civilization by acts of courage, generosity and vision, unparalleled in the history of man" (Jones 78), the United States appears in *Hocus Pocus* as a country whose aspirations are frozen—a land that promised much but delivered little. John Leonard tells of taking a walk with Vonnegut in New Hampshire: "We happened, in an orchard, upon stricken boughs of black apples. Helicopters had spayed Stop-Drop on these apples during the October picking season, and then an early frost had killed them off, and so they hung there, very Japanese" (301). *Hocus Pocus* focuses not on the aesthetic beauty but on the waste and inedibility of those black apples on those "stricken boughs." At the center of the novel lie the preserved black apples of several crucial, if disastrous, events in the twentieth century that vividly illustrate humanity's inhumanity rather than any human "progress": the Atomic Bomb, the symbol of sudden total destruction of life; Auschwitz, the symbol of human ingenuity in the service of such destruction; Vietnam, the symbol of the utter futility of war; and the Athena prison break modeled on the famous Attica prison uprising in New York state, the symbol of rage and frustration caused by the failure of American society to give meaningful work, life, or hope to all citizens. These twentieth-century events become linked to the first-century binge of six thousand crucifixions that resulted from the slave revolt under Spartacus and to "the orgy of butchery . . . by the Japanese Army on the Chinese city of Nanking in 1937" (Vonnegut, *Hocus Pocus* 318). Behind such appalling events, selected from two thousand years of human history, lies "the futility of ignorance" that leads people to dream of impossible perpetual motion machines that look lovely but do nothing. In day-to-day life that ignorance more generally may lead to humans practicing brutality, choosing ugliness, indulging in mind-numbing drugs, and willingly following orders to perform the most inhuman and inhumane acts. "The lessons I myself learned over and over again when teaching at the college and then the prison was the uselessness of information to most people, except as entertainment," says Hartke, the narrator of *Hocus Pocus* (67).

At the end of the twentieth century and well into the new millennium, it becomes clear in Vonnegut's fiction, especially in *Hocus Pocus*, that Mars is in the ascendant—Mars, the God of War, not Venus, the Goddess of Love, rules human affairs. After he dies, Hartke wishes to have engraved on his tombstone "a number that represents both my 100-percent-legal military kills and my adulteries" (322) and not, as one critic contends, "the names of the women he has loved" (Broer 191).[20] Only a number. Nothing else. The number dedicated to Venus and the number dedicated to Mars. His epitaph neglects completely to mention the poor, the criminals, or those imprisoned—all prominently featured in Eugene Debs's epitaph. But Eugene Debs had convictions by which he lived his life and Debs died early in the century (1922)—a century that would become tyrannized by Hitler, Stalin, and a host of all-too-successful dictators. In the closing years of that century, like the first years of the twenty-first century—tired, worn out by wars, racism, the pandemic, the breakdown of social services and democratic government, and living on an endangered planet—Americans could yet reverse each of these disasters if they had

---

20. Lawrence Broer writes: "Just as the words on his namesake's tombstone reflect decency and caring, Eugene projects as his own epitaph the names of the women he has loved" (191). But nowhere in *Hocus Pocus* does Hartke say that is what he is doing. In the novel he plans for only a number to be carved enigmatically on his tombstone. That number will be over eighty and results from the list Hartke makes consisting exclusively of the names of those women with whom he has had sex but excluding prostitutes and his wife (30), with whom he was indeed in love, at least for the first four years of their marriage.

the will. Vonnegut's novel, like Emerson's oration "The American Scholar," is his attempt to awaken his fellow countrymen to action and to possibilities in the present that are fast disappearing into time-past. Although the national or even planetary elevator may stall, effective action could still be taken to get it going again and to take it down to reality away from the fantasy and distraction of a never-ending department store sale. But if action is to be taken, then it must be taken by ordinary, responsible people who, overcoming indifference and inertia, leave the distraction of the sale and instead work together to do maintenance, to help save the child and those stranded on that stalled elevator. No one from management will arrive to apologize for the inconvenience.

In the film *2001*, despite HAL, the rogue computer, humans do arrive on Jupiter's moons where a warm welcome awaits them prepared by cosmic beings who have solved not only most of the problems humanity has identified but also many of the problems that humans have not yet even begun to identify. But by the end of the twentieth century and the first decades of the twenty-first life on Earth resembled far more a Vonnegut novel than it did the Kubrick film. All the promise of space flight, of going from the moon to Mars to the planets to the galaxy and beyond, withered under the loss of imagination, the loss of will, the loss of investment (and the investment in manned flight would have had to be huge, as Vonnegut pointed out several times). If, in much science fiction the universe is but a playground for human beings as they carry their wars, phobias, and diseases out beyond the solar system, in Vonnegut's fiction humans are redirected to look again at themselves and their planet. What they will see is not progress over time but conditions that should give them pause:

> Apart from the possibility of nuclear immolation of the Earth and human time, there are the extraordinary ways in which industrialized-consumerized humanity has, in its preoccupation with immediate gratification and immediate profit, hastened the processes of evolution: expending in days the solar energy that took millenia to store in the Earth's horde, destroying ecosystems in weeks that took an ice age to evolve, accelerating the processes of extinction with use-it-up technology and pollution, speeding the processes of mutation (and speciation) through radioactive contamination. (Gifford, *Farther Shore* 95)

As a character emphasized in Vonnegut's millennial novel, "We could have saved it but we were too doggone cheap" (*Hocus Pocus* 143).

Progress in time, Vonnegut maintains, is but an illusion of motion going somewhere (*The Sirens of Titan*), a delusion of society advancing (*Deadeye Dick*), or a series of chimerical detours through life (*Hocus Pocus*). C. P. Snow's reformulation of the three laws of thermodynamics appears as appropriate an epigraph for Vonnegut's novels as it is for the America at century's end pictured in them and for all those who continue to believe in human progress over time:

> *You cannot win.*
> *You cannot break even.*
> *You cannot get out of the game.*

Chapter 4
The Fullness of Time and the Cancer of Time

Time, for the most part, is a constant companion. Impermanence underlies experience. We revere the absolute but are bound to the transitory. Even those features of the cosmos that may present as enduring—the expanse of space, the distant galaxies, the stuff of matter—all lie within the reach of time.
———*Brian Greene*

Time is of paramount importance in all of the world's religions whether a religion finds revelation within history as Judaism and Christianity do, aligns itself with the cycle of the seasons as most ancient religions did, or focuses on a world or state of being outside time as Buddhism does. The reverse is also true: that religion greatly influences our view of time. So much so that it would be difficult to overestimate the impact religion has had on our various conceptions of time. For those living in the West the dominant influence on their thinking about time has been Christianity's building upon a foundation inherited from Judaism. A great ninth-century Jewish narrative placed the passage of time as the very cornerstone of belief:

> The passage of time. . . [was] the field in which their God [made] manifest his power and his providence on their behalf. . . . history was interpreted as the revelation of the divine purpose so that a teleological *Weltanschauung* [worldview] emerged, according to which the whole cosmic process was regarded as the gradual unfolding or achievement of God's plan, the destiny of Israel being its central theme. (Brandon 148)

Christianity and in particular Roman Catholic Christianity, especially under Pope Gregory, adopted this teleology and as a result came to view time not as cyclical but as linear (see chapter 1) with "the birth and death of Christ and the Crucifixion as unique events, unrepeatable." Their placement at the center of all events in history meant that "Western civilization came to regard time as a linear path that stretches between past and future. Before the advent of Christianity only the Hebrews and the Zoroastrian Persians preferred this progressive view of time" (Coveney and Highfield 26).

Over centuries this arrow of time moving from Creation through the advent and death of Jesus of Nazareth and ending in the future with the Eschaton (see chapter 3) became the norm not just for Christian believers but also for Western society in general.[1] During this process Christianity's belief in sacred history (*Heilsgeschichte*) inherited and/or adopted from Judaism became foundational; that is, the Judeo-Christian belief in the paramount importance of history as the medium that provides the record of God's acting in time became central (see Brandon 148).

W. H. Auden in *For the Time Being: A Christmas Oratorio* (1944) bases this long poem on just such a notion of sacred history, on this record of God acting in time. Additionally, several Protestant theologians whom he was reading while contemplating and/or writing his sacred oratorio also advocated placing this idea of sacred history centrally in Christian thought and theology. These theologians included the nineteenth-century Danish churchman Søren Kierkegaard,

---

1. In the United States 71% of the population identified themselves as Christian and 40% of Americans identified as some form of Protestant, according to the Pew Research Center for Religion and Public Life survey in 2014.

the twentieth-century theologian and political activist Reinhold Niebuhr, his brother, the ethicist-theologian H. Richard Niebuhr, and the philosopher-theologian Paul Tillich. All four of these thinkers, starting from a belief in sacred as opposed to secular history, placed major emphasis on the religious concept of "the fullness of time"—a metaphor based on human parturition. "The Fullness of time" in philosopher Nathaniel Lawrence's definition, for example, refers "to the point of closure of a pregnancy and the opening of a separate life" (35-36). For these theologians, as for Auden, this birth of "a separate life" has a specific religious reference to the Incarnation. Tillich, for instance, contrasts this concept of the fullness of time when the Incarnation occurred with the dominant Western methodological line of thinking about time: "In this dynamic thinking in terms of creation, time is all-decisive, not empty time, pure expiration; not mere duration either, but rather qualitatively fulfilled time, the moment that is creation and fate. We call this fulfilled moment, the moment of time approaching us as fate and decision, *Kairos*" (*Interpretation of History* 129). James Luther Adams clarifies Tillich's use of the term *Kairos* and its relation to the fullness of time by contrasting the Greek usage with that of the early Christians:

> The historical development of the word "*Kairos*" illustrates the two conceptions of time characteristic of the two contrasting outlooks. In Greek linguistic usage the word meant time as pure duration; in its transformation under the influence of the historical consciousness of early Christianity it acquired the meaning of fullness of time. And thus in its two meanings it symbolizes the two types of thinking. (203)

The necessary conditions for what Tillich called "*Kairos*" or "the moment [of time]" that leads to this birth and its consequences for individuals, society, art, science, and comedy is central to Auden's oratorio, in which he contrasts the fullness of time with what he sees as the concept of time as duration whether time is viewed as linear or as cyclical. In the oratorio's opening choruses, for example, durational time, symbolized by "the clock on the mantelpiece," is seen as linear stretching from the past through the point of the present into the future. The clock indicates to the observer where he or she may be in relation to this time line of duration. The limitations of this secular view of time Auden had earlier explored through another clock symbol in "We're Late," a poem he appended to the "New Year Letter" in *The Double Man*:

> Clocks cannot tell our time of day
> For what event to pray
> Because we have no time, because
> We have no time until
> We know what time we fill,
> Why time is other than time was. (*Collected Poetry* 26)

Because the members of the chorus in *For the Time Being* also believe that they "have no time" in the sense that they do not "know what time [they] fill," but only experience the mere passing of time, they despair. Because the clock can only record the passing of the present into the past of "time was," it "has nothing to recommend" (407). There is, moreover, neither hope nor comfort to be found in a future where, the chorus believes, past failures and mistakes will merely be repeated. In this bleak vision their individuality becomes blotted out as "darkness and snow descend / On all personality," leaving only a faceless, inarticulate crowd shuffling "off through the snow" (407).

In addition to employing "darkness and snow" as the traditional symbols for death and desolation, the poem uses them to indicate the death of an age, the inadequacy of political solutions, and the lifelessness of the old religious answers. The symbolic darkness and snow become reinforced in the opening "Chorus" not only through their repetition in the last line, but also through the use of images of decay ("ruined temples") and danger ("fanatical eyes"). The Roman Empire is rotting and instead of being reinvigorated and purified of evil by the energy of a larger-than-life Hercules, its vitality is being sapped by a fat, contented, indolent ruler indifferent to the pleas of his subjects. Drained of emotion and energy, the chorus describes its crucial loss with a worn-out cliché, "Love is not what she used to be," and pleads for something extraordinary: that this linear order of time be superseded by another order, one where despair may be overcome: "We who must die demand a miracle" (407). The chorus comes to believe that the miracle they demanded has indeed happened in the Incarnation, which brought into the world a radical new order, especially of time. The Incarnation has, they believe, freed "our future . . . from our past" in the sense that their future now need no longer be merely like the past or, worse, a repetition of the past, but instead could now be filled with possibility, with "new life."

In contrast to the opening choruses, the urbane Narrator—this model of modern man—rejecting the "Fullness of Time" presents instead yet another secular concept of time, this one a series of unending cycles perhaps best exemplified by the ubiquitous cycle of birth, death, and rebirth. Throughout the oratorio the Narrator will survey the world and brag about human progress through the ages. He exudes optimism and confidence, for, judged by human standards, people have not done badly, nor are human accomplishments inconsiderable. If a few difficulties remain unresolved, or if disasters occasionally occur, he suggests that such may be attributed to "the political situation" or to "the subnormal temperatures prevailing" (409). But his and other humans' *savoir faire* is shaken by the birth of the Christ—this "outrageous novelty," as he puts it, that brings "all in doubt" including the old assumptions about both linear time and cyclical time. These assumptions are no longer self-evidently true and may very well become invalid.[2] The Narrator experiences a "Void" instead of

> . . . . the natural world where
> The occupation of space is the real and final fact
> And time turns round itself in an obedient circle . . .
> (409)

He attempts to explain the enormous change that has taken place, and concludes:

> . . . . I mean
> That the world of space where events re-occur is still
>   there
> Only now it's no longer real; the real one is nowhere
> Where time never moves and nothing can ever happen
> . . .

The Narrator thus sees himself as caught between two worlds: the old world of cyclical birth, death, and rebirth, where season followed season as time turned "round itself in an obedient circle," is gone; that circle has been broken. Disconcerted he attempts to describe his confusion and anxiety by comparing it to Alice's experience on the other side of the mirror by saying he feels like he has passed "through the looking glass." But into

---

2. This paragraph and much of the following discussion is greatly indebted to Tom F. Driver's "Auden's View of History in *For the Time Being*," 3-8.

what or into where has he passed? The nature of the new world has not yet been fully revealed and thus he is left in "this Void." Tom F. Driver, after analyzing this speech of the Narrator, concludes:

> Auden is speaking here of the general run of things in human existence—the world of common sense, the world of scientific principles, the world of all rhythmic regularity—but he is also speaking of the classical, pagan world that preceded Christianity, a world for which reality was manifest in cycles of recurrence, as in the thinking of Pythagoras, Parmenides, and Plato. Thus, the Horror that Auden mentions is the result of a step forward into time-consciousness, whether this be thought of historically as something done by the Jews or psychologically as the emergence of the question of meaningful existence in the life-journey of any . . . [person]. It is a Horror because it is an intolerable half-way house. Time is breaking the circle of endless repetition, but time has not yet come into its own as something to give meaning to the here and now. ("View of History" 4)

In order to leave the "half-way house" of just developing time-consciousness, humans, whether represented by the Narrator or the Chorus, must take the next "step forward," which for Auden means recognizing in the coming of Christ the redemption of the future from the past and the giving of a new religious perspective to the natural cycles so that humanity need no longer see time either as linear or cyclical but instead experience it as redeemed.

Auden thought that the denial of the cyclical nature of time was necessary if the radical meaning of Christ's birth as a unique event in time is to be perceived. He agrees with many biblical scholars, such as James Muilenburg, for example, who in "The History of the Religion of Israel" maintains, "In Judaism and Christianity history and faith are inextricably related . . . . When we try to discern the character of Israel's religion . . . we are confronted first of all not with doctrines or principles or even ideas, but with the activity of God in events." For Christians, Christ becomes the culmination of a series of historical events crucial for faith that began with God's Promise given to the Patriarchs, Abraham, Isaac, and Jacob-Israel (see Genesis 12, 24, 28, 32). If as Muilenburg, among others, contends "history is . . . the area of maximum interest and concern" for Jews and Christians, then Christ will be "foolishness to the Greeks" and all others whose religion is non-historical, because they will fail to see the importance of "saving history" (*Heilsgeschichte*) as the arena for God's action.[3] This point of view is reflected in *For the Time Being*, where the old order must be destroyed so the new may appear, for, as Auden believes, "historical time is real and significant, not meaningless [as in the opening choruses] or an endless series of cycles [as in the Narrator's first speech]" (untitled essay in *Modern Canterbury Pilgrims*). While events still occur in linear and cyclical time, the framework of "saving history" now becomes determinative.

Auden thus discerns the true meaning of time in the paradox of the Incarnation. God acts and the kingdom of God appears "not in our present and not in our future, but," as the Narrator describes, "in the Fullness of Time." Probably any

---

3. 1 Corinthians 1.23. See also 1 Corinthians 1.18-25. For a discussion of the importance of history in Old Testament interpretations, see Martin Buber, "Saga and History," 150-56. For a discussion of the importance of *Heilsgeschichte* in New Testament thought and Christian theology, see Reinhold Niebuhr, *The Nature and Destiny of Man*, 62-67.

attempt to explain or describe the paradox of the Incarnation must appear as paradoxical as the event itself and Auden's description is no exception. In an untitled contribution to the *Partisan Review* series "Religion and the Intellectuals," he defines the "Fullness of Time" as "the right moment for the eternal vow to be made Flesh and the Divine Sacrifice to take place."[4] This definition, like the whole Oratorio, draws heavily on the thought of Kierkegaard, who earlier had defined the importance of the fullness of time as "[t]he concept round which everything turns in Christianity" (Auden, *The Living Thoughts of Kierkegaard* 175). The Danish theologian then elaborated by adding that this concept "makes all things new, . . . the *fullness of time*, is the instant as eternity, and yet this eternity is at once the future and the past" (175; emphasis added). (Auden would later edit Kierkegaard's work in *The Living Thoughts of Kierkegaard* [1963].) In his poem "Kairos and Logos," Auden elaborates on this view that there was a "right moment" for the Incarnation to occur as the time when "Predestined love / Fell like a daring meteor into time, / The condescension of eternal order " (lines 28-30, page 12). The Fullness of Time induced by this intimation of an "eternal order" include "[a] ground and possibility of order" and "the certainty of love" (35-36). But the largest changes are also the most profound as this order reflects a new reality that "never, like its own, condemned the world / [o]r hated time, but sang until . . . death / O Thou who lovest, set its love in order" (37-39, 12).

Paul Tillich gives another definition, but in prose, of this Kairoic moment as used by Auden in both "Kairos and Logos" and *For the Time Being*:

---

4. See Auden's untitled essay in *Modern Canterbury Pilgrims*, ed. James A Pike, 173-77.

Kairos is fulfilled time, the moment when time is invaded by eternity. But Kairos is not perfect completion in time. To act and wait in the sense of Kairos means to wait upon the invasion of the eternal and to act accordingly, not to wait and act as though the eternal were a fixed quantity which could be introduced into time, as a social structure which represents the end and goal of history, for instance. The eternal is that which invades; it is not something tangible and objective. (*The Religious Situation* 129; see also *The Interpretation of History*)

H. Richard Niebuhr, another theologian contemporaneous with Auden, describes this concept of the fullness of time in less philosophical and, perhaps, clearer language: that "Jesus had been born in the fullness of time meant that all things which had gone before seemed to conspire toward the realization of this event" (112). Auden follows Niebuhr's line of reasoning and in that same untitled contribution to "Religion and the Intellectuals" defines the "Fullness of Time," as noted earlier, as "the right moment for the eternal vow to be made Flesh and the Divine Sacrifice to take place" (120).[5]

---

5. Auden here is quoting from his review of Reinhold Niebuhr's *The Nature and Destiny of Man* reprinted in *The Complete Works, Prose*, vol. 2 (133). For a full discussion of Kierkegaard's influence on Auden's poetry during the 1940s, see Justin Replogle, "Auden's Religious Leap," especially 49-51 and 58-64. For a point of view opposite Kierkegaard's, see Oscar Cullmann, who in *Christ and Time* (1950) criticizes Kierkegaard because his conception of "contemporary" mistakes the significance of the present for redemptive history. According to him, faith transfers us back into the time of the Incarnation; it makes us contemporaries of the apostles. In this view it is correct that faith permits us actually to survey the entire redemptive line and to share in its fruits. . . . But the concept of contemporaneity presupposes that basically time as redemptive time has already come to a standstill with Jesus Christ; hence, we can only go back to him in order to enter the realm of salvation. (146)

In the "Meditation of Simeon," the central prose section of *For the Time Being* (448-54), Auden gives three conditions that he sees as necessary before time may be "fulfilled" or "before the Infinite could manifest Itself in the finite" (which may be his phrasing for Tillich's "time . . . invaded by eternity"). Humans must first thoroughly explore other avenues of meaning and find them wanting, but they must have no excuse for the lack of meaning or for the consequent despair in which they find themselves: "the mirror in which the Soul expected to admire herself must be so perfectly polished that her natural consolation of vagueness should be entirely withdrawn" (449). (This idea is evident throughout the oratorio; for example in the initial speech of the first Wise Man (429) and the opening chorus previously discussed.) Second, people must try philosophically to ascertain the true nature of the world and to see themselves as unfulfilled (see the Second Wise Man's first speech: "We anticipate or remember but never are" [430]). Finally, people must explore their own consciousness and come to know themselves psychologically to the point "where there remained but one thing to know, [their] . . . Original Sin" (450). From Auden's point of view, as reflected in Simeon's "Meditation," the first century after Jesus's birth met all of these conditions. In a parallel statement in the essay, "The Means of Grace," he gives his reasons:

> The special Christian revelation, the Incarnation, occurred precisely at that moment in history when an impasse seemed to have been reached. The civilized world was now politically united, but its philosophical dualism divided both society and the individual personality horizontally, the wise from the ignorant, the Logos from the Flesh; the only people who did

not do this were the Jews, but they divided society vertically,
themselves from the rest of the world. (765)[6]

This historical "impasse" is removed by the Incarnation, where
the possibility of uniting society and the individual personality
becomes present in the "certainty of love" ("Kairos and Logos"
12). Time is not "hated" by God, nor is He "indifferent" to it, but
He has "illuminated the time in which . . . our freedom is
realized or prevented" (*For the Time Being* 452). The result is
the important recognition of humanity's natural element,
which in Auden's religious understanding is time, more
particularly history.[7] In *The Dyer's Hand* (1962), Auden argues
that "[m]an is a history-making creature who can neither
repeat his past nor leave it behind; at every moment he adds to
and thereby modifies everything that had previously happened
to him" (278). Similarly, Simeon concludes that "the course of
History is predictable in the degree to which all people love
themselves, and spontaneous in the degree to which each. . .
[person] loves God . . ." (*For the Time Being* 452). In the words
of the Wise Men:

---

6. *The New Republic* 104 (2 June 1941): 765. The thought and vocabulary of
   Auden's reviews, essays, and poetry of the early forties parallel to a
   remarkable degree that of H. Richard Niebuhr's in *The Meaning of
   Revelation* (1941). Niebuhr's brief volume is especially valuable in
   interpreting Auden's theological point of view in *For the Time Being*.

7. "We are in history as the fish is in water and what we mean by the
   revelation of God can be indicated only as we point through the medium
   in which we live" (H. Richard Niebuhr, *Revelation* 48). Auden following
   H. Richard Niebuhr delineates one understanding of time and history,
   which in this instance becomes a religious understanding of time as the
   medium of human life. How humans comprehend and/or experience that
   "medium" as the medium of human life is the subject of this book.

> Love does not fear substantial anarchy,
> But vividly expresses obligation
> With movement and in spontaneity. (446)

The spontaneity latent in history is similar to what the Chorus describes as the "magic secret of how to extemporize life" (414). The "secret" is not to be found within a person, through solitude, but is revealed to the individual from outside him or herself. Auden believes that once individuals become aware of God's love for them as revealed in the Incarnation, they become freed from the petty desires and fears that otherwise entrap and block any uncalculated response to life. The Incarnation thus provides an antidote to "the error bred in the bone," which Auden dwelt on in "September 1, 1939":

> . . . the error bred in the bone
> Of each woman and each man
> Craves what it cannot have,
> Not universal love
> But to be loved alone. (61-65)

The "faces along the bar" (44) of "September 1, 1939" agree with the Narrator of *For the Time Being* that universal love is not satisfactory because it does not recognize each person as an individual hence, each appears to have "no importance to love" (410), except as part of an aggregate. Yet in the paradox of God's action in Christ, the "universal love" is directed towards all people and, at the same time, towards each person alone. As Simeon later says in his "Meditation": "the Truth is indeed One, without which is no salvation, but the possibilities of real knowledge are as many as are the creatures in the very real and most exciting universe that God creates with and for His love . . ." (454).

God's revelation in the fullness of time is, thus, paradoxically both universal and personal. Christ comes to and for *all people* in the Incarnation, yet in this same act each person learns that he or she is "loved alone," for, as Simeon says echoing Martin Buber, "that which hitherto we could only passively fear as the incomprehensible I AM, henceforth we may actively love with comprehension that THOU ART" (451). In the first edition of *For the Time Being*, Auden had written "HE IS" rather than THOU ART. The poet then changed the wording based on his reading of Martin Buber's highly influential *I and Thou* (1937), where Buber distinguishes between two very different basic forms of human relations: the I-It relation, which is his description of a person relating to a thing or to another human being treated as a thing, and the I-Thou relation where the person's, the "I's whole being is fully realized through a dialogue with God, the 'eternal Thou,' and in consequence with the 'Thous' of his fellow human beings as well" (Kirsch, *Auden and Christianity* 49). On the basis of this individual, personal experience, the Wise Men and Shepherds celebrate the end of human isolation:

> Released by Love from isolating wrong,
> Let us for Love unite our various song,
> Each with his gift according to his kind
> Bringing this child his body and his mind. (445)

The knowledge of God's purpose in acting in the "Fullness of Time," which is revelation, becomes the basis for the religious understanding of time as redeemed. Instead of seeing time as a series of events to which humans are disinterested spectators, every person, thanks to the Incarnation, can experience time through what H. Richard Niebuhr calls "internal history":

> In internal history . . . our time is our duration. What is past is not gone; it abides in our memory; what is future is not non-existent but present in us as our potentiality. Time is here organic or it is social. . . . Time in our history is not another dimension of the external space world in which we live, but a dimension of our life and of our community's being. We are not in this time but it is in us. (69)[8]

This claim that "[t]ime in our history is . . . a dimension of our life and of our community's being" helps explain why the Wise Men and Shepherds conclude joyfully, if somewhat enigmatically:

> Space is the Whom our loves are needed by,
> Time is our choice of How to love and Why. (447)

In the Fullness of Time and in response to the encounter with the Incarnation "for once in our lives / Everything became a You and nothing was an It" (compare Buber). The effects of this religious view of time, as Auden describes them in *For the Time Being*, are as profound as they are far-reaching and lead to a new, religious understanding of the primary importance of history not as external, but internal; of space not as impersonal, but personal; and of time not as linear or as cyclical, but as redeemed. In the Fullness of Time, "We are not in this time but it is in us" (H. Richard Niebuhr 8).

---

8. H. Richard Niebuhr also says: "Events may be regarded from the outside by a non-participating observer; then they belong to the history of things. They may be apprehended from within, as items in the destiny of persons and communities; then they belong to a lifetime and must be interpreted in a context of persons with their resolutions and devotions" (63). Later he adds, "In our history all events occur not to impersonal bodies but to selves in community with other selves and they must be so understood" (65).

"The Cancer of Time"

> *Time passes.*
> *That is all.*
> ——*Samuel Beckett,* What Where

Samuel Beckett is also a deeply religious writer whose work raises, what Paul Tillich calls, "ultimate questions" about the meaning and/or purpose of life, but unlike Auden he is in no sense a believer in any orthodox religion. Time for Beckett was indeed "a metaphysical problem" (Deane 64), but not a theological one. Examining the several representations of time in Beckett's early plays reveals just how continuously and how exhaustively he wrestled with this metaphysical problem, which came to pervade his work. From his first produced play, *Waiting for Godot* (1952), to his last, *What Where* (1983), he returned again and again to explore—not what Auden called "The Fullness of time," but—what Beckett called the "cancer of time" ("Memory and Habit are the attributes of the Time cancer" [Beckett, *Proust* 7]).

In western thought, art, and language since the advent of Christianity, the most common image of time, as previously outlined in the introduction and in the first part of this chapter, is of a line stretching from the past through the present into the future. Most of Beckett's early plays, especially *Endgame* (1957), *All that Fall* (1957), *Happy Days* (1961), *Act without Words I* (1957) and *II* (1960), along with the brief dramaticules follow this expected path; that is, characters and events move from somewhere in the past through the present into the future—even if that future, like all futures, remains indeterminate. In other early plays, however, the image of time shifts away from the traditional line, to become best represented by other geometric forms, such as a series of concentric circles in *Krapp's Last Tape* (1958), a closed circle in *Play* (1963), a spiral in *Waiting for Godot,* and even—I will claim—a Möbius strip in the radio play *Embers* (1959).

In *Act without Words II,* for instance, two characters clearly distinguishable as unique individuals move horizontally across the stage from stage right to stage left. Their action suggests that traditional image of time as a line on which human beings are stuck, but their actions also convey to an audience a sense of the inexorable passing of the only time there is. "Was there any other time but that time," remarks a character in *That Time,* not really asking a question so much as asserting a commonplace (*Complete Plays* 395). That there is no other time only increases the poignancy of *Act without Words II,* because although the two characters may move continuously, they fail to go anywhere or do anything. Thus the imagery of this mime strongly implies the futility of all human action because all action proves repetitive, empty, and meaningless.

Endgame builds on this image of characters moving on a line as throughout the play time does progress until at last it comes to an end. "Me to play," says Hamm (*CP* 93, 132). Like a story which has a beginning, middle, and end, Hamm's life-story, which began with his "accursed progenitor" (96), then moved through various stages until it arrived, finally, at immobility and the impossibility of acting. Hamm and company are in the "endgame" with only a few final moves left as time winds down to those instants that immediately precede immobility. "Old endgame lost of old, play and lose and have done with losing," he advises himself in the play's closing moments (132). He then accurately sums up his situation: "Moments for nothing, now as always, time was never and time is over, reckoning closed and story ended" (133). Curtain. Play's over, story's done. Time that proved too brief to understand or accomplish anything now is ended. "Outside of here it's death" (96).[9] Perhaps there is a Hell next door, perhaps not. It does not matter as the "story" has ended. Having gone on until there is no more to do, no more to say, no more to feel, Hamm ends his play. "It's finished . . . ," he announces (116), echoing Jesus's last words on the cross. Then adds, "Nearly finished," echoing Clov's opening line (115, 93).

For Clov, too, time runs out though at the end he appears dressed for the road and ready to leave—perhaps to "fresh fields and pastures new," but more likely to more of the "muck" of which Beckett speaks in interviews and in *Godot*. Clov's poignant line "I say to myself that the earth is extinguished, though I never saw it lit" (321) suggests that he will continue to see and experience only "ashes" (113) in his physical, moral, emotional, and mental landscape. "Something . . . [for him, too, has taken] its course" (98, 107), "reckoning closed and story ended" (133).

Endgame is clearly an eschatological play about the end of time, of "last things" in Beckett's universe. Like a chess game—or any game—like the journey through life, like the living of a day, time progresses through the knowable present on into the unknowable future. While there is repetition in *Endgame*, as there is in *Godot* and in *Play*, the repetition here is more background against which the play's action, which does move forwards from the past through the present and into the future, takes place. Nagg *does* die. Clove *does* get dressed for the road. The painkiller *does* run out, the story Hamm tells *is finished*, and

---

9. The mention of the boy off in the distance who as a "potential procreator" could begin "this" all over again does not alter the ending, for in Hamm's bleak assessment: "If he [the boy] exists he'll die there or he'll come here. And if he doesn't . . ." (131).

the end *is an end*—a conclusion without any real possibility of additional action, unlike in *Godot.*

Time is also experienced as linear in most of Beckett's other early plays including the radio play *All that Fall* and the mime *Act without Words I.* For example, in *All that Fall,* something happens before the play begins—a murder has been committed; an action takes place in the present moving the characters towards the future in much the same way as the comic, improbable bulk of Maddy Rooney moves inexorably, if with considerable difficulty, to the railway station to meet blind Mr. Rooney. Her struggle to arrive takes on epic proportions and occupies all of the listener's attention as "something [there, too] is taking its course" (*Endgame* 98).

In *Act without Words I,* a lone mime faces a Pavlovian world where he is expected to salivate and respond on cue, yet where he cannot possibly meet such expectations because the cues appear to be arbitrary, and even contradictory. Events, orders, and rewards appear at random, unpredictably, and finally seemingly out of control. It is as if a Pavlovian psychologist in charge of this particular experiment intended to drive his subject mad. Because there is no discernible pattern to events, no reason why certain ones occur before or after others, time may have the appearance of a line but if so, it is one that closely resembles Franz Kafka's notion of there being "no way, only a wavering." Yet here the "wavering" dissolves into isolated random points without meaning. The mime's situation itself more closely resembles the dog's situation in Kafka's wonderfully deadpan short story "Investigations of a Dog," in which the hero, a precocious dog, attempts, through the use of reason, observation, and experimentation, to predict what action on his part will result in bringing food down from the air. Similarly, the mime in *Act Without Words I* attempts to guess which action on his part might, for example, bring the carafe of water within reach. Kafka's dog concludes that "we find our food on the earth, but the earth needs our water to nourish it and only at that price provides us with our food, the emergence of which, however, and this should not be forgotten, can also be hastened by certain spells, songs, and ritual movements" (215). This dog conducts his "scientific" experiments and carefully makes his observations, but without certain crucial information about time, such as what happens before the food appears that makes it appear, and, as a result, his observations remain partial and his conclusions cannot possibly be accurate. For him to assess accurately his situation he would need access to information about human beings, their actions and their motives—information which is forever and completely denied him by his very nature, his dogginess.

In the same way, for the mime in *Act without Words I* to respond "correctly" to a given stimulus he would need to know what purpose or plan, if any, the manipulator of objects might be following. Without such knowledge he is left with the extraordinarily frustrating task of attributing purpose and meaning to what must remain for him entirely random, often maliciously arranged, events. He is, as Lance St. John Butler points out, an almost perfect illustration of what Heidegger meant by humans being "thrown" into time (Butler 36-37): "From my 'state of mind' I look backwards, as it were, at my throwness into facticity; from my understanding I look forwards into my possibility" (Butler 36). But like Kafka's dog, it is impossible for the mime to act on the basis of any "under-standing," for he has no real knowledge of past events, nor does he have any clear anticipation of future "possibility"; therefore, whenever he succeeds in making a few correct predictions, it is purely accidental and ultimately misleading, for his chain of reasoning is always based upon a faulty premise. What is worse, the mime's desire to predict in the present by reasoning from the past to the possible future—in order to be in a position to satisfy whatever demands are being made upon him—works to his own frustration and defeat. As Thomas Postlewait observes,

> in terms of the temporal sequence there is no orderly principle of cause and effect that unifies memory and expectation. . . . Time and space may be apriori conditions for understanding, as Kant argues, but for Beckett's characters neither things next to each other nor one thing after another provides a modal basis for demonstrating interconnection. (480)

The wavering line of time thus holds no meaning, nor does it offer a secure purchase from which to evaluate the past, let alone predict the future.

Time in *Krapp's Last Tape* appears to correspond to a clear line progressing from the past, before the curtain rises, through the present of the performance to the future of the final curtain scene. A closer examination reveals, however, that there is not one but three times present in the play: 1.) the time of the performance itself set in the future when "the aged Krapp-to-be, an Irishman incapacitated by time" makes his "last tape" at age sixty-nine (Bermel 160); 2.) the time of "that stupid bastard I took myself for thirty years ago . . ." (Beckett, *Krapp's* 222), when he believed he had "every reason to suspect at the . . . (*hesitates*) . . . crest of the wave—or thereabouts" (217); and, finally, the time of Krapp, " . . . that young whelp" (218) who must be about twenty-seven or—more likely—twenty-nine years old. Those three times in this play may best be represented not by a straight line or even by a "wavering," but by a series of concentric circles with the Krapp of about twenty-nine in the center, then Krapp of thirty-nine in the first circle, followed by an outermost ring of Krapp at sixty-nine. In between are all forty of the Krapps represented by the "spools" (read "stools"?) of recorded tape piled up in his "den." The shape of these concentric circles itself forms an image of a spool or reel of tape.

Krapp's project of recording, that is, capturing his memories each year, on a spool of tape proves predicated on two relatively shaky premises: first, that the year will be a significant unit of time, and second, that he knows the significance of events as they happen in that year. As each year passes, Krapp takes time on his birthday to evaluate the past year's events or, as he puts it, to separate "the grain from the husks" (217). He then records these achievements "against the day when my work will be done and perhaps no place left in my memory warm or cold, for the miracle that . . . (*hesitates*) . . . for the first that set it alight" (220). What Krapp failed to realize is—to borrow the Hungarian-American writer Eleanor Perényi's insight—first, that "one passes insensibly from one part of life to another, from the past into the future. . . . You are never given so much as a glimpse of what you will become," and second, that "[f]or a long time, the memory of the past sustains you, and when it no longer does, you are already a different person" (169). The older sixty-nine-year-old Krapp has ironically no patience for his recorded, freeze-dried memories, nor does he have much patience for the younger Krapp of thirty-nine, whose aspirations he sees as pretentious and whose language he finds riddled with jargon and hard words. That "memory of the past" fails utterly to sustain him. In fact the elder Krapp, "already a different person," loses all interest in the very project itself: "Last fancies. (*Vehemently.*) Keep 'em under! . . . Ah finish your booze now and get to your bed. Go on with this drivel in the morning. Or leave it at that. (*Pause.*) Leave it at that. (*Pause.*)" (222-23).

In the past year, the event he enjoyed at sixty-nine above all others was reveling in pronouncing the word "Spooool! Happiest moment of the past half million" (222). Otherwise life, for him, has been reduced to "[t]he sour cud and the iron stool" (222). Like Emil Jannings's clown in *The Blue Angel* (1930, dir. Josef von Sternberg), Krapp now waits only for death with little or no curiosity about his former years' activities. His earlier excretions, the "crap" of his life captured on spools of tape, all neatly packaged, labeled and filed, surround him in his den, but hold no interest for him. Instead, he thinks of how it might be to recall earlier moments of physical activities, rather than mental achievements:

> Lie propped in the dark—and wander. Be again in the dingle on a Christmas Eve, gathering holly the redberried. (*Pause.*) Be again on Croghan on a Sunday morning, in the haze, with the bitch, stop and listen to the bells. (*Pause.*) And so on. (*Pause.*) Be again, be again. (*Pause.*) All that old misery. (*Pause.*) Once wasn't enough for you. (223)

Like the dog in Kafka's story, Krapp drew up his plans, created his project, and constructed his argument all upon a false premise: he thought he knew when young what would be valuable to him when old. But his assumptions prove false. At the end he turns back to an earlier tape in which he said "farewell to love" but which also has a clear description of his lying "across her [Bianca] with my face in her breasts and my hand on her" (223). Gone are the claims to be "at the crest of the wave," to be engaged in meaningful, significant life work, and in their place are memories of physical events: sights, sounds, smells, and human contact. Thus *Krapp's Last Tape*, this "piece of Protestant sentimentality," as one critic called it and Beckett did not disagree (Murray, "Productions" 111), concludes as it began with "moments for nothing" (Beckett, *Endgame* 133) as Krapp in the future listens to and comments disparagingly upon Krapp in the present, who in turn listens to and comments disparagingly upon Krapp in the past. Finally, the last Krapp in the future abandons the project entirely in order to listen to moments that recall the sensual pleasure in an incident which earlier he had rejected, saying, "No, I wouldn't want them back [now]" (223).

In *Play*, the concentric circles of time in *Krapp's Last Tape* become replaced by a single closed circle forever revolving through the same events described in the same words. Here, three dead characters find themselves in Beckett's version of Dante's version of Hell where the damned are condemned to travel forever in an endless circle, continually reminded of the evil that led them to this infernal place and always faced with the knowledge that there is no exit, there is no hope since they have no more time. In contrast to Krapp, who is free to choose whatever tape he wishes to listen to and if he is not free to "be again," then he is at least free to recall again whatever portion of his "old misery" he desires, the three characters in *Play*, like those in Dante's *Inferno*, are condemned to repeat the same action over and over, speak the same speeches over and over, and have the same thoughts over and over.

Such endless repetition signals the impotence engendered by the absence of hope, the absence of a time-future. That any of the three characters "become aware of the pressure on them from an 'invisible inquisitor' to see the story differently," as one critic maintains, remains doubtful (Worth 261). Nor can "they . . . recognise the others' point of view, feel twinges of pity for them, entertain visions of a more civilized relationship" (261). Instead, their lives go on in endless repetition. As Katharine Worth observes: "the whole process is repeated, word for word, and of course this makes a strong impression of circularity . . ." (261), a circularity that implies absence of change and, by extension, the assumption that there never can be, nor ever will be, any change in their condition. The man of the trio is the only one of the three to use the word "change," and the context indicates that he is referring to his own death: "Down, all going down, into the dark, peace is coming . . . at last . . . when first this change" (*Play* 312). Moreover, he and the two women react in traditional, even predicable, ways to their "change" of death: the Man is grateful for the peace death brings; the First Woman pleads for mercy, while the Second Woman is angry and ready for a fight. Time for each has stopped: nothing new happens; no new events occur; no new emotions, no new idea or perception intrudes; there is only endless, complete repetition of their "Moments for nothing." The three are "trapped in a post mortal limbo chewing the dry bones of mutual memory," as Lance Butler succinctly summarizes the action or lack of it (164). To represent visually this negation of any progress in or of time, Beckett chose, as did Dante before him, a closed and endlessly revolving circle reflecting the truth of the motto over Dante's hell, "Abandon all hope ye who enter here." As the voice in *Embers* says—and he could well be speaking of the characters in *Play*: "that's what hell will be like, small chat to the babbling of Lethe about the good old days when we wished we were dead" (Beckett, *Embers* 256).

In *Embers* itself, however, time appears not as a closed circle but as almost a reflection of the chaos in a mind. Eugene Kaelin in "Voices, in English, on the Air," declares that *Embers* is "as clear a presentation of schizophrenia as Beckett has devised" (187):

> Henry has only one last ray of hope: to tell a story clearly so
> that others may understand who and what he is. But the
> alienation and self-entanglement of his inauthenticity is
> such, and the turbulence it creates so overwhelming, that he
> shall never find either the end or the significance of his tale,
> to which only the sea is a fitting background. (187)

A different approach to time in the play and the surface chaos
of the story might account for the "turbulence" of which
Kaelin speaks by observing that there is in the play only one
character even though there may appear to be several
characters performing discrete actions within and without the
main tale. There is really only one tale, one time, which is the
present moment of Henry's telling his story, as Kaelin also
suggests. All time in the play is Henry's—the lone
character's—time. Within that present moment, he creates
through recall or through imagination the various characters
and brings them not into conscious existence, but into his
consciousness. Nothing in the play exists except what exists in
Henry's head. Time in *Embers* may thus be best represented not
by a traditional, but by an untraditional geometric shape: that
of the Möbius strip—a figure which appears to have two sides
but in reality has only one; a figure which also appears to have
only one side but which in reality has two, exactly as the play
appears to have many characters, and several times, but in
"reality" everything is located in Henry's mind as he remains
the play's only character and all time remains his time.

If *Play* leaves no room for possibility, since no change is
possible within a closed circle, and *Embers* presents a closed
system within one man's head, *Waiting for Godot* in contrast
presents a different image of time—one that offers genuine
possibility, if within some well-defined limits. The German
round song which begins act 2 is a good example of the limited

action possible within the play. According to Ruby Cohn, this song is "an old favorite of Beckett (who translated it from the original German) . . ." (40):

> A dog came in the kitchen
> And stole a crust of bread.
> Then cook up with a ladle
> And beat him till he was dead.
>
> Then all the dogs come running
> And dug the dog a tomb
> And wrote upon the tombstone
> For the eyes of dogs to come:
>
> A dog came in the kitchen
> And stole a crust of bread.
> Then cook up with a ladle
> And beat him till he was dead.
>
> Then all the dogs come running
> And dug the dog a tomb— (52-53)

Cohn argues that the song "exemplifies a Chinese-box structure through time and words: the dog's tombstone . . . commemorates a dog who has been beaten to death and so on ad infinitum" (40). But seen in light of the whole play, the movement of that song sung as a round suggests not so much a series of nesting boxes as it does a spiral circling round itself, which, in turn, mirrors the time of the play where the same or identical actions are repeated with the same or identical characters who make use of the same or identical props. Each act begins with a pair of boots on the stage, for example, that look exactly like the pair of boots on stage at the beginning of the other act; each act follows a similar pattern: the two tramps meet, greet, and talk to one another; Pozzo and Lucky arrive, encounter the tramps, and depart; night falls suddenly; and each act concludes with a small boy who arrives to announce— inevitably—that "Mr. Godot . . . won't come this evening but surely tomorrow" (48). As each day a dog rushes into the kitchen to be beaten, buried, and a tombstone erected with its story written upon it, so each "day" the tramps meet, pass the time in waiting, and having "waited long enough [they] will wait forever" (*Malone Dies* qtd. in Deane 62). "We are not saints," says Vladimir, "but we have kept our appointment" (*Godot* 73). Yet he is also correct when he observes near the beginning of act 2: "Things have changed since yesterday," to which Estragon adds: "It's never the same pus from one second to the next" (55). In *Godot*, the Heraclitian flux shifts from the river of time as the river of life, to the "pus" of time as the "pus" of life. Within this constricted view tiny distinctions between dogs, cooks, boys, and tramps performing similar actions, singing similar songs, saying similar or sometimes seemingly identical things become important, as does an improbable tree with no leaves and one with "four or five" (52); between a blind and a seeing Pozzo; or between a speaking and a silent Lucky.

The opposing view, that there are no distinctions that become differences, is eloquently maintained by Pozzo:

> Have you not done tormenting me with your accursed time? It's abominable. When! When! One day, is that not enough for you, one day just like any other day, one day he went dumb, one day I went blind, one day we'll go deaf, one day we were born, one day we'll die, the same day, the same second, is that not enough for you? [*Calmer*] They give birth astride of a grave, the light gleams an instant, then it's night once more. (82)

Ironically, Pozzo confuses the infinitely slow progress of time in which nothing happens with the infinitely fast progress of time where everything blurs together. Ihab Hassan cogently argues that "[i]n Beckett's work . . . time runs out at an infinitely slow pace. At the beginning and at the end, we still wait for Godot, but things become a little worse . . . . This is the world of entropy" (188). But the term "entropy" might be better applied to *Endgame*, where everything appears to run out, rather than to *Godot*, for in *Godot* there is the positive action of the tramps waiting, which both the play's action and the German round song mirror. Lance Butler maintains that

> [w]aiting is how we comport ourselves towards possibility, according to Heidegger, and for Vladimir and Estragon this is roughly the case too. . . . the tramps are authentically keeping their options open while waiting for possibility. Meanwhile it is essential that they do nothing that will preclude their genuine availability for possibility. In other words they must do nothing. Which is why nothing happens in the play. (54)

Or, as one wag put it, why nothing happens twice in the play. Go Go and Di Di do indeed wait for "possibility" by doing nothing, and in their waiting lies hope. Unlike Dante's sinners, who can never change, and unlike his *Inferno*, where any suggestion of freedom is merely a hideous delusion designed to increase torment, the tramps in *Waiting for Godot* experience some movement as they wait for possibility. They are, as Vladimir says, "inexhaustible" (57), which is an appropriate description of them and their time which may best be represented not by a closed circle of the damned as in *Play*, nor by a line moving from the past through the present into the future as in *Endgame* and the mimes, but by a spiral where action repeats, but not in quite the same way, as the spiral comes round to the same position but never exactly in the same place. In that slight shift of the spiral lies possibility. Because the spiral "is perpetually turning in on itself, expanding and contracting, [and] has an interchangeable centre and circumference, and has neither beginning nor end . . . ," it is often used symbolically to represent the joining of "[t]he universe and man's consciousness in a continuum and a dynamic whole . . ." (Puce 7).

To paraphrase the American theologian H. Richard Niebuhr, all of Beckett's characters, like all human beings, "are in [time] . . . as the fish is in water" (48). Whether that ubiquitous time is represented by a closed circle signifying a completed, unchanging, and unchangeable condition or by a series of concentric circles of diminishing and diminished meaning rippling out from a center or by a spiral of endlessly repeating actions in slightly changed positions or by the more traditional line stretching from a beginning to the inevitable end—whatever the most appropriate image may be, the characters in Beckett's early plays are stuck in time as a fly becomes stuck on what Langston Hughes once poignantly called "the sweet flypaper of life" (DeCarava and Hughes, 1955), and none is able to overcome its limitations. As Maddy Rooney so cogently observes, as earlier quoted, "It is suicide to be abroad. But what is it to be at home, . . . what is it to be at home? A lingering dissolution" (*All that Fall* 175). Hence the progression in Beckett's early plays from the options for action or inaction in *Waiting for Godot*, which remains his most optimistic and occasionally even hopeful play, to the other plays where characters are driven into immobility, as the author reminds audiences again and again that "[i]n the Beckettian universe, no man can shuttle off his mortal coil. We are beings who exist in time; death is inescapable" (Kearney 273).

Yet even that realization will not satisfy his most memorable characters, Di Di and Go Go, who refuse to curl up in the fetal position taken by the mime in *Act without Words I* when faced with an arbitrary universe that appears without possibility. The tramps instead insist on moving through that universe at their own pace and with their own style despite their knowledge that they, like the mime in *Act without Words II*, are not going anywhere significant. They continue to speak and act, for they are, unlike Winnie in *Happy Days*, not reduced to immobility because of being buried up to the neck in sand, or unlike Mouth in *Not I*, not reduced to a mere mouth, nor are they, unlike the characters in *Play*, reduced to playing a part in Hell in their funereal urns. Their time may become "Moments for nothing," but in those moments they will assert their presence as persons.

This juxtaposition of empty moments and the inexhaustible quality of character may best be seen in the fragment of poetic dialogue in *Godot*, which begins: "All the dead voices."

> ESTRAGON. All the dead voices.
> . . .
> ESTRAGON. They talk about their lives.
> VLADIMIR. To have lived is not enough for them.
> ESTRAGON. They have to talk about it.
> VLADIMIR. To be dead is not enough for them.
> ESTRAGON. It is not sufficient.
> [*Silence.*]
> . . . (57)

Nor is it sufficient for the two tramps.

Adrift amidst the shards of civilization, Di Di and Go Go attempt to create in their consciousness what one critic terms a "higher order, purely positive aesthetic value" (Kaelin 12). Thus they "pass the time" in conversation, argument, invention, abuse—in talk, although they realize that time "would have passed in any case" (Beckett, *Waiting* 45). For them, these are not so much "moments for nothing" as they are moments for waiting, and in waiting there is indeed "possibility" (Lance St. John Butler 36, 54). The spiral of time turns and turns as we are left with what Kaelin calls "the starkness of the tragedy" (161). But as he is also quick to point out, such "starkness" in Beckett "is relieved by the humanity of its expression" (161). Thrown into facticity, Beckett's characters are thrown into time, into existence, "where . . . suffering and . . . being are one" (Kaelin 11), and where upon reflection we may come to under- stand that "[a]ll our individual times will pass away; and when they do, so will we. Our dignity is to know this to be a fact" (Kaelin 161). Or, as Beckett will later write in one of his very last plays, *Ohio Impromptu*: "The sad tale a last time told. . . . Nothing is left to tell" (448). (This final line of the play is then repeated and reinforced by the visual image of Reader closing the book [448]). Yet in affirming mortality Beckett also affirms the human dignity that is derived from accepting such mortality.

But what of the destructive, infectious "cancer of time" that Beckett first broached in his critical work on Proust? The early plays appear to wrestle with the experience of time under several different aspects rather than appearing to suffer from its infection. It is true that all his characters are on Earth and that there is no help for that, but it is equally true that all creatures including all humans live in time. Beckett's early plays give us images of how humans may live in time from ignoring it as in *Act without Words II* or being unaware of it as the tramps are for much of *Waiting for Godot* to misjudging it as Krapp does in

Krapp's Last Tape to filling it with whatever scraps or shards of civilization they may find at hand (*Godot*). This tale of time begun with Beckett's first produced play, *Waiting for Godot*, ends with *What Where*'s concluding lines, which suggest his frustration with the puzzle of time. Like Borges, his conclusion is that time could be a riddle to which humans will never find the answer, so having explored the problem thoroughly he concludes that all we can know or deduce is that "time passes." Therefore, it is better to leave it alone and accept it as an unsolvable riddle:

> Time passes.
> That is all.
> Make sense who may.
> I switch off. (*Complete Plays* 476)

Chapter 5
Time, Memory, and Dementia

Looking back, we cannot see,
Except for its blurring lights
Like underwater stars and moons,
Our starting-place.
Behind us, beyond us now
Is phantom territory . . .
        ——*Robert Hayden, "Traveling through Fog"*

We are our memory, we are
this chimerical museum of shifting forms,
this heap of broken mirrors.
        ——*Jorge Luis Borges, "Cambridge"*

Without time there would be no memory and without memory we would lose our sense of time. The two are inseparable for time is "the landscape of experience" (Boorstin 1) and memory is the record of that experience (and much more). Memories are how we recall and understand past events in the present after they have become "blur[ed]" and receded down the course of time both in our own lives and in those of others into what Robert Hayden called the "phantom territory" ("Traveling through Fog" 6). Often we call upon our memory as we reconsider our own or others' behavior that may have puzzled and disturbed us. Yet, as previously discussed in chapter 2, no memory can be an exact duplication of past events but rather each appears as a broken reflection of past events brought forward into present time. Borges described this phenomenon eloquently in his poem "Cambridge," also quoted in the epigraph to this chapter, as that "chimerical museum of shifting forms" (46). This chapter discusses the effect time has on memory using first an example taken from Marina Carr's play *The Mai* (1994) of a person who attempts to understand another now dead. In this instance the understanding is especially difficult as it involves a child attempting to comprehend a late-parent's seemingly incomprehensible action. The second example, taken from Frank McGuinness's play *The Hanging Gardens* (2013), examines what happens to a person when over time memory begins to deteriorate in cases of dementia of whatever form and how this loss of past-time affects an individual's identity, leaving that unfortunate person in limbo and those around him or her in desperate straits.

Time and Memory

> *[T]he astonishing phenomenon of memory, the foundation and abiding stockpile of things past and yet strangely present.*
> ———*Nathaniel Lawrence*

In W. P. Kinsella's novel *Shoeless Joe* (1982)—later made into the film *Field of Dreams* (1989, dir. Phil Alden Robinson)—two young men meet their father not as they will know him as his children but as he was before he married and became their father. This fantasy manipulates time so that the two siblings encounter their parent as he was before either of them was born and that enables them to pay him a great compliment. Their father, a catcher on a professional baseball team, has just finished a game when his future sons meet him and one says, "I admire the way you catch a game" (254). Besides facilitating the fantasy, the time slip also helps dissipate the inevitable mystery of parental motivation and values for the two sons. In ordinary everyday experience time denies such a meeting to all children who must instead fall back on their memory and the memories of others as they attempt to understand their parents. In Carr's play *The Mai*,[1] Millie at thirty attempts to understand the troubling memory of her mother, known as The Mai, who abandoned her children for high-paying summer work in London in an Arab hairdressing salon when Millie was fifteen. When her mother returned home she used that income plus other resources unknown to her daughter to build a magnificent house in the hope and, perhaps, expectation it would call back her feckless, unfaithful husband, Robert. But something even more puzzling and traumatic for Millie occurred a few years later when she was eighteen and her mother, then forty, committed suicide. For the next dozen years Millie had been haunted by this seemingly inexplicable act of her mother.

Millie narrates events in *The Mai* much as Tom Wingfield narrates those in Tennessee Williams's *The Glass Menagerie* (1945), but unlike Tom, who struggles with his memories of his sister and his mother, whom he abandoned a good few years before, and about which he feels considerable guilt, Millie struggles to understand through memory her dead mother's motivation that is intimately related to her mother's identity as

---

1. *The Mai* was voted Best New Play of the 1994 Irish Life Dublin Theatre Festival. Already acknowledged as one of the brightest new Irish playwrights (see Roche, *Contemporary* 6 and especially 286-88), her plays were, however, clearly derivative of Samuel Beckett. With *The Mai* Carr found her own voice leaving behind what she described as "my Beckett phase" (Interview C23). For a clear discussion of contemporary research on mind and memory, see Isaac Rosenfield, *The Invention of Memory*, a book that has greatly influenced my own thinking about memory.

a woman.[2] Millie's most significant memory, because the most
powerful and disturbing one, is, therefore, of The Mai's suicide,
which intrudes into other less emotionally fraught memories.
For example, in the middle of act 1, as Millie describes the
summer that Robert, The Mai's husband, who had absconded
some five years earlier, returned as abruptly as he had left, she
leaps ahead eighteen months to describe a trip to town she and
Robert took "to buy a blue nightgown and a blue bed jacket for
The Mai's waking . . . . No shroud for The Mai" (28). The play's
complex sequence of events culled from Millie's childhood
memories occurs not in their original chronological order in
which they happened but in the order of their emotional impact
on and importance for Millie, now thirty. In addition, part of
this sequence includes "the act of shared memory," which
Anthony Roche argues "is the play itself, the thread of affil-
iation which binds Grandma Fraochlán [The Mai's one-
hundred-year-old grandmother], the Mai and Millie together
across time, space and the absence of death" ("Women" 162).

Millie explores her first memory, which is of the grand
house her mother built in the belief that it would bring her
errant husband back, or, more precisely, she recalls "a *room with
a huge bay window*" (Carr 11) that has over time become her
memory of the house. This visual image of the huge bay
window dominates her memories of her mother as it dominated
the Abbey stage in the 1994 production of *The Mai* from the

---

2. Carr says she has read Tennessee Williams's *The Glass Menagerie* many
   times (Interview C23). Other well-known instances in contemporary
   Irish drama of an on-stage narrator who participates in the action are
   Michael in the successful Brian Friel play *Dancing at Lughnasa* (1990, for
   further comparison see Roche, "Women" 160) and Hugh Leonard's
   Stephen D (1964), a dramatization of James Joyce's *A Portrait of the Artist
   as a Young Man* conflated with *Stephen Hero*. For a full discussion of the
   failings of *Stephen D* see Lanters, especially 31-43.

raising to the lowering of the curtain.[3] This window, according to Millie's recall, frames The Mai's expectations, which appear fulfilled when Robert enters at the beginning of act 1; it also frames Millie's other strong memories of her mother's longing for him and her summoning him back to her side heard early in act 1 (14), as it will frame the tableau of Robert with The Mai dead in his arms at the end of act 1 (42). In act 2, the window frames Robert's betrayal—epitomized by the impersonal birthday card he gives The Mai with, worse, a ten pound note enclosed. At the end of act 2, Millie recalls a "memory" she could not have had because she was not present when the event happened, of The Mai looking through that window one last time before either going to bed or going off to commit suicide by drowning herself in Owl Lake, her own lake of tears.[4]

The repeated references to Owl Lake, of which the window affords a view, coupled with Millie's telling of its legend in a splendidly dramatic fashion has the effect of having that lake, though invisible to the audience, increasingly and ominously dominating the play as it increasingly comes to dominate Millie's memories. The verbal imagery coalesces with the powerful visual image framed in the window of the dead woman carried in Robert's arms backlit by ghostly light (42).

---

3. Commenting on Kathy Strachan's stage design of the 1994 Dublin production Roche notes about the "dream house she has constructed" that "[i]ts central feature in terms of the staging and . . . design is a huge window center stage which gives out to Owl Lake, the pattern of the lake reflected around the stage" ("Women" 161).

4. The 1995 production, a revival of the original 1994 production, differed from the published playscript in that The Mai did not "turn and drift from the room" (72). Instead, she clearly looked through the window, and only then went outside to reappear directly behind the window. Thus the audience's last glimpse of her was as seen through the window when she walked outside the house presumably to go down to Owl Lake and drown herself.

The sexual-sensual imagery begun with Robert playing The Mai's body with his cello bow followed by The Mai's appearing in her slip to get the whiskey bottle also culminates here with The Mai dead wearing the same or a similar slip: her unattainable, idealized love for unfaithful Robert now consummated in death and all framed in the very window she built to summon him back to her side. As Oscar Wilde wrote, imitating the sardonic style of the Latin satirists, "When the gods want to punish us, they answer our prayers," they answered The Mai's oft-repeated prayer of "Come home—come home" (Carr 14).

What Millie comes to understand in her present time and at her current age, and through her memories of past events that happened when she was too young to comprehend adult motivation, is that although Robert bears her dead body in the tableau, he could not bear The Mai's all-consuming passion. Like Hickey in Eugene O'Neill's *The Iceman Cometh* (1940), he could not live with The Mai's unshakeable faith in his ultimate fidelity. "There's a limit to the guilt you can feel and the forgiveness and the pity you can take!" cries Hickey (239), and surely Robert would not disagree.[5] Because Carr focuses on the wife and not, like O'Neill on the husband, we catch only glimpses of Robert's side of the conflict and these occur mostly in the arguments he has with The Mai. (The exception occurs in act 2 when Robert flaunts his tawdry infidelity before her and the small town where they live.)

---

5. Robert, like Hickey, wanders, seeks out other women because of boredom, curiosity, or no reason at all except they are there and available. The key distinction between the women in these two plays lies in Evelyn's pathos as opposed to The Mai's tragedy. Evelyn's naive, if unshakable, faith in Hickey's ability to reform—"you couldn't shake her faith that it had to come true—tomorrow!" (238)—contrasts with The Mai's final understanding of Robert's weak personality and her acknowledgment of his self-deception.

The structure of act l is, therefore, organized to reflect not the order in time of past events but their emotional impact on Millie in present time. As Israel Rosenfield rightly asserts in *The Invention of Memory: A New View of the Brain* (1988),

> Emotions are essential to the creation of memory because they organize it, establishing its relative importance in a sequence of events much as a sense of time and order is essential for a memory to be considered a memory, and not a thought or a vision of some particular instant, unrelated to past events. (72)

Thus the first, because the most important, event Millie recalls when she is thirty happened when she was sixteen and her father, Robert, returned to his deserted wife and family. The second most important event for Millie lies further back in time: it chronicles Robert's departure five years earlier when Millie was eleven. Then she recalls events of the summer of Robert's return—again, in the order of their emotional importance for her—after that The Mai's suicide by drowning, and so on through the act.[6] But the time of the play expands

---

6. Chronologically, events in the play occur as follows: 1.) The Mai and Robert fall in love, marry, have children, and after years of marriage one day Robert leaves. (All of these events occur before the play's action begins and are, therefore, recounted as memories by various participants and/or witnesses.) 2.) The Mai leaves her children with another woman and goes to work in London to earn money to build her house (early in act 2). 3.) Five years later Robert returns (opening scene of act 1). 4.) The Mai "celebrates" her fortieth birthday (opening scene of act 2). 5.) The Mai talks with Millie (closing scene of act 2). 6.) Robert carries the dead Mai in his arms (closing scene of act 1). 7.) Millie and Robert drive to town to buy a blue bed jacket to wake The Mai in—"no shroud for the Mai" (middle of act 1). 8.) Millie tells of her life after the death of her mother and of her attempt to understand events in her own life. (Millie's telling these details provides the frame for the play.)

greatly as added to Millie's recollection of events and people are other people's memories, which often go back another three generations in the family (compare Roche, *Contemporary* 247). As Millie tries to understand her mother, how she lived and why she died, she establishes the criteria by which she judges the importance of events, reflects upon how, where, and even why she knows what she knows about her mother, and in the process confronts her own identity as it is bound up in that "how" and "why."

Events that once appeared ambiguously clouded for Millie when they happened to her as a child now frequently appear clarified years later as she herself approaches The Mai's age, when those original events happened. For instance, Millie believes that she at thirty understands The Mai's motive for moving to and working in London that summer, which appeared unfathomable when she was a child and felt terribly deserted by her mother's leaving. Similarly, some events which appeared clear when they occurred now seem ambiguous, such as the stories Grandma Fraochlán told of her lover/husband, the nine-fingered fisherman, or those she told of her daughter Ellen's husband or about Ellen's marriage. Years afterward, tall tales about local characters have, perhaps, an unexpected relevance they lacked before, particularly tales about Sam Brady and his legendary cow, Billy the Black, which he would ride "like a horse . . . naked except for a pair of red bloomers" (50).

Dreams, whose content had been ignored or laughed at when dreamt, now are seen as hauntingly prophetic. Especially significant in thirty-year-old Millie's estimation was The Mai's dream the night before she and Robert were married as it foretold Robert's desertion of her a decade or so later. In that dream they both appear as children: she smiling and waving and he passing by her saying, "Not yet, not yet, not for thousands and thousands of years" (26). As he disappears she "see[s] a black cavern [she says] and I know it leads to nowhere and I start walking that way because I know I'll find you [Robert] there" (26). But Robert heads towards somewhere else, while she, determined, dedicated, follows searching for him. Her effort "leads nowhere" except to the blackness of her own death. Also, all those ancient local legends about Owl Lake, that all of them neglected and/or ignored in their youth, now appear in retrospect as dire warnings of impending doom which Robert, The Mai, and Millie all ignored at their peril "like sleepwalkers along a precipice . . . [they] walked on and on . . . not listening" (42).

Carr strongly believes that the needs of her drama, especially its use of time, should shape the sequence in which events occur rather than the more usual notion of a chronological sequence of events structuring the drama—all of which coincides with memory's continual rearrangement of the chronology of events. In her program note to Tom Mac Intyre's play *Good Evening, Mr Collins* (1955, revived in 1996), Carr describes how the playwright "plays with Time in the piece." She might well have been describing her own fantastic "playing" with time in *The Mai.* She emphatically declares in the same program note: "Time as we understand it, with all its imposing logic, is merely a construct of The Fallen World and therefore to be treated with suspicion" ("Bandit" n. pag.).[7] Similarly, in *The Mai*, precipitous non-mimetic shifts of subject, scene, and language occur as the time sequence is broken up and/or rearranged—most memorably at the end of act 1. There, immediately after she recalls a conversation between

---

7. In *Portia Coughlan* (1996), Carr continues playing with time by radically rearranging the sequence of events.

The Mai and her aunt Julia about Ellen (The Mai's mother) and her marriage, Millie abruptly shifts subject and language to narrate the legend of Owl Lake. Following this mythic narrative an audience is dramatically confronted by the sudden, arresting tableau of Robert with the dead Mai in his arms, which is succeeded in turn by Millie's verbally interpreting the Owl Lake legend in relation to her mother, father, and herself in highly poetic language.

   In writing of Mac Intyre's story "the lap of hay" inserted into *Good Evening, Mr Collins*, Carr describes vividly the quality of that story but also of her own legend of Owl Lake in *The Mai*: "Firstly it's the lyricism of it, then it's the simplicity. Finally it's how Mac Intyre uses the story, how it resonates through the whole piece, how all of Michael Collins' life and death is in that story. This is craftsmanship at its best" ("Bandit" n. pag.). The name "Owl Lake," like almost all anglicized place names in Ireland, is an English misreading of the Irish name, *loch cailleach oiche*, which means "Lake of the Night Hag or Pool of the Dark Witch" (41).[8] In the legend of Owl Lake, "Coillte, daughter of the mountain god, Bloom, fell in love with Biath, Lord of all the flowers" and they lived happily through the spring and into the summer. Then "one evening approaching autumn," he mentioned that he had to go to "live with the dark witch of the bog," but would return in the spring which he did do, but too late, for by that time the Hag had pushed Coillte into the lake formed from the copious tears she shed on his leaving (41). This legend, like Mac Intyre's story, "resonates through the whole piece," that is, through the whole play.

---

8. Compare the many erroneous translations of Irish place names in Brian Friel's *Translations* (1980).

The legend of Owl Lake not only parallels the story of The Mai and Robert falling in love, marrying, having children, his sudden leaving and equally sudden return, but the image of the god's daughter drowning herself in her own lake of tears also foreshadows the play's conclusion when The Mai will drown herself in Owl Lake. The startling image of The Mai dead, which immediately follows the telling of the legend, visually confirms this ending: "*Ghostly light on the window.* ROBERT *stands there with* THE MAI'S *body in his arms, utterly still.* MILLIE *watches them a minute. Ghostly effect*" (42). Following this shocking tableau, Millie eloquently articulates the implications of the legend of Owl Lake for The Mai, Robert, and herself in language often elevated as is appropriate to such legends. Her warning of dark, inevitable things to come verbally underlines the visual tableau: "I knew that story as a child. So did The Mai and Robert. But we were unaffected by it and in our blindness moved along with it like sleepwalkers . . . and all around gods and mortals called out for us to change our course and, not listening, we walked on and on" (42).

That tableau with which act 1 ends (as emphasized earlier) appears far out of order in the time sequence of the play's chronological events. By placing the suicide—chronologically the penultimate event of the play's action—not near the end of act 2 but at the end of act 1, Carr compels her audience to see all of The Mai's acts and words, including those still to come in act 2, as leading inevitably to this tableau of her drowning. This is the kind of "daring and invention" that Ionesco praised as "freedom of imagination [which] is not flight into the unreal, . . . [and] not escape" (qtd. in Hesson and Hesson 196), but rather a re-shaping of "the reality we thought real" (Malekin 41). Like Tennessee Williams Carr also scorns "the exhausted theatre of realism," employing instead various fantastic stage techniques and set pieces—such as the presentation of events in a non-chronological sequence, the use of mythic and/or prophetic narratives, the violent shifts of subject, and the sometimes arbitrary mixture of times, people, and places—all of which are fantastic in that they depart from a chronological time sequence or what is acknowledged as consensus reality and are employed in order to better explore the natural, the possible, the mortal as held in memory. In no sense, however, can *The Mai*, a true memory play, be considered a fantasy, which Colin Manlove, among others, has carefully defined as "[a] fiction evoking wonder and containing a substantial and irreducible element of supernatural or impossible worlds, beings or objects with which the mortal characters in the story or the readers become on at least partly familiar terms" (ix). There is no supernatural element in *The Mai*.

Throughout the play, Millie probes her memories in an attempt to understand and to gain knowledge of how and why events happened the way they did and how and why people behaved the way they did. For example, although her father, Robert, professes his undying love for her mother (Carr 27), Millie now examining her recollections as an adult realizes that he is no Romeo who, finding his Juliet dead, will commit suicide rather than face life without her, but is, instead, a latter-day Jason who, for all his professions of love such as "you are and were and always will be the only one" (27), will yield easily and repeatedly to temptation, especially if it is ego-flattering, such as a younger woman's attraction to him.

At the beginning of act 2, an audience can neither evade nor disregard the palpable inevitability that now hangs over the play. As J. M. Synge's *Riders to the Sea* (1902) must end with the last man of all the men in the house drowned and buried in a coffin made of "the finest white boards" (5), so *The Mai* must end with Robert unfaithful, The Mai drowned in the lake of her own tears, her dead body carried in his arms. This sense of tragic inevitability working its way through time, against which the events of act 2 play themselves out, partakes of what Carr calls "the Greek idea of destiny and fate and little escape" (Interview C23). However inevitable that tragedy may be, it nevertheless differs markedly from that of Greek classical drama such as *Oedipus Rex* or, more appropriately for this play, *Medea*. Unlike Carr and her contemporary audience, Sophocles and Euripides could count on their audiences knowing and remembering at least the outline of the story of their plays, thus instantly creating tragic irony as soon as, for instance, Oedipus appears on stage announcing himself as "I . . . of the famous name," or inducing fearful anticipation as when Medea off-stage rages, "Wronged, wronged, I am wronged / in every deepest corner of my being" (20). Carr's invented legend of Owl Lake, however, coupled with her playing with time, especially with the tableau at the end of act 1, does create in act 2 the "idea of destiny and fate and little escape" by establishing for the audience a memory of an event which has not yet occurred, an event still to come. As the Greek audience would recall throughout Euripides's play those dead children from the familiar legend of Medea, so a contemporary audience— thanks to·Carr's fantastic stage technique—recalls the dead Mai in Robert's arms throughout act 2. The cause of The Mai's tragic death—her single-minded passion for Robert—is strikingly similar to that of a Greek heroine, especially when Robert proves incapable of returning such highly charged commitment. His wistful belief that "not everything has to be final and tragic . . . not everything" (25) rings increasingly hollow coming from a weak, philandering man, especially when spoken to The Mai, this strong, deeply ardent, and totally committed woman, for whom events will prove both "final and tragic." Grandma Fraochlán sees Robert as a man who leaves, returns, and leaves again. When he objects, she recalls how "[y]a'ar own father left ya'ar mother, didn't he?" (23),[9] to which Robert replies by drawing a fine distinction between one who leaves never to return and one who, like his father and himself, leaves, then returns: "He never left her! He went to America for a few years. It was after the War, he had to get work, but he came back, didn't he?" But his argument falls on deaf ears, for as Grandma Fraochlán points out:

> An' thousands sted, war or no war, or brung their wives an' childer wud em. Buh noh you, no, an' noh ya'ar father, an' sure as I'm sittin' here, ya'll noh be stoppin' long, because we can't help repeatin', Robert, we repeah an' we repeah, th' orchestration may be different but tha tune is allas tha same. (23)

Grandma Fraochlán's contention that the passing of time changes nothing, for "we repeat and we repeat," rests on the Sophoclian assumption of character as fate. Against this fate humans living through their time are, if not powerless, then at least close to helpless.

Millie attempts to understand the impotence her parents experienced in the grip of fate working through time by puzzling through the various remembered incidents and recalled stories of her mother's life; such as The Mai's leaving her four children with another woman who already had ten of her own in order to take that job in a London hairdressing salon (45, 46). There she met an Arab princess. She and The Mai

---

9. Some of the play's dialogue is in an Irish midlands dialect Carr favors and uses in this and other plays.

"were two of a kind, moving towards one another across deserts and fairytales and years til they finally meet in a salon under Marble Arch. . . . Two little princesses on the cusp of a dream, one five, the other forty" (46). Only years later did Millie understand that her mother in the grip of her all-consuming passion left her children in order to work to finance her dream: "nothing was going to stop that house being built for Robert" (46). With the grand house completed, The Mai sits in that huge window "her temples throbbing as her lips formed two words noiselessly. Come home—come home" (14). Everything will be sacrificed for this passion, this dream, even the children.

"Memories," as Rosenfield contends, "are the procedures that are responsible for the organization of perceptions. They are therefore *generalizations* of previous experiences, ways of organizing sensory stimuli that permit them to be related to past experience" (62). Thus, in our present time we organize our "past [that is, our previous experience]." What emerges for Millie out of this process is her understanding of the total desire and complete unwavering commitment of these women, Grandma Fraochlán and The Mai, for their men.[10] At one hundred years old, Grandma Fraochlán had always dwelt on her great love, her husband, the nine-fingered fisherman, then dead some forty years. Asked to choose between him and her children, she would always choose her lover:

> There's two types a people in this worlt from whah I can gather, thim as puts their childer first an' thim as puts their lover first an' for whah it's worth, tha nine-

---

10. There is, however, a great difference between Grandma Fraochlán's passion for a husband who returns her love, even performing a heroic feat to be with her during childbirth, and Robert, who does not return The Mai's ardor and who can offer only a lame excuse for not showing up when their son, Stephen, was born.

-fingered fisherman an' meself belongs ta tha labber a these. I would gladly a hurlt all seven a ye down tha slopes a hell for wan nigh' more wud tha nine-fingered fisherman an' may I roh eternally for such unmotherly feeIin. (69-70)

Medea, Grandma Fraochlán, and The Mai all put their lovers first ahead of their children, but only Grandma Fraochlán never regrets doing so.

The Mai is, therefore, not about "the new woman" like, say, Ibsen's Nora in *The Doll's House* (1879), nor is it like so many contemporary plays about the difficulty of being a woman in the contemporary world. It is, rather, a play focusing on a daughter's attempt to understand her mother's seemingly inexplicable acts by going back in time through not only her memories but also those of others as well as those of the setting, the last place where events occurred. As Millie confesses towards the end of the play, "I wear Owl Lake like a caul around my chest to protect me from all that is good and hopeful and worth pursuing" (71). Through the painful process of piecing together memories of the past she arrives at a new view, a new understanding of her mother as a woman trapped in a one-sided relationship which could only—and inevitably must—end in disaster. The Mai will come to a tragic end no matter what she does or does not do, no matter how well she builds her house, raises her children, or selects and keeps her friends, because the object of her monopolizing passion is clearly not worthy of her: the man is weak where she is strong, he will betray her again and again, whereas she will choose to remain loyal to him. Medea, confronted by the infidelity of Jason, a similarly weak man, turned her great passion from love to rage and enacted a horrible revenge on him by killing their children to spite him.[11] The Mai in an almost identical situation discovers her passion turning to despair and so commits suicide: "The ground is gone from under me," exclaims The Mai. Nor is time her friend. "I'm forty years of age. . . . I'm on the downward slope. . . . I'm trapped" (54). At age thirty Millie understands what the preteen Millie could not when she asked her mother what to her is the obvious question, "Why don't you leave him?" A nonsensical question if, like The Mai, one cannot "think of one reason for going on without him" (72). Even the cello playing with which the play opens—beautiful and rich as played by John O'Kane in the Dublin production of 1994 suggesting elegance, romantic lushness, civilized behavior, order—becomes transformed into something ugly, vicious, mechanical as time springs the trap closing in on The Mai. The opening romantic sound image is overtaken by an overtly erotic, physical, sexual one as Robert shifts from playing the cello to playing The Mai's body with his bow—"softer," she enjoins (11). Both images contrast in intensity with the cello playing later in act 2, where it is The Mai who does the playing in one of the drama's most unforgettable, violent visual/verbal images:

> She moves around the study, sounds a note on the cello, takes the bow, begins screeching it across the cello to annoy ROBERT . . . THE MAI sits down and plays a few phrases

---

11. Brendan Kennelly in his introduction to his translation of *Medea* reveals that he began his translation at the imperative suggestion of a woman who meeting him in the Peacock Theatre after the production of his translation of *Antigone* admonished him: "You understand women's rage. Do *Medea* next. Many people say the play is about jealousy. It's not, it's about rage" (6). Kennelly adds: "This is the rage I tried to present in *Medea* . . ." (7). His version was first performed on 8 October 1988 and revived in July 1989. Marina Carr's play clearly parallels Euripides's in Kennelly's translation at several points, as discussed in this essay.

> *expertly. . . . She brandishes the cello bow all over the place.*
> ROBERT.   Look, will you put that down, you'll break it.
> THE MAI.   And so what, you'll replace it, you're good
>   at replacing things.
> *She taps the bow along her toes, stops, pulls a string from it,*
> *looks at Robert, looks away, resumes playing herself: knees,*
> *thighs, stomach. Then she stops to snap a string as it suits her.*
> *She plays her breasts and makes notes on her throat with her*
> *other hand.* (48-49)

The Mai's anger over Robert's betrayal, evident in the sound image of the screeching cello bow and the implications in the verbal image "you'll replace it," precedes the visual image of her playing her body with the bow, an image of her angry frustration caused by his indifference to her, which itself culminates in the highly charged, potentially violent sexual image of her playing her breasts while fingering the frets of her throat, which intimates possible obliteration.

Assembling these memories, Millie as an adult comes to understand that The Mai loved beyond measure, beyond reason, beyond thought, and far beyond the advice of her well-meaning, devoted friends and family. Her mother chose deliberately to eschew moderation, what Euripides called "heaven's fairest gift, the very sanity of the gods, . . . Moderation keeps the demons of excess at bay, and makes us grateful for the gift of limits" (*Medea* 49). No one would willingly place themselves in The Mai's unenviable position outside "the gift of limits," but part of her tragedy lies in her belief that she has no choice but to love this unfaithful man. "I cannot think of one reason for going on without him" (72).

The passions and their inevitable tragic or pathetic outcome at the center of *The Mai* are the stuff of myth and legend. If ordinary people do not behave that way, those in the grip of fate, such as The Mai, Oedipus, and Medea, do. Oedipus did kill his father and marry his mother, while, as Iocasta added, most men only dream of doing so. Medea did kill her and Jason's children because "passion strangles all my love" (66). And, The Mai did choose suicide rather than going on alone without Robert. Grandma Fraochlán, the one-hundred-year-old matriarch of the family, ignoring the parallel to her own all-consuming passion, speaks for many viewers and reviewers when she says to The Mai: "Ya survived this long without him, why'a ya bringin' all this an ya'arself agin?" (16). This question or one like it may well have motivated Millie to try years later to piece together from her own memory and others' memories the story of her mother. As Medea concluded at the end of Euripides's drama: "there's nothing left but memory. Some griefs deepen with memory, become more real than when they happened first" (74).

To tell this story of "griefs deepen[ed] with memory" Carr violates chronological time in *The Mai*, disrupting the sequence of events to better illuminate the link between Millie and her mother "across time, space and the absence of death" (Roche, "Women" 162). Millie's attempt involves what may be one of the most mysterious of all subjects for a child, the relationship between her parents before she was born and before she came of age—an attempt which she sees as crucial for her own identity. Unable to meet her mother as she was when she married Robert, since such events happen only on the "field of dreams," Millie nevertheless discovers that she remains linked by blood, experience, and—even more importantly—by memory these "constantly evolving generalizations—recreations—of the past," which leads in turn to her mature understanding of her mother and to her own "sense of continuity, . . . [her own] sense of being, with a past, a present, and a future" (Rosenfield 76).

Time, Memory, and Language

> *To imagine the future was no more possible for Clive than to remember the past—both were engulfed by the onslaught of amnesia [dementia].*
> ——*Oliver Sacks*, Musicophilia

Time, memory, and language are so intertwined in human growth and experience that the loss of any one of them will almost inevitably, although not always, lead to the loss of all three. As Toni Morrison remarked in her Nobel Prize acceptance speech, "we do language. That may be the measure of our lives" (1993). For people suffering with dementia in whatever form, however, language, memory, and therefore time become fragile and in danger of disappearing. Being unable to "do language" means that time-future holds not the prospect of comfort derived from a lifetime of memories but, for the victims of dementia, the terror of forgetting, of losing time-past, and therefore of becoming unable to function within their former world in time-present. Through the various forms of dementia the Wolf of Time "that sucks the memory from our tongues" (Kastenbaum 178) robs aging and older people of their memories of their time-past, "those shards of broken mirrors that time leaves to us" (Borges, "Cambridge"). Concurrently, as the Past begins to slip away not into memory but into oblivion, other, false memories may appear to take its place. Luis Buñuel in his book of memoirs, *My Last Sigh* (1983), reflects on the implications of this kind of impending loss having witnessed his mother falling deeper into dementia with one of its consequences being her inability to recall past events and people, while replacing her actual memories with false ones. He concludes from observing her decline that "[y]ou have to begin to lose your memory, if only in bits and pieces, to realize that memory is what makes our lives. Life without memory is no life at all . . . . Our memory is our coherence, our reason, our feeling, even our action" (4–5). Facing what he believes erroneously will be his own "final amnesia" he bleakly assumes: "Without it [memory], we are nothing" (5). Such statements provoked Oliver Sacks to ask: "what sort of a life (if any), what sort of a world, what sort of a self, can be preserved in a man who has lost the greater part of his memory and, with this, his past, and his moorings in time?" (*The Man who Mistook* 24).

The Irish playwright Frank McGuinness in *The Hanging Gardens* provides a compelling example of confronting just such a loss of memory and "moorings in time" as life for Sam Grant, a reclusive aging novelist, descends into dementia. As the play opens, Sam holds center stage exalting over his extraordinary gardens audaciously comparing them to the ancient Hanging Gardens of Babylon as he proclaims his proud ownership of them and invokes the gods' blessing on himself. His is a kind of "biblical invocation of the ancient city [of Babylon] as 'a dwelling place for demons / a haunt for every unclean spirit" (O'Toole).[12] but, tragically, the demons are all within Sam:

> SAM.   Fetch me the moon shining on Babylon. Let its
> gods shower blessings on me. Fetch me diadems

---

12. Fintan O'Toole is quoting the Book of Revelation 18:2, English Standard Version: "And he called out with a mighty voice, 'Fallen, fallen is Babylon the great! She has become a dwelling place for demons, a haunt for every unclean spirit, a haunt for every unclean bird, a haunt for every unclean and detestable beast.'"

of sun and stars. Let me wear this crown of rain,
rain that's drenched me. For these lands are my
Kingdom, my Hanging Gardens.
(McGuinness 11)

The Hanging Gardens of Babylon—one of the seven wonders
of the ancient world![13] The figure of Sam flooded with light
appears to be at the very center of power and while there are
other people present on stage who attempt to interrupt his
pirouette, they appear to be merely obscure, indistinguishable
figures, relegated to the shadows. Yet an audience may sense
that something is not quite right, for Sam's appearance
standing in the pouring rain incongruously wearing now-
saturated pajamas seems at odds with this bravura performance
invoking gods and powers. For his appearance seems closer to
that of the "poor bare . . . unaccommodated man" King Lear
encountered on the heath (act 3.4) than it does to that of
Nebuchadnezzar, the great Babylonian emperor of the famous
Hanging Gardens. Suddenly, a strong but resigned female voice
cuts in puncturing all his high-flown-rhetoric by saying simply,
"Sam, get in—you're soaked" (She *takes him by the hand,*" and he
goes meekly with her exiting the stage [12]).

As the narrative of *The Hanging Gardens* unfolds, an
audience comes to realize that Sam's brave speech in the

---

13. The Hanging Gardens of Babylon, one of the seven wonders of the
ancient world, are traditionally attributed to Nebuchadnezzar, who ruled
Babylon from 604 to 562 BCE during its Golden Age and built the
gardens for one of his wives. Stephanie Dalley in *The Mystery of the
Hanging Gardens of Babylon: An Elusive World Wonder Traced* (2015)
argues, however, for the gardens being built by the Assyrian king
Sennacherib at Nineveh in an earlier century. A more likely chronology
might have those Assyrian gardens providing a model for
Nebuchadnezzer. For a lengthy discussion of the history of both
gardens see Timothy Potts, "Looking for the Hanging Gardens."

prologue commanding the moon, the sun, and the stars is "full of sound and fury, / Signifying nothing"—a speech of empty rhetoric, suggesting, if anything, only wishful thinking. For although Sam long ago named these gardens after the seventh wonder in the ancient world—those fabulous Hanging Gardens of Babylon—and daringly named the house itself "Babylon," these gardens are a "wonder" only in the tiny Irish hamlet of Buncrana, where Sam and his wife live and even more ironically, these gardens are not even his but belong to his wife, Jane. The gardens are her life's work, for she is a "distinguished gardener" (5), a financially successful author of garden books, and an equally successful investor. Appearances are often deceptive and central to this play is the tearing away of one appearance after another exposing the work of "[t]he wolf of time that . . . will not be fooled or deterred" (Kastenbaum 180). The consolation of self-knowledge derived from memory, from knowing and valuing, for instance, that the person will be remembered, especially within the family, will be denied Sam by this wolf as it sucks his memory and the blood from his vitality.

The late Bertam J. Cohler, a well-known clinical psychologist at the University of Chicago and author of numerous books and articles, speaking of the cumulating effects of dementia, which someone such as Sam Grant exhibits again and again, cautioned against viewing these effects too narrowly: "we must consider whether the [resulting] depression isn't markedly worsened by memory loss and the inability to recall the past, which is so essential for being able to use the life-story construct as a continuing source of solace and comfort" (122). Sam in *The Hanging Gardens* will participate in this larger pattern of lost, irretrievable memories coupled with the tragic "inability to recall the past," which will rob him of his life-story, thereby eliminating one of the significant comforts for most humans at the end of life, if not before—the loss of time-past.

While McGuinness never identifies the precise condition from which Sam suffers, he does provide enough examples and symptoms for an audience to realize that Sam is plunging deeper and deeper into some form of dementia, which, although it may have several quite different causes, has a uniformly bleak result. The Irish "Living with Dementia Research Programme," published as *Dementia in Ireland 2012*, defines dementia—from the Latin *de mens* "from the mind"—as an "umbrella term used to describe a group of diseases that have common symptoms but different causes" (Cahill et al.). Each of these "common symptoms" will be exhibited by Sam in the course of the play including "impaired memory, language, ability to communicate, mood and personality" (Appendix D). He will also exhibit "these challenging behaviours . . . agitation, aggression, wandering, sleep disturbance, inappropriate eating, inappropriate sexual behavior, delusions, hallucinations and paranoia" (Appendix D). During *Hanging Gardens* we see Sam *agitated* as he searches for his lost non-existent because imaginary daughter, who he hears continually whispering to him (31), *aggressive* as he punches Jane *"hard in the stomach"* (32), *wandering* about aimlessly unable to sleep (11), suffering from *delusions* of Jane as a hairdresser and of their stillborn black daughter (21, 30), *hallucinating* that Jane is turning into a bush or tree (28), and experiencing *paranoia* when he fears Jane will hit him (27). Besides these behaviors, the play also chronicles the deepening development of his inability to use language, to recognize the time, or make decisions—a process that James H. Schulz and Robert H. Binstock describe with considerable authority in their book *Aging Nation* (2006):

> the symptoms of the disease gradually become more pronounced. They typically include difficulties with language, time disorientation, difficulty in making decisions, depression and aggression, lack of initiative and motivation, and—of course—significant short-term memory loss. Finally, . . . loss of speech, and eventually an inability to walk or even sit up. (172)

Sam's dementia robs him of time-past, time-future, and eventually will rob him of time-present. But the play also delves into the concomitant problem of care-giving, of those people—in this case, Sam's immediate family of wife and three adult children—who may be charged with caring for an elderly person in the grips of dementia and in the process have their own time radically altered as well. The care-giver problem in twenty-first century Ireland was already significant when McGuinness wrote his play as it was and remains unsolved in many other countries, including the United States and most of Europe. All indications were and are that the problem will worsen as the population of western countries continues to age. "Unless a cure is found dementia is set to become a worldwide epidemic" (Cahill et al.). To take the example of Ireland, as the Irish population continues to age, the percentage of those "older people aged 65 and over [susceptible to dementia is] expected to double [between 2006 and 2041] . . . from approximately 0.5 million today [2012] to over one million by 2031."[14] There is also a subset of the population under 65 who currently suffer from Younger Onset Dementia in Ireland, which may number 4,000 or more, according to the London *Daily Mirror* for 28 April 2010 (de Burca 23). Clearly,

---

14. McGuinness testified in an interview with Roche that he works to insure that all his plays, including this one, derive their "resonance . . . from the events that they are reporting and from the events that form the backdrop to them" (Roche, "Interview" 23).

this is a problem that will not go away but being so widespread can only become progressively worse. McGuinness's play holds a "mirror up to [an aging] nation" (Murray, *Twentieth Century*)—a nation that might perhaps just as soon ignore or avoid this problem.[15]

The backdrop for *The Hanging Gardens* becomes thus both an aging population and the increasing incidence of dementia. Sam illustrates both as his disease enters a new and alarming phase where symptoms that might have been accounted for by the normal time-bound aging process and, therefore, been overlooked can now no longer be ignored as they become more and more prominent. Unfortunately, in such situations reason as an agent of change becomes itself helpless. Jane may plead with Sam to go back to work, his son Charlie may implore him to eat his breakfast, and the other two adult children entreat him to do various "normal" tasks, but none will have their pleas answered: Jane will be violently punched in the stomach, Charlie will be humiliated, and the others ignored or ridiculed. The world of the demented is not governed by reason but irrationality and appears one where what previously was seen as abnormal has now become the norm. It is also one that this family is particularly ill-equipped to deal with.

The Grant family in *The Hanging Gardens* is Tolstoy's archetypal "unhappy family" unlike any other and "unhappy in its own way" (*Anna Karenina* 1), where time is not a benign medium. A series of seemingly right, perhaps even good,

---

15. McGuinness devoted *Gates of Gold* to what he called "the politics of aging," about which he said in 2002: "That's something I wouldn't have been interested in 20 or even 10 years ago" (Joe Jackson 2). *The Hanging Gardens* joins a series of plays by McGuinness about aging which includes *Factory Girls* (1982), *Dolly West's Kitchen* (1999), and *Gates of Gold* (2002) and culminates in *The Visiting Hour* (2021). The first three focus on "the politics of aging" (qtd. in Jackson 2).

choices made by Sam and Jane when young lead over their lifetimes to the claustrophobic dysfunctional situation with which the play opens, where Sam, as husband and father, is increasingly at the mercy of whatever form of dementia is robbing him of time-past and time-present as he progressively loses his stability, his history, and his precious words while pushing his partner in this life-experiment beyond endurance. Yet Jane also shows herself as a product of, as well as a proponent of, their earlier agreement to form "a nation of two" against the world.[16] Now, faced with this crisis caused by Sam's imploding dementia she cannot admit the desperate nature of her plight. She wants to act, wants Sam to return to his old self, wants their old way of life back, wants him to affirm their "tangled, exasperated but enduring relationship" (O'Toole), but none of that is remotely possible, for time does not run backwards. While Jane has the strength and the "anarchic spirit" of Rima in McGuinness's earlier play *Dolly West's Kitchen* (1999) ("An Irish Writer" 3), who also was unquestionably in charge of the household, she lacks Rima's flexibility. As the products of this chosen rigid isolation, each of the three children in turn asks of their parents what each believes their parents have never given: their unmerited acceptance and love, or what Victor Hugo once called "[t]he greatest happiness of life" and which W. H. Auden defined as the craving for "Not universal love / But to be loved alone." ("September 1, 1939")[17] But neither Sam nor Jane is capable of giving such love.

---

16. "Nation of Two" is taken from Kurt Vonnegut's novel *Mother Night* (1961).

17. See chapter 4, "The Fullness of Time." Victor Hugo was quoted in the *New York Times* 26 Nov. 2013, D3 as saying: "The greatest happiness of life is the conviction that we are loved, loved for ourselves—say rather, loved in spite of ourselves."

McGuinness succeeds in creating an idiosyncratic and convincing nuclear family, howbeit a distinctly dysfunctional one where the three children have at best a distant relationship with their parents. And, where all four—mother and children—must somehow against very high odds attempt to cope with their husband/father under extremely difficult conditions.

Character, as the Greeks knew only too well, is destiny, and in *The Hanging Gardens*, the character of young "reclusive" Sam along with that of young Jane lead over their lifetimes to the intransigent, demented Sam and the stubborn, insular Jane we now encounter. With their "nation of two"—or two standing against the world—they both cut themselves off from society and thus from help. Sam will not hear of their getting a nurse in and Jane is similarly adamant about no stranger entering their fortress. Together Sam and Jane created these conditions in their early married life that return to haunt them in later years. Still, as Cohler has argued:

> Across the course of life, individuals rely upon others as a source of both meaning and solace in their lives. From the initial experience of the infant, comforted by his mother's very presence, to the older adult maintaining continuity of past and present through memories of a lifetime of relating to significant others, the psychological significance of relationships is intertwined in the remembered story of a life that answers the question of meaning. . . . and that works to preserve morale. (123)

Sam is losing the "story of [his] life," and Jane rejects relying on others, leaving the two of them alone and isolated as the Wolf of Time relentlessly advances. All three of the children understand their parents' chosen route of isolation, which has also had a profound effect on their own inability to interact with others (Charlie), to find a place for themselves socially (Maurice), or to engage in meaningful interpersonal relationships (Rachel). Rachel's parody of the town's questioning of Maurice about his father—"still writing?"; writing that no one in town has read—and mother—"toiling away in her big garden?"; a garden that none of them have seen (13-14)—clearly has the core of truth in it. The children as adults may now understand their parents' chosen route of isolation, but that isolation has also affected them profoundly.

While we know nothing of Sam's fiction—no conversation quotes a sentence or a phrase and there is a notable absence of references to any fictional title, plot, or character—we do see Jane's garden every minute of the play, since all action and every dialogue takes place there. As Jane's workplace for testing her gardening methods and ideas, the garden denotes her successful financing of the family and, especially, her financing of Sam's novel-writing. Her garden also proves emblematic of the Grants' isolation from society in that no one outside the family has seen or ever will see it. That isolation appears most starkly in the physical manifestations of Rachel's pregnancy, which was accomplished without any human partner but through artificial insemination (39, 42-43).

Unlike the writer Tom in Brian Friel's *Give Me Your Answer, Do!* (1997), who must struggle with the artist's core question whether the work has value, the issue for Sam in *The Hanging Gardens* is neither the quality nor even the quantity of his writing, about which we learn nothing, but rather how does this man whose identity has been completely bound up with words and his ability to write face the gradual and continuing loss of words? Having neglected to put on any socks, he attempts to describe what happened: "Did not wearing them" (64). Having spent a lifetime acknowledging "the profound and hidden power . . . in words," he realizes in a brief lucid interval that they have deserted him, thus ending his career as a writer:

> SAM. Books. Best out of it. Writing. Well out of it. Let it go. And it's gone. It will never come back. What grief. (29)

Daring words. The loss squarely faced and accepted. Or is it? Having communicated through words both publicly in his writing and privately in his family, Sam now senses that he is losing control over them and that loss will in turn inevitably entail the end of his career as a novelist and worse. What he does not fully realize, however, is that this loss also means for him the end of memory and of all meaningful human connection. Although Sam has limited to a single person—his wife Jane—those people he relies on "as a source of both meaning and solace" (Cohler 123), nevertheless, even that relationship is now under threat of erasure as he replaces real memories with false ones. For example, he insists that Jane once worked as a "hairdresser," which she firmly and flatly denies, and that they had a fourth child as mentioned earlier, a stillborn black baby girl, which is pure fiction (21). By substituting such false memories for real ones, while at the same time forgetting actual past incidents and people, Sam engages in acts that threaten his very identity and contribute to the diminishing meaning of his life as his dementia destroys the "continuity of past and present [and] . . . the remembered story of a life," the very time of his life (Cohler 123).

Dementia is especially cruel in that self-reflection and self-knowledge, instead of offering a respite from the fear of the end, only adds to it. As Schulz and Binstock conclude from their gerontological study: "To experience and be aware of the gradual deterioration of ones [sic] brain, losing first mental and then physical function, is horrible" (172). Thomas De Baggio—a real, not a fictitious, person diagnosed with Alzheimer's at the relatively very young age of fifty-eight—eloquently describes the terror he faces as he anticipates his future—a future Sam shares:

> I am on the cusp of a new world, a place I will be unable to describe. . . . I must now wait for the silence to engulf me and take me to the place where there is no memory left and there remains no reflexive will to live. It is lonely here waiting for memory to stop and I am afraid and tired. (*Losing My Mind* qtd. in Schulz and Binstock 172)

Both DeBaggio and Sam have descended into W. B. Yeats's "foul rag and bone shop of the heart," but robbed of words they are unable to locate "where all ladders start" and instead face only the rag and bone shop's endless silence ("The Circus Animals' Desertion" 392). The only possible exit from this silent world remains death, but not Keats's "easeful Death" ("Ode to a Nightingale" 52). Instead, both must envision an end conditioned by their dementia, which adds its own terrible dimension. As Cohler further argues, "The fear of death arriving in the context of personal fragmentation [such as McGuinness depicts in *The Hanging Gardens*] may well represent the ultimate terror confronting the older adult in our postmodern society" (117).

Sam, like Oswald in Ibsen's earlier play *Ghosts* (1882), faces complete debilitation.[18] Oswald had implored his mother to end his life when she would see him descending into this state "becoming . . . a helpless child again" (Ibsen, act 3), while Sam, also sensing what lies ahead, confesses that "[t]here is no

---

18. McGuinness translated *Ghosts* in 1988, and his version was published years later in 2010. His translation of that play premiered 30 January

remedy for what afflicts me" (68) and asks first Jane then each of the children to help him end his life at the time when he becomes unable to function. Each in turn refuses as Oswald's mother had earlier also refused.

Following Ibsen's example, McGuinness compresses time in *The Hanging Gardens* as Sam at first only intermittently begins to understand his situation, then definitely realizes he has lost the ability to write and no amount of cajoling by his well-meaning family will bring it back. This loss leads inevitably, inexorably by the play's end to a second deeper and very real fear of losing words completely: "I forgot the song for word" (80), he laments before being plunged into a world where he will be forever silent and where time will cease to exist. As critic Emer O'Kelly observed of Sam in the Abbey Theatre production, "he knows he is lost because words are lost to him" (19).

In the last scenes of the play, as the Grant family gathers together in an attempt to cope with this extremely difficult situation, McGuinness, following his "beloved Ibsen" in *Ghosts*, compresses some of the late stages of the dementia into one sharp decline which, while not unheard of, remains clinically somewhat unusual, but dramatically very effective ("An Irish

---

2007 at the Bristol Old Vic. In an interview with Mária Kurdi, he discusses his work on translating Ibsen.

When *Ghosts* premiered originally in the nineteenth century, it caused outrage and was roundly condemned as too inflammatory, too graphic, too scandalous as well as being untrue in its portraits of a toadying clergyman, a hypocritical father willing to prostitute his daughter, and a syphilitic pillar of society. But the greatest outcry was over the sexual content. Ibsen performed a public service in exposing such hypocrisy, in painting a graphic picture of the mental deterioration caused by this sexually transmitted disease, and in bringing into the light what society would rather have hidden.

Writer" 17, 21). In the final scene, Sam in a moment of lucidity becomes once more the family's story teller (74). He makes up a story that he tells with the aid of Jane, who starts him off with "[o]nce upon a time," and then she, along with Rachel and Maurice, play his game of insisting on the telling details, while Charlie less successfully attempts to contribute. Similarly to the earlier and much longer interval where Sam engaged with each of the children individually as a loving father, Sam here presents a side of his character ignored by many reviewers who saw only a "manipulative patriarch" (Meany) or the "tradition[al] . . . Irish . . . cruel father" (Keating). The story Sam invents builds on an old folk tale of the father who sacrificed his child/children in order to build a mansion-fortress-palace—a story that has obvious parallels with Sam's sacrificing everything including his children to his ambition of becoming a novelist. Sam's version of the tale includes a fantastic happy ending that also runs parallel to the play in that both the man in the story and Sam earlier in the play receive back their children. With such an ending to his story, the play itself might appear to also be heading toward a similar happy ending (76). But there is an ominous sign just before the whole family led by Jane, minus Sam, joins together in singing "The Moon behind the Hill." Sam, rather than participating "looks very far away" (77) as he contemplates the onslaught of the last stage of dementia when he will fail to recognize bird song—something which occurs moments later, after the family finishes singing.

The singing itself during this quiet interlude presents the play's one modicum of hope for this family as they—without Sam—unite in singing. Yet the song occupies only a brief "near-normal" interval, which proves to be but a lull before the storm about to break, emphasizing both the temporary nature of this lull and the contrasting but inevitable bleak end as Sam egregiously fails to recognize the song Jane sings—one that he must have heard dozens if not hundreds of times over many years since it was Jane's mother's song. His guess that she sang "Danny Boy" is patently absurd since "The Moon behind the Hill" is melodically light years removed from "Danny Boy." "Do I know that?" he asks. "Did I know the words?" "The words— the words—." And words desert him: "'I forgot the word'" (79). Worse still is his failure to recognize the song of the bird, mentioned earlier: "'I forgot the song for word'" as "*A bird sings somewhere in the distance*" (80). But Sam no longer recognizes either the bird's song or his wife, Jane—"Who are you," he asks plaintively.

> CHARLIE. It's all starting.
> MAURICE. Beginning of the end. (79)

Unable even to utter the word "word," Sam descends into unintelligible muttering as night falls, "*turning the family into shadows*" (80). What was familiar is gone and in its place is the terror of a living death. Sam as played by Niall Buggy in the Abbey production appeared physically fit, which only added to the terror of a prospect of years to be lived out in silence without identity, personality, memory, or history—without words, without time. This is an event "that shows the terrifying aspects of existence," to borrow Karl Jaspers's definition of the tragic (14).

This last scene also is symmetrical with the play's opening scene in the rain in that both feature Sam center stage with the family on the periphery "*turning . . . into shadows*" (80), and in both scenes rain falls.[19] Rather than completing a full circle,

---

19. The Abbey production omitted the rain during the closing scene, thus foregoing the symmetry of the opening and closing scenes.

however, the play's structure more closely resembles that of a spiral as seen most vividly in the contrast between Sam's grand performance in the prologue, where he welcomes the rain— "Let me wear this crown of rain"—proclaiming himself the rightful owner of the Hanging Gardens—"these lands are my kingdom, my Hanging Gardens. . . . My palace is Babylon, and you walk in the Hanging Gardens" (11-12)—and his pitiful figure at the end of the play unable to rise and unable to speak. In the play's final tableau, Buggy, giving a thoroughly convincing portrait of dementia, attempted again and again to sit up. "[T]his is Horror starting already to scratch Its way in" (Auden, *For the Time Being* 410).

Erik Erikson in his several studies of adult development postulated a teleological development over a lifetime where at the end of life the task left remaining becomes to achieve serenity by accepting both what happened in life and the inevitability of death. The alternative to such serenity is the despair that arises because of regrets over what did or did not happen coupled with futile protests against the inevitability of death. Sam's dementia short-circuits any such movement by destroying memory. As all cognizance disappears, any assessment of the past becomes impossible, as does any anticipation of the end. The invisible Wolf of Time through dementia has stolen Sam's "time and eat[en his] . . . dreams" exactly as that wolf also stole the time and ate the dreams of Oswald in Ibsen's *Ghosts* and of those of Buñuel's mother and waits to feast on Buñuel himself and on Ireland's increasingly aged population.

Chapter 6
Time, the Life Cycle, Immortality, and Mortality

Put us all into it. . . . Father Son and Holy Ghost
and Jakes Mᶜ Carthy.
——*James Joyce*, Ulysses

Most writers work by exclusion rather than inclusion. Almost alone among prominent authors writing in English, William Shakespeare and James Joyce, practiced inclusion; that is, they "put us all into it," as Joyce proclaimed in *Ulysses* (135). Encountering either Shakespeare or Joyce a reader cannot then retreat to a smaller, more comfortable, and much more manageable plane of thought, emotion, or experience, for both Shakespeare and Joyce aim at giving readers nothing less than all of human life lived in time. John Middleton Murry in reviewing *Ulysses* in 1922 became one of the first readers to notice and object to this very quality. He proclaimed that "⌈t⌉he curse of nimiety, of too-muchness hangs over it as a whole" (qtd. in Dettmar 49n58), for Joyce, like Shakespeare before him, wrote works of "excess" (to borrow Tom LeClair's useful term) or "what Thoreau in *Walden* called 'extravagance'" (LeClair 4). Theirs is the art of mastery. LeClair enunciates "three essential criteria of mastery, mastery of the world in which they were written, mastery of narrative methods, and mastery of the reader" (5). With Joyce and with Shakespeare, their mastery of all three enables them to explore in depth the human life cycle lived in time. Where Shakespeare dramatized the "seven ages of man" throughout his plays, Joyce explored the various stages of life in his fiction. While Joyce emphasized the continuing nature of the cycle as phoenix-like, where everything begins again, although with different actors, Shakespeare tended to emphasize the absence in the new cycle of the old cast of characters. Both acknowledge that each person's cycle must—obviously—be lived in time since humans live in time as the fish lives in water, and as Lyall Watson, the author of *Supernature* (1973), once quipped, "if you want to know what water is—don't ask a fish." But humans do ask about the nature of time as they go through the cycle of life, since each person's cycle must be lived in time. James Joyce in his fiction ambitiously attempted to capture the whole of the human life cycle "from infancy through maturity to decay," as he graphically phrases it in *Ulysses* (697). Beginning with the child's earliest memories in *A Portrait of the Artist as a Young Man* (1916) and progressing through the vicissitudes of childhood, recorded in that novel along with the early stories in *Dubliners* (1914), Joyce went on to analyze adolescence and early adulthood in the middle stories in *Dubliners*, as well as in the bulk of *A Portrait of the Artist as a Young Man*.[1] He then memorably depicted the middle mature years in his portrait of Leopold and Molly Bloom in *Ulysses*. Finally, he pictured the evening of life in the long short story that ends *Dubliners*, "The Dead," and its end and re-beginning as an on-going, never-ending cycle in *Finnegans Wake* (1939).

Following in Carl Jung's footsteps the American developmental psychologist Erik H. Erikson spent a productive lifetime studying and reflecting upon the human life cycle. Each step on life's way, he concluded, involves its own challenge to be faced, its own task to be done. For example, the task faced by

---

1. Colin McCabe provocatively declares that "*A Portrait* inaugurates a new relation between time and meaning" (57), but this claim lies outside the scope of this chapter.

adolescents, such as Stephen Dedalus faces in chapters 2 to 4 of *A Portrait of the Artist as a Young Man,* is to achieve identity. Part of that task must take place socially, or as Erikson defines the problem: "To be oneself (or not to be) [and] to share being oneself'" (*Identity* 178). Stephen struggles with being himself and with sharing being himself throughout the last section of the novel and into the first chapters of *Ulysses.* Offered several different role models from which to choose, he declines to choose any. Nor has he friends that might by any stretch of the definition be grouped under Erikson's rubric "Partners in Friendship" (178). Buck Mulligan, for instance, is no friend of his but one who will use him for his own ends, such as taking the key to the tower where they live, by which means he asserts ownership. Having drunk Stephen's money, Mulligan deliberately loses Stephen on the way to Nighttown. Worse, according to Bloom, Mulligan may have put a narcotic in Stephen's drink in the Lying-In Hospital. Clearly, Mulligan will ignore Stephen when he is no longer of any use to him. But I've gotten ahead of the story of the human life cycle.

Joyce pictures the cycle beginning with Stephen's growth of consciousness in *A Portrait of the Artist*: "Once upon a time and a very good time it was there was a moocow coming down along the road" (176). This is Stephen's earliest memory. "His father told him that story. . . . The moocow came down the road where Betty Byrne lived: she sold lemon platt" (176). This first recollection of Stephen's obviously partakes in its innocence of what Jung describes as "the paradise of unconscious childhood" (5). Yet, even this early, the problem of self-identity begins to surface, if at first simply: "*He* was baby tuckoo [emphasis added]." Then it emerges more complexly as Stephen's barely acknowledged identity comes up against the question of his father's identity: "his father looked at him through a glass: he had a hairy face." As does the identity of Betty Byrne: "she sold lemon platt" (176). Separating himself from his father and then, in turn, his father from other humans, represented by Betty Byrne, begins for Stephen what will become a life-long process of comparing like or similar people and things while contrasting unlike people and things. Making distinctions between like or similar things—two adults in this instance—so basic to the acquisition of human language, the growth of knowledge, and the stimulation of learning, moves Stephen along the cycle of life as he gains greater consciousness.

Joyce records a second process in Stephen's attitude towards "his song" by which he takes those first steps towards increasing consciousness.

> O, the wild rose blossoms . . . .
> He sang that song. That was his song.
> O, the green wrothe botheth. (176)

When Stephen speaks of himself "objectively, in the third person" (Jung 7), as in "that was *his* song" (emphasis added), then we, as readers, share in his dawning sense of himself as a discrete individual, which derives from his recognition of his self in relation to this particular song. "*He* sang *that* song." Stephen's seemingly unconnected discrete memories in the opening paragraphs of *A Portrait* record what Jung calls an "initial series of contents" (7). Only later as memories become continuous will Stephen develop strong feelings of subjectivity.

In the next stage of growth, Stephen will begin to make connections between memories. This process extends his perception of connections as well as extending his drawing of distinctions through comparison and contrast and will continue throughout *A Portrait*. A similar progress occurs with the various characters in *Dubliners*, from the young boy confronting death in "The Sisters" to the schoolboy learning of evil in "An Encounter," from the young woman paralyzed unable to act in "Eveline" and the young men acting without thinking of the consequences in "After the Race," through those in middle years, such as Little Chandler in "A Little Cloud," until we reach the elderly sisters in "The Dead."

Because all life is a process of change and change takes place within and over time, when change ceases, the process stops, the individual's time ends, and death occurs. Only at that end point can we in retrospect meaningfully view that life against one of the dominant time metaphors, such as the seven ages of life (Shakespeare) or the stages of life (Jung) or the life cycle (Erikson). Stephen's growth from boyhood to adolescence remains the compelling human story of the coming of age of a young man in a highly repressive society. Within the whole oeuvre of Joyce's fiction, however, it forms the early part of Joyce's depiction of the human life cycle, where each stage becomes recapitulated, examined, probed, and illuminated.

The Mid-Life Crisis and *Ulysses*

Joyce's great artistic achievement remains the complex fictional portrait of Leopold and Molly Bloom in mid-life. When Mr. Bloom was conceived as a character, male life expectancy was under fifty (Joyce himself would die before reaching sixty).[2] Bloom, therefore, although relatively young by twenty-first-century standards, is a model of a person in mid-life at the end of the nineteenth through the beginning of the twentieth-century. Without exaggeration he muses, "Soon I am

2. Tom Kirkwood describes the large increase in life expectancy between the 1880s and 1990s: "life expectancy at birth in England and Wales has nearly doubled from some 46 years in the 1880s to around 76 years in the 1990s. . . . Life expectancy has doubled because many fewer people are dying young" (5).

old" (285). Much has been written of the Blooms as fictional characters, as "humors," as symbols, such as Mr. Bloom as The Wandering Jew and Molly Bloom as the Earth Mother, as classical motifs, such as Bloom as Ulysses/Odysseus and Molly as Penelope, and so on and so forth, but the true power of their portraits rests on their humanity and it is this "sound of humanity that reverberates throughout . . . *Ulysses*," as Morton Levitt observes (5-6).

Characteristically of those in mid-life, both Molly and Bloom recall their dead parents, who can no longer shield them against the knowledge of the end that will now become more and more present. With their parents' death, each has become the exposed link in the family chain. A second characteristic of mid-life adults shared by Molly and, more especially, by Bloom lies in their sense of pervasive loss. Loss rather than opportunity will come more and more to dominate the remainder of their lives. Third, the Blooms experience what Americans call "the empty nest syndrome," which occurs when children leave home. Rudy died several years before the novel begins while his sister, Milly, has recently gone to live and work in Mullingar. Yet both children are present to both parents in thought and memory. The memory of Rudy shadows Bloom's day as the dead son proves never far from the father's thoughts and feelings. Moreover, Rudy may well be the reason for the present-day crisis during which Molly will commit adultery for the first and only time since they were married.[3] Her mixed motives range from physical, sexual desire—"Thanks be to the great God I got somebody to give me what I badly wanted to

3. José Lanters summarizes Bloom's feeling of guilt over Rudy's death and its effect on his relationship with Molly: "it is evident that the event [of Rudy's death] was a crucial factor in the deterioration of the Blooms' sexual relationship and that Leopold Bloom feels he is somehow to blame for his son's demise" (530).

put some heart up into me" (758)—to the possibility of shocking Poldy (her affectionate nickname for her husband) into returning as her sexually active partner in their marriage. She wants him back. Not least she wants him back as her sexual partner because, as she insists using a low Dublin idiom, "Poldy has more spunk in him [than Blazes Boylan]" (742).

But Bloom cannot return; the life cycle goes in only one direction. The "years dream return," but for him the reality of his dead son, Rudy, and the responsibility he assumes, if not for his death, then for his failure to survive, overwhelms all else: "Could never like it [sexual intercourse] again after Rudy [died]" (168), he reflects honestly. Thus, within Bloom the necessity to procreate conflicts with the impossibility of his procreating. As father he is responsible for the health of his newborn son and that son died—"my fault perhaps. No son" (285). In effect, Bloom assents to the ancient Jewish belief that "if it's [the child is] healthy it's from the mother. If not the man" (96). Or, more specifically: "the health of the child is a reflection on the virility of the male" (Gifford and Seidman 111). As husband, Bloom does not wish to participate in sexual activity that might result in procreation. Molly's later miscarriage only confirms him in this feeling. And yet he recalls with pleasure and affection making love with his wife. "The most moving event in the book, for both Molly and Bloom, is their love-making at Howth, which took place sixteen years previously, but which ends the book with its resounding affirmation," as Joseph Ronsley argues (118). Anxiously anticipating Molly's adultery Bloom reconciles himself to this "inevitable" event by returning in his mind to those past events on the hill of Howth, where he and Molly first made love. By recreating that moment in the present, by bringing it into the present through memory, he acquires "a sense of continuity

[in time], a sense of being, with a past, a present, and a future"
(Rosenfield 76) that leads to his equanimity. Molly in her
monologue with which the book ends also returns to exactly
the same moment of their love-making on Howth (782):
"and then I asked him with my eyes to ask again yes" (783). The
task of the reader is to join these memories—one of Bloom's
and the other of Molly's widely separated by hundreds of
pages and many hours of reading time—first by recalling them
and then by actively linking them. Bringing both together in
the present will of necessity alter that very present as the
reader reads those famous last words of *Ulysses*. Thus a reader's
reading time spent in reading the end of the novel partakes of
all three of Augustine's time present as noted in the
"Introduction": "the present of things past, . . . the present of
things present, . . . [and] the present of things future (273)."[4]

Ulysses remains one of the great books of memory in
several senses. Among them is the knowledge that life must be
lived forwards in time but can only be understood backwards,
as Kierkegaard once observed. Great epics, such as *Ulysses*,
begin traditionally *in medias res* or at that moment when there
is enough of the hero's lifetime to begin to discern patterns or
perhaps tentatively to attempt an assessment. Yet the unity of
narrative embodied in a single life's time becomes fully
apparent only after that life is over; that is, after its time is done.

---

4. In *The Confessions*, Augustine concludes,

> It is, now, however, perfectly clear that neither the future nor the past
> are in existence, and that it is incorrect to say that there are three
> times: past, present, and future. Though one might perhaps say:
> "There are three times—a present of things past, a present of things
> present, and a present of things future." For these three do exist in
> the mind, and I do not see them anywhere else: the present time of
> things past is memory; the present time of things presents is sight;
> the present time of things future is expectation. (273)

Bloom and Molly continue to move forwards in time while also remembering. "I remember that I was happy when I am not happy now, and I recall my past sadness when I am not sad now; . . . I can recall a desire I had once, when I have it no longer" was Augustine's now classic formulation of the problem of remembering in present time events that occurred in the past (223). During his long day and night, Bloom pauses several times to observe "Me. And me now" (*Ulysses* 176). "I was happier then. Or was that I? Or am I now I?" (168). The Heraclitian river of time flows in one direction only, yet "the way up and the way down are the same," as both Heraclitus and St. Augustine knew full well. Heraclitus refers to the future as "the way up" the river in that to be experienced the person must go forwards into the future; that is, the future must become the present while a person must go into the past; that is, go back down the river of time in order to bring the past into the present through memory. Thus the "way up and the way down are the same" in that either or both must be brought into the present to be experienced. Both Bloom and Molly attempt to understand their lives by calling up memories of one another from their earlier, perhaps less complicated and certainly less troubled, life together and those recollections color their present.

Through memory Bloom proves exceptional, even heroic, in being able to integrate the suffering, pain, and loss he has experienced in the past ("generativity" in Erikson's terms), while at the same time avoiding the emotional pitfall of becoming self-absorbed (Erikson, *Identity* 129). "The past is not to be repeated but *redeemed*, because it has the power yet to redeem the future" (Kiberd 475), and the key to such redemption, according to Erikson, lies in generativity without self-absorption (*Identity* 129). Carrying with him his memories

of all his days and ways, Bloom proceeds energetically from the
known to the unknown, or as Joyce more wittily wrote, "from
the unknown [that is, the mystery of birth] to the known [the
certainty of death]" (*Ulysses* 572).[5] He aspires—like many
people do in mid-life—to do a day's work even under
demanding circumstances. At the end of the day, his accounts
balance. He has done works of charity and mercy that when
added together demonstrate that he has performed not just one
but all seven of the works of corporal mercy and all seven of
the works of spiritual mercy. Don Gifford contends that

> in retrospect the significance of trivial things and of things
> understated, omitted, or neglected [in *Ulysses*] suggest that
> Bloom, the heterodox Jew-Protestant-Catholic-Freemason,
> is the only reasonably fallible, unself-consciously devout,
> practicing Christian (or, rather, "anonymous Christian" in
> Karl Rahner's phrase) in Dublin. . . . Devout Catholics were
> instructed by the Maynooth Catechism that each morning
> they should pray to be able to perform one or more of the
> seven corporal and seven spiritual works of mercy during
> the day. . . . Bloom [has] performed . . . all fourteen.
> ("Memory" 45)

Rather than the transient futile sensation of triumph, however,
Bloom's day ends calmly and with "equanimity" (*Ulysses* 433).
He accepts himself with all his limitations, Molly with all of
hers, his children both living and dead, as well as his lot in life
for which he blames no one and for which he offers no excuses.
Bloom neither despairs nor appears resigned. Nor is he
disgusted with himself, his lot in life, or with life itself. Instead,

---

5. "Life, he himself said once, (his biografiend, in fact, kills him verysoon, if
   yet not, after) is a wake . . . a phrase which the establisher of the world by
   law   might   pretinately   write   across   the   chestfront   of   all
   manorwombanborn" (*Finnegans Wake* 55).

he remains a picture of integrity. Unlike his fellow Dubliners, he spends his energy not in "reinforcing their narrow range of consciousness [but] . . . in shattering it in the tension of opposites and building up a state of wider and higher consciousness" (Jung 10). And in that "higher consciousness" lies the key to Bloom's attractiveness not merely as a fictional character, but also as an available example of right conduct.

A devoted husband and father, Bloom uses his time wisely as he opposes evil, stands up and speaks out, however haltingly, for justice and love, mourns his dead son, attends to his daughter's needs, and returns to his wife at the conclusion of that arduous day. Throughout he displays a marvelous ability to function as a whole, healthy, and productive adult—Joyce's "competent keyless citizen" (*Ulysses* 697). Bloom recognizes, however intuitively, the truth in Jung's assertion that "the meaning and purpose of a problem seem to lie not in its solution but in our working at it incessantly. This alone preserves us from stultification and petrifaction" (11-12). The serious problems life presents as most adults discover can never be solved fully or resolved once and for all. The gifted American psychotherapist Sheldon Kopp remarked ruefully that given his talent and worth he expected as a young adult to be invited to sample the cream of life but instead was given a bucket of sour milk with some sketchy instructions on how to make yogurt. Bloom similarly works at his problems incessantly. Yet he realizes there can be no solution to his greatest problem; that is, the death of his son in infancy. It is Rudy's death rather than Blazes Boylan's sexual conquest that becomes the event that shadows the Blooms' marriage. Boylan is, after all, merely a distraction from, or at most a symptom of, that shadow, whereas the death of Rudy inevitably and substantially altered Leopold and Molly's relationship with one another (*Ulysses* 168). And that alteration became their first step into what Jung aptly calls "the afternoon of life" (17): "we cannot live the afternoon of life according to the program of life's morning; for what was great in the morning will be little at evening, and what in the morning was true will at evening have become a lie," as he astutely observed (17). It becomes self-defeating for adult development to continue on the same trajectory into the afternoon of life "with the false assumption that our truths and ideals will serve us as hitherto" (17). Similarly, Leslie Fiedler acknowledges that "in the middle of life, as the day wears on, we who began as sons and lovers look around to discover that we have become fathers and husbands; that somehow we have learned that exile is not what must be sought but what must be endured, and what therefore joins every man to every other man" (207-08). New conditions call for new actions and reactions. Bloom "as a competent keyless citizen . . . had proceeded energetically from the unknown to the known through the incertitude of the void" (*Ulysses* 697). Acting in existential knowledge of life's "parenthesis of infinitesimal brevity," which becomes more and more apparent the longer a person lives in "irreversible time" (728), Bloom "in the afternoon of life" as father and as husband successfully devises different strategies and affirms different values from those of his youth. His equanimity (433), for example, arises from his intimate knowledge acquired at some cost in the afternoon of life of "the futility of triumph or protest or vindication: [and of] the inanity of extolled virtue: the lethargy of nescient matter: the apathy of the stars" (734).

Bloom also illustrates Erikson's contention that, for adults, the temptation to social or individual isolation must be resisted in favor of "solidarity" with others and intimacy within relationships (*Identity* 178). The deepening crisis in the Bloom's marriage centers on the nature of his and Molly's solidarity with one another as well as on their failure to communicate with one another over the past nine months. Both solidarity and communication figure enormously in what Erikson would describe as the intimacy or lack of it, that "isolation" within their relationship (*Identity* 129).

In discussing works of mastery, LeClair insists that "books that know and show what we as a people and a species need to understand in order to have a future [are those that have] survival value" (viii). Joyce's *Ulysses* has, I believe, enormous survival value for ordinary, everyday life.[6] In his deeply etched portrait of personal heroism in an ordinary life, Joyce demonstrates that "the ordinary is the extraordinary" (Ellmann 3). "The ordinary is the proper domain of the artist," Joyce once asserted, "the extraordinary can safely be left to journalists" (Ellmann qtd. in Kiberd 470).

---

6. Like Leslie Fiedler "I have been living Joyce for a long time now, and especially I have been living *Ulysses*, not outside of but within the very texture of my life, as a part of a process of growing up and growing old. *Ulysses* was for my youth and has remained for my later years not a novel at all, but a conduct book, a guide to salvation through the mode of art, a kind of secular scripture" (196-97). I am not wholly convinced by that last pirouette, but I certainly do agree with Fielder's description of *Ulysses* as a "book of conduct" in large measure, because I have found Joyce's extremely detailed, intimate portrait of Bloom in mid-life to be a good guide to living in time. For an extended, similar argument, see Declan Kiberd, *Ulysses and Us.*

The Cycle of Finnegans Wake

> *But, Holy Saltmartin, why can't you beat time?*
> ——*James Joyce,* Finnegans Wake

Joyce, having himself set foot on the "sill of shade" in the afternoon of life, would spend the next seventeen years after the publication of *Ulysses* enduring considerable emotional and physical pain and suffering. Facing the known end with neither disgust nor despair, he energetically—some would say, possessively—wrote his great comic epic *Finnegans Wake*. A work more discussed than read but one that faces squarely and unflinchingly the ultimate end of any individual human life; that is, the end of a person's lived-time, without despair but with great equanimity as a natural part of the life cycle.

The challenge of *Finnegans Wake* lies, I believe, in its vision of the totality of all life lived in time seen from the perspective of a most creative life. Going beyond the intellect, Joyce employs "primordial images[,] . . . symbols which are older than historical man, which . . . still make up the groundwork of the human psyche" (Jung 21), to give readers the whole of the human life cycle. His single story in the *Wake* is, in fact, that very cycle of life: birth, growth, maturation, fertility, decline, and death, and then the cycle repeats like Vico's road "to end where it began." "There extand by now one thousand and one stories, all told, of the same" (5). "Hush! Caution! Echoland!" (13). Hence the heart-wrenching sadness of the ending of *Finnegans Wake* mixed with the joy of the re-beginning. "Soft morning, city! Lsp! I am leafy speafing" (619). "There'll be others but non so for me" (626). Anna Liffy, the river, the woman, the wife, and mother at the very end of her time knows her end is near, but the story of which she has been a part is far from over. As she replaced her mother so another is now about to replace her:

> Yes, you're changing, sonhusband, and you're turning, I can feel you, for a daughterwife from the hills again. . . . And she is coming. Swimming in my hindmoist. Diveltaking on me tail. Just a whisk brisk sly spry spink spank sprint of a thing theresomere, sultering. Saltarella come to her own. I pity your oldself I was used to. Now a younger's there. Try not to part! Be happy, dear ones! May I be wrong! For she'll be sweet for you as I was sweet when I came down out of me mother. . . . End here. Us then. Finn again! Take. Bussoftlhee, mememormee! Till thousandsthee. Lps. The keys to. Given! A way a lone a last a loved a long the . . . (627-28)

In undermining and even doing away with traditional notions of time and character in *Finnegans Wake* Joyce attempts to capture the essence of action rather than the more traditional novelist's goal of reproducing or creating a single action. He also chooses to concentrate on the life cycle itself, "the movement [in time] from birth through maturity to death, with the renewal of movement resulting from the seed planted in each completed cycle" (Peake 354). Charles Peake rightly contends that

> The terms, "birth," "maturity," "death" and "seed" are metaphors; the same cycle is followed by inorganic as by organic existence; it applies equally to the atom and the physical universe, to all objects, plants and animals, and to man, his groupings, his institutions, and to all he creates or experiences. . . . It depends on the interplay of opposites and illustrates their underlying identity, since the first moment of birth is the first moment of dying and the same cyclic

movement produces simultaneously ascent and descent. (354)

Similarly, at the end of *Finnegans Wake*, A.L.P., Anna Livia Plurabelle, is leaving life as the river Liffey flows out to the sea to return via evaporation in the life-giving rain. That rain in turn fructifies the earth allowing seed to grow and the cycle of birth, life, death—the regeneration that continually occurs in time—to begin again as reflected in the end of the book joined back to the beginning of the book: "Us then. Finn again! . . . A way a lone a last a loved a long the [This is the last line on page 628.] riverrun, past Eve and Adam's, from swerve of shore to bend of bay, brings us by a commodius vicus of recirculation back to Howth Castle and Environs" [line 1 on page 3]. Phoenix-like the cycle begins again but this time with different players: "there'll be others but non so for me" (626). "It's Phoenix, dear And the flame is, hear! Let's our joornee saintomichael make it" (621). So one cycle of life comes to an end as a new cycle begins, much like a spiral turning round to the same spot on the circle but slightly higher or lower than the last one.

Wisdom and the Life Cycle

"Where is the wisdom of our old people, where are their precious secrets and visions?" Jung asked at the beginning of the last century (18). Not surprisingly, it is this wisdom maturing from what Erikson describes as "[t]he dominant antithesis in old age . . . [of] *integrity* vs. *despair*" (*Completed* 61) that Joyce reflects, however obliquely, in *Finnegans Wake*, as well as throughout the rest of his previous work taken as a whole. Erikson insists that

> [t]he dominant antithesis in old age . . . we termed *integrity*
> vs. *despair*. . . . Integrity, however, seems to convey a peculiar
> demand as does the specific strength that we postulate as
> maturing from this last antithesis namely, *wisdom*. This we
> have described as a kind of "informed and detached concern
> with life itself in the face of death itself" . . . . wisdom rests
> in the capacity to see, look, and remember, as well as to listen,
> hear, and remember. (*Completed* 61, 112)

Remembering is, therefore, crucial. "Our eyes register the light
of dead stars," André Schwarz-Bart so memorably wrote in
Le dernier des justes [The Last of the Just] (1960), as our days
and nights are lived by the light of all our and others' previous
days and nights and by the faint glow of the anticipation of
whatever time we may have remaining. The person we are
today is, in part, made up of the memory of all previous days:
"In a man's single day are all the days of time," as Borges wrote
in "James Joyce."[7] Or, as he vividly pictures in "Cambridge,"

> Those odds and ends of memory are the only wealth
> That the rush of time leaves to us.
> We are our memory,
> We are this chimerical museum of shifting forms,
>   this heap of broken mirrors. (43-47)

As Borges claims in "Cambridge," "We are this chimerical
museum of shifting forms" in the sense that today we are the
sum total of all our previous experience, yet that experience is
held but imperfectly in memory waiting to be brought forward
into today (see chapter 5). Memory becomes more important

---

7. For a detailed discussion of Borges's complicated relationship to James
   Joyce and his work, see Thomas J. Rice, who discusses at length "Borges'
   anxious relationship to the influential figure of James Joyce . . ." (56).

and more treasured the longer life continues.[8] Having experienced little the infant can recall little: "there was a moocow coming down the road," for instance, is a charming but infantile memory. Those in mid-life, such as Leopold and Molly Bloom, have, in contrast, much to recall as they wrestle with loss and the memory of what has gone before. Those at the end of life, like Anna Livia Plurabelle, have, however, the most to recall and so become almost totally preoccupied with memories of what they will shortly leave.

> What has gone? How it ends?
> Begin to forget it. It will remember itself from every sides, with all gestures, in each our word. Today's truth, tomorrow's trend.
> Forget, remember! (*Finnegans Wake* 614)

"To grow old is a great privilege," writes Erikson at the end of a very long life. He continues:

> It allows feedback on a long life that can be relived in retrospect. With the passing of years, retrospect becomes more inclusive; scene and action become more real and present. Sometimes the distant scenes and experiences are close to bewildering, and to relive them in memory is almost *overwhelming*. (*Completed* 128)

"Forget, remember!" exhorted Joyce at the end of his last book expressing a similar sentiment. Both suggest the wisdom to be found in old age as time becomes more precious because more limited.

James Joyce's works taken as a whole from *A Portrait of the Artist as a Young Man* and *Dubliners* through *Ulysses* and *Exiles* to *Finnegans Wake* embody Erikson's "meaningful interplay

---

8. See chapter 5 on dementia for the human cost of losing memory through contracting one of the various forms of dementia.

between beginning and end as well as some finite sense of summary and, possibly, a more active anticipation of dying" (*Completed* 63). If inclusion, together with mastery of the world and narrative methods, sets Joyce apart from other twentieth-century writers, so does his depiction of the totality of the human life cycle lived in time so evident throughout his work.

The Chimera of Immortality

> *Immortality, forever beyond our reach . . .*
> *[T]hinking about life that never ends clarifies the*
> *relevance of life that does.*
> ——*Brian Greene*

"O let not Time deceive you / You cannot conquer Time," cautioned W. H. Auden in "One Evening," a poem often acknowledged as perhaps the finest twentieth-century lyric in English (1.23-24). Yet many people try to do exactly that: to conquer time and achieve immortality with usually disastrous results. For example, the first-century Roman author and provincial governor Petronius has an extended set piece, "Dinner with Tramalchio," in his *Satyricon*: this longish chapter satirizes the obnoxiously rich parvenu Trimalchio, who loves bad puns and exudes bad taste, while entertaining or, rather, boring his guests at his endless dinners with gossip and stories. In one such story, he claimed—somewhat extravagantly— to have once seen the famous Sybil of Cumae reduced to a tiny shriveled-up woman trapped in a bird cage hanging outside a shop. His audience would immediately recognize this Sybil, because her story was so famous: when young this Sybil was so beloved by the god Apollo that he gave her the gift of foresight which brought her fame. Later, when he attempted to seduce her in return for the gift, she resisted demanding that the god now also grant her a new wish in return for their making love. When Apollo agreed she said, "I wish to become immortal." The god tried to dissuade her, advising her to ask for anything but not that. She remained adamant, however, and would not give him what he wanted until finally he reluctantly gave in and granted her wish. So she became immortal. Unfortunately, she then also became so proud of her godlike status that she refused to make love to Apollo. So he cursed her and her immortality. He could not take back from her his gift of eternal life because gods cannot break their oaths, but Apollo realized what the Sybil did not, that it would be only a matter of time before she would deeply regret her rash act, for in stating her wishes she had neglected a terribly important detail: when she asked the god for immortality she had neglected to also ask for eternal youth. The result as seen in that bird cage was that over the many centuries since her transformation she had simply withered away. Trimalchio reports that some local boys had asked the tiny wasted figure, "if you now had a wish, what would you wish for?" Without any hesitation, she answered, "I want to die!" She had found to her sorrow that immortality or endless time without eternal youth was not worth having, and—to quote once more the Wildean imitation Latin epigram—"When the gods want to punish us, they answer our prayers."[9]

---

9. The Sybil of Cumae became famous in the twentieth century when T. S. Eliot in "The Waste Land," quoting Petronius, gave her reply to the boys' question, "I want to die." Eliot then repeated her story in the Notes to "The Waste Land." For an excellent contemporary and unexpurgated translation of Petronius, see William Arrowsmith's *The Satyricon* (1959).

Many centuries later Jonathan Swift applied a kind of philosophical logic to the question of immortality in his savage satirical portrait of the Struldbruggs in book 3 of *Gulliver's Travels.* As usual, in that book Lemuel Gulliver brings his great naiveté and superficiality to this encounter as he once more lives up to his name as "gullible" Gulliver. Hearing that some people in the land of Luggnagg, where he now finds himself, are immortal, his enthusiasm for them and their extraordinary condition knows no bounds:

> I cried out, as in a rapture, "Happy nation, where every child hath at least a chance for being immortal! Happy people, who enjoy so many living examples of ancient virtue, and have masters ready to instruct them in the wisdom of all former ages! but happiest, beyond all comparison, are those excellent STRULDBRUGS, who, being born exempt from that universal calamity of human nature, have their minds free and disengaged, without the weight and depression of spirits caused by the continual apprehensions of death! (book 3)

But rather than immortality conferring wisdom and virtue on those fortunate few, endless time instead breeds boredom and indifference, since such people having been given all the time in the world to try or do everything and anything in the world discover that nothing in the world is worth doing; that is, there is for them no one thing important or distinctive enough to entice them to act. The Struldbrugs are, in fact, a sorry lot, as Gulliver reports upon seeing them:

> They were the most mortifying sight I ever beheld; and the women more horrible than the men. Besides the usual deformities in extreme old age, they acquired an additional ghastliness, in proportion to their number of years, which is not to be described; and among half a dozen, I soon

distinguished which was the eldest, although there was not above a century or two between them. (book 3)

The conclusion he draws from seeing them is as enthusiastic and as effusive as his first reaction, but now in the opposite direction: "The reader will easily believe, that from what I had heard and seen, my keen appetite for perpetuity of life was much abated. I grew heartily ashamed of the pleasing visions I had formed; and thought no tyrant could invent a death into which I would not run with pleasure, from such a life" (book 3).

Unless we are the immortal and eternally youthful gods, Time does mark our bodies, especially our faces as we age, as it did to both the Sybil of Cumae and the Struldbrugs. Denying this fact of life in our contemporary world has become for some almost a way of life, creating a huge market for crèmes and potions, tablets and diets, and most prominent of all, plastic surgery, as each "remedy" promises to postpone if not reverse at least a portion of the aging process. Oscar Wilde envisioned yet another possible remedy for aging which promised eternal youthfulness, if not immortality, in his novel *The Picture of Dorian Gray* (1891). Dorian Gray sat for his portrait to be painted, and when the picture was finished, he discovered to his shock that this portrait had a strange property that would enable him to avoid any physical sign of aging no matter how extravagantly or badly he behaved and no matter what kind of diet or hours he kept. Rather than his body and face showing the sum total of his aging, his utterly lifelike realistic portrait would record as part of its image of him the result of each of his excesses as he committed them as well as show the effects of the aging process itself. Having discovered the fantastic portrait's secret he quickly reveled in the new possibilities of a life lived without any worry about the increasing and visible effects of aging:

> This portrait would be for him the most magical of mirrors. As it had revealed to him his own body, so it would reveal to him his own soul. And when winter came upon it, he would still be standing where spring trembles on the verge of summer. When the blood crept from its face, and left behind a pallid mask of chalk with leaden eyes, he would keep the glamour of boyhood. Not one blossom of his loveliness would ever fade. Not one pulse of his life would ever weaken. Like the gods of the Greeks, he would be strong, and fleet, and joyous. What did it matter what happened to the coloured image on the canvas? He would be safe. That was everything. (120)

After such contemplations, Gray decides to hide the painting in an empty attic, thus revealing that he realizes the extent of its strange power. Now, thanks to this portrait, he has no need to fear time, which would effect his growing old, growing weak, and losing his good looks: "the face painted on the canvas could grow bestial, sodden, and unclean. What did it matter? No one could see it. He himself would not see it. Why should he watch the hideous corruptions of his soul? He kept his youth—that was enough" (136). But such bargains come at a price and the one Dorian Gray pays for his "magical mirror" proves high; his attempt to hold back the aging process ends tragically not only for him, but also for many who knew him, as "Time will have his fancy / Tomorrow or today" (Auden, "One Evening l.33-34).

These three stories which span about two thousand years from Petronius, who lived under Nero and the Roman Empire, to Swift in eighteenth-century England to Wilde at the end of the nineteenth and beginning of the twentieth century—along with so many more—suggest that humans cannot evade time. When a person embarks on an impossible quest for an eternal life of endless time, as the Sybil of Cumae did, receives unsought-for immortality as happened to the Struldbrugs, or when one suddenly has the opportunity for a never-ending springtime of life, as Dorian Gray did, then they miss out on an essential and most natural part of human life—its terminal years—with terrible and often ironic results. Heather Ingman's perceptive comment on Wilde's novel applies equally well to the fiction of Petronius and Swift: "*Dorian Gray* reveals the danger of trying to impose on life a form it does not have, particularly in Dorian's [and the Sybil's and the Struldbrugs"] attempt to hold back time" (34). Only the gods are immortal; that is, they do not live within time and, therefore, are profoundly unserious as they appear forever young, for they never suffer any serious consequences of their actions. By contrast, most of us at least at some point or points in our life, share with the great eighteenth-century hymnist Isaac Watts the sense of time that

> Time, like an ever-rolling stream,
> Bears all its sons away;
> They fly forgotten, as a dream
> Dies at the opening day.
> ("Our God, Our Help in Ages Past" [1708], 25-28)

Humans having to live within time discover as they age that their very nature proves mortal and they are, therefore, inherently tragic in that they pay, and often pay dearly, for their mistakes and, however they live their lives, they'll "pass and be forgotten with the rest" ("The Whiffenpoof Song," 1909).

Shakespeare and the Smell of Mortality

In Shakespeare's *The Tragedy of King Lear* (1606), Gloucester, now blind but recognizing Lear's voice, says: "O, let me kiss that hand." To which Lear replies: "Let me wipe it first; it smells of mortality" (4.4). The whole of Shakespeare's play reeks of mortality—the pervasive "smell" generated by time-bound lives lived in partial knowledge of the way things and the way people are or by the—often faulty—perception of the way things are and the way people are. In the apocalyptic world of *Lear* time will have a stop as one by one the characters die: Gloucester dies of a heart attack "[t]wixt two extremes of passion, joy and grief" (5.3; 199), Cordelia hanged by some perfidious slave[10]; Edmund bested in a duel by Edgar; and at last Lear either deceived into believing that Cordelia revives— "This feather stirs; she lives" (5.3; 266)—or in deep despair over the injustice of the world ruled by inhuman arbitrary powers— those "justicers above"—gives up the ghost. As Kent observes, "[t]he wonder is he hath endured so long" (5.3; 317).

George Steiner in *The Death of Tragedy* found *King Lear* "the most comprehensive image of man's estate in Shakespeare's entire work" (257), and that estate is mortality since human life must be lived in time. Frank Kermode more specifically concluded that the play "is about suffering represented as a condition of the world as we inherit it or make

---

10. Frank Kermode discussing the play's cruelty notes that

> although several versions of Cordelia survive in chronicles and other poems, including the old *King Leir*, on which Shakespeare drew, no Cordelia except his is murdered. [Dr.] Johnson seems to be expressing dismay at a cruelty inflicted on him personally, and I think he is not alone in feeling that. There is a cruelty in the writing that echoes the cruelty of the story, a terrible calculatedness that puts one in mind of Cornwall's and Regan's suffering to be protracted and intensified, as it were, without end. (Kermode 197)

it for ourselves" (184), while Terry Eagleton sees it as focusing on "flesh . . . frailty and finitude" (183). However we formulate it—with or without comic alliteration—the play quite possibly remains the most comprehensive image of suffering with all its myriad causes in Western literature since the Book of Job. Kermode goes further:

> Much of the effect of *King Lear* seems to me to arise from its own unsparing cruelty, which can sometimes seem to be an almost sadistic attitude to the spectator, an attitude enhanced by the coolness with which we are manipulated, forced to deal with a pain that does not hinder the poet from playing his terrible games. (193)

In this view, "you justicers . . . above" (4.2; 78-79) are conspicuous for their neglect of human affairs and—worse—for their seeming delight in human suffering:

> As flies to wanton boys are we to th' gods.
> They kill us for their sport. (4.1; 36-37)

And the "sport" enacted on the stage, before an often-horrified audience, inflicts its pain in scene after scene after scene.

W. H. Auden may well be right that Lear is not "a person I might meet, but . . . is a state which in the life of [hu]man[s] everybody at one time or another experiences. . . . We get a picture of a human heart and of every human heart together" ("King Lear" 220). And in that sense, all four—Steiner, Kermode, Auden, and Eagleton—clearly agree with Dr. Johnson, who famously thought *King Lear* unactable on the stage for the very reason that its vision of mortal humanity was so unblinkered, so unforgiving, so stark. Small wonder the next generation edited it for pity's sake and Cordelia and Edgar could at last be married and Lear be pensioned off. Lear may or may not be "a man / More sinned against than sinning" (3.2; 59-60), but in the non-bowdlerized version of the play, he is one doomed to drink the last bitter drop to the lees. The greatest of Shakespeare's tragedies, *King Lear* presents an uncompromising view of the world steeped in injustice and fratricide where—handy-dandy!—the fool and the king change places, where—handy-dandy!—the children and the parents change places, and over all is that ubiquitous smell of mortality, for "time must have a stop" (*Henry IV*, part 1 5). Like in the Book of Job, upon which Shakespeare drew so extensively, the good and innocent suffer while the evil appear to prosper.

King Lear presents a tragedy of last things, the last moments of old age, the last days of warring families, and even the last days of a fracturing nation—each a terrible subject in and of itself. But in what sense is it, as Auden claims, a condition or state "which in the life of ... [humans] everybody at one time or another experiences"? ("King Lear" 220). I would guess that Auden finds the commonality of *Lear* in the picture of the human heart breaking in those last days. Lear finds himself in a situation only partly of his own making. He surely is responsible for naïvely imagining that he could prevent civil war by the simple expedient of himself as sovereign dividing his kingdom, and he certainly is at fault as a father for jumping to unwarranted conclusions about all three of his daughters' regard and love for him. But just as clearly there is no sense in which he deserves, or in which he provoked, the determined evil of Goneril, Regan, and Edmund. Yes, Lear is weary and wants to "unburdened crawl towards death," "where every third thought shall be of the grave" (1.1; 41, xx). Lear is old—he is an old king, an old father, an old man. In a memorable North American production, Christopher Plummer by all accounts played Lear brilliantly as an old pensioner growing increasingly senile (see O'Brien, Brantley). Age certainly does enter into the tragic mix as Lear's options narrow, his world flies apart, his time runs out, and events do indeed race downhill like the Fool's justly famous "Great Wheel" (2.4; 69), but does that justify the transformation of that wheel into an instrument of torture? *The Tragedy of King Lear* leaves the answer up to each individual in the audience, but the question itself has provoked extensive commentary over the centuries with each age giving answers that reflect that age's values and/or prejudices. Whatever the answer, the image of the "wheel of fire" remains seared in most readers' imaginations:

> . . . I am bound
> Upon a wheel of fire, that mine own tears
> Do scald like molten lead. (4.7; 46-48)

Time Comes to an End

It may be a measure of the age in which we live that, in contrast to the tragedy of *King Lear*, contemporary plays that treat of these same subjects, such as the last moments of life or the last days of fratricidal families or the fracturing of nations, do so usually not as tragedy but as comedy. Traditionally, comedies end with either a marriage or a dance or preferably both as the old or natural order reasserts itself and those who have made war or bickered or fought find themselves now reconciled and happily ensconced within that order. For instance, in Jean Giraudoux's *The Madwoman of Chaillot* (1945), Evil and the Seven Deadly Sins lie defeated banished by an imminently sane Madwoman to languish in the sewers under Paris where they belong. Yet this potentially happy ending still remains in jeopardy as long as the young lovers in the play remain apart. This young pair under threat of not acting in time are the future of Paris and also symbolically of France and of the human race itself. Their fate, therefore, becomes extremely important as well as the determining issue of whether the play ends tragically or comically. Defeating evil is not enough, suggests the playwright, it is also imperative to support, defend, and further love. Only when such positive values win out—however momentarily or however fantastically—is the comedy assured. The young couple in the play heed the Madwoman's warning that "[i]f two people who love each other let a single instant wedge itself between them, it grows—it becomes a month, a year, a century, it becomes too late," and so they kiss. And the play ends happily.

But such an affirmative reordering of priorities in time as Jean Giraudoux achieved in *The Madwoman of Chaillot* at mid-twentieth century appears now impossible in this twenty-first century. Comedy, like light verse, is under a cloud relegated to the superficial, the frivolous, or to the disconnected quip epitomized by the powerful, ubiquitous stand-up comic. Yet tragedy fares no better. Late twentieth-century drama in English featured little or no tragedy. Instead of *Hamlet* (1609) there was Tom Stoppard's *Rosenkrantz and Gildenstern Are Dead* (1966), instead of *Othello* (1604) Harold Pinter's *Homecoming* (1965); instead of *Coriolanus* (1609) David Hare's *The Great Exhibition* (1972). Then there is theatre in the United States featuring an abundance of melodrama from Mary Tyrone's hair-raising entrance at the end of Eugene O'Neill's *A Long Day's Journey into Night* (1956) to Rip Torn memorably capitulating to the frenzied mob in the Broadway production of Tennessee Williams's *Sweet Bird of Youth* (1956) to Tilden's muddy march up the stairs to confront Hallie in all the many versions of Sam Shepard's *Buried Child* (1978), and, perhaps most obvious of all, Beth Henley's repetitive plays. Perhaps tragedy became more than problematic in a fantastic world with no Great Men such as Lear or Othello or no Great Women such as Medea or Hedda Gabler. (See chapter 5 for an exception in The Mai.) In American drama many post-war critics maintained that tragedy could no longer accommodate Aristotle's great person falling from a great height but instead must focus on a small person, a Low-man, doing a pratfall from off a low joint stool. Yet Arthur Miller's *Death of a Salesman* (1949) was no tragedy. Despite Charlie's white-washing disclaimer that "nobody dast blame this man," many in the audience wisely did so. On the occasion of the play's fiftieth anniversary Arthur Miller wrote at some length in *The New York Times* about how Willie was pitiable but not tragic.

What did appear to flourish often in the last half of the twentieth century and into the twenty-first was a mixture of comedy and tragedy, especially in Samuel Beckett's plays, most memorably in *Waiting for Godot* and *Endgame*. If Shakespeare had emphasized the comedy side of tragicomedy with "The Most Lamentable Comedy and Most Cruel Death of Pyramus and Thisby," as did Ionesco when he confessed that "the comic alone is able to give us the strength to bear the tragedy of existence" (*Notes and Counter Notes* 113), Beckett's emphasis often falls on the first term of *tragi*-comedy in a world where "[n]othing['s] to be done" (*Waiting for Godot* 10) and where "habit is a great deadener" (*Waiting for Godot* 83). Where everything is but "play" (*Play* 305) during each "happy day" (*Happy Days* 135), and characters exist locked in isolation "burning to be gone" (*Krapp's Last Tape* 222). Beckett, our chronicler of dissolution, our great playwright of minimal theatre, challenged almost every aspect and facet of the theatre, creating innumerable dramatic images of the late-twentieth-century terminal world—a world under threat of erasure where time is running out and all choices lead to dead ends (see chapter 4). A character in O'Neill's *The Iceman Cometh* might well be speaking for Beckett when he concludes, "All things are the same meaningless joke to me, for they grin at me from the skull of death" (128). Without genuine choice that leads to action and without all the consequences that follow such choice, true tragedy appears impossible. Maddy Rooney, Beckett's magnificent comic creation in *All that Fall*, sums up this absence of choice admirably when she wryly observes as previously quoted: "It is suicide to be abroad. But what is it to be at home . . . ? . . . A lingering dissolution" (175).

The plays of Edward Albee go at least somewhat against this grain as his characters often face real choices in real time with severe consequences from Peter's accepting Jerry's challenge to fight in *Zoo Story* (1959) to George's shielding Martha at the end of *Who's Afraid of Virginia Woolf?* (1962) to Stevie's slaughtering her rival in *The Goat or Who Is Sylvia?* (2002) to the mother banishing her son in *Three Tall Women*. Rather than *Lear*'s apocalypse of last things or Beckett's world under threat of erasure, Albee's *Three Tall Women* shares with tragedy the focus on last moments as the time of life runs out and shares with comedy the move towards resolution and affirmation. Several contemporary plays share some superficial features with *Three Tall Women*, such as the cast of three women in David Mamet's *Boston Marriage* (1999), or a cast of three women featuring a mother unable to be reconciled with a disaffected child in Tomas Kilroy's *The Shape of Metal* (2003). But there resemblances end.

What is extraordinary about Albee's play—besides its unflinching look at the end of life and its luminous language— is his daring mixture of realism in act 1 and the fantastic in act 2. The play demonstrates the truth of Robert Brustein's arresting proposition that "modern dramatic realism is usually a subterfuge" (*Revolt* 15). Without explanation the play moves from the realism of act 1 with its dialogue among three distinctive characters, the old woman, the caretaker, and the young lawyer, to the fantastic staging of act 2 with its embodiment of three stages of the old woman's life: the dying woman and two "younger versions of [herself]" (Sacharow 120).[11] As Lawrence Sacharow, the distinguished director responsible for the American production of *Three Tall Women*, observed: "The story [of *Three Tall Women*] moves in dimensions outside of time and into an imaginative realm that poses great mysteries" (120). Using a fantastic means of presentation reminiscent of Pirandello's *Six Characters in Search of an Author* (1921) and his *Henry IV* (1922), Albee solves the extremely difficult problem of putting on stage the physical, emotional, and mental reality of old age while simultaneously presenting the woman's memories of three quite different times in her life along with the internal dialogue of her last moments—and all of these not as abstractions but as embodied.

The first act centers on a highly realistic depiction of old age and its limitations together with those of the people involved in looking after the elderly. The three nameless women characters are designated in the script simply as A, B, and C. A, a once very tall woman, who is now almost 90 and

---

11. To say as one critic does that "*Three Tall Women* presents three figures who construct themselves as three different characters in the first act . . . and by the end of the second act discover themselves to be three depictions of the same woman at different ages" (Jenckes 107), is to endow a character on stage with volition—something no stage character *by definition* can have since such characters are already "constructed" in a script to be interpreted on stage. Even Pirandello's famous six characters are so constructed before the curtain goes up.

stooped with age, suffers from osteoporosis, incontinence, and all the other vagaries, inconveniences, and embarrassments old age brings in its wake. Visually, in addition to the stooped posture, she nurses a bandaged broken arm that refuses to mend and which the doctors wish to amputate. As a result she is in constant pain. B, her middle-aged caregiver, appears remarkably patient with A's problems and understands her attempts to maintain a shred of dignity in her decrepit condition. She also understands A's pride that continually gets tripped up over details forgotten, neglected, or overlooked. C, the young woman lawyer, does not empathize with A, nor does she show much patience with her problems. She merely wants to do her job, go back to the office, and, generally, get on with her life. This first act is painfully realistic in its unremitting vision of the vicissitudes of old age, their effects, and the reactions of others.

The brilliance of Albee's play lies, however, not in this realism which proves but an example of Brustein's "subterfuge," but in his using it as a means to set the audience up for the fantastic second act. As act 2 begins, we in the audience remain comfortable—B and C are on stage engaged in dialogue. We've seen this before in act 1. Yet within a short space we may grow uncomfortable or be simply puzzled, for although B and C look the same as they did in act 1 except for wearing different dresses, and although B and C are played by the same actresses, they appear to be almost entirely different characters. C, still young, has become the Tall Woman's self at twenty-something full of expectations and plans, while middle-aged B has become the Tall Woman's self in mid-life who, aware of the passage of time, understands that most of her choices have been made and now she must live with them. At the end of act 1, elderly A had suffered a stroke and so appears at the opening of act 2 bed-ridden, unconscious, with a breathing mask for oxygen over her face. That prominent, if silent, figure lies immobile in bed waiting for death and the end of time—her life basically over, her lived-time completed. Although somewhat more complicated than perhaps expected from the first act, an audience should be able to make the necessary adjustments to this altered presentation. But then, A makes a stunning, dramatic, and wholly unexpected entrance— a true *coup de théâtre*. She appears no longer stooped or forgetful and no longer suffering from a broken arm or incontinence or other embarrassing bodily failures. Instead, she appears as what she must have been for most of her lifetime, an energetic truly Tall Woman, one who speaks with verve and gusto as one who commands the present, recalls the past, and anticipates the future. This portrait results from the magic of theatre as rooted in Jan Kott's paradox of the theatre as the illusion of reality and the reality of illusion.[12] In this "reality of illusion" what we encounter embodied on the stage is an "illusion of reality" of an internal, mental dialogue of the woman's final moments before death as her time runs out. Her physical body meanwhile remains throughout the act visibly immobile and comatose on the bed in order to emphasize the internal nature of this last dialogue. Also visible but silent is her alienated son.[13] (Although the son appears physically onstage, he remains

---

12. Kott in *The Theatre of Essence* maintains: "We watch a performance and, therefore, everything that happens onstage is not 'for real'; we are in the theatre, we sit in a seat and look at the stage and so everything that happens there, happens 'for real': the actors are alive and the props are real. The theatre is both the illusion of reality and the reality of illusion"(133).

13. The Son, as stubborn as his mother and as philandering as his father, became enmeshed in a test of wills with his mother during adolescence, which resulted in her throwing him out of the house and his leaving home for good. In an interview with Bruce Mann, Albee confesses,

mute throughout the act since he obviously must be outside A's internal dialogue.)

Eric Bentley observed that "every art is the baring of the human soul, but it is only in the theatre that the baring of the soul takes place through the physical presence of human bodies on stage" (qtd. in Kott 132)—a process that Albee's play illustrates at every turn. In act 1, the three women embody three reactions to the process of aging over time that leads to death. The "smell of mortality" that hangs over the act is at first rejected, then defied, until at last listened to. In act 2, the three women embody three of the seven ages of the Tall Woman: the young "twenty something," the middle aged matron, and the old woman. The dialogue in the play echoes Charles de Montesquieu's witty epigram: "Lamentably, there is too short an interval between the time when one is too young and the time when one is too old."

The three ages being simultaneously on stage represent not only each age as itself but also, and, at the same time, each age as a part of the memory of a whole life. These last reflections and memories are the Tall Woman's last thoughts articulated and acted out by the three vertical Tall Women against the background of her horizontal worn-out body at the end of her time. Albee's creative artistry illustrates Blaise Pascal's rueful conclusion that " [a]ll our dignity consists, then, in thought. By it we must elevate ourselves, and not by space and time which we cannot fill" (qtd. in Auden, "King Lear" 225).

G. Wilson Knight once described Shakespeare's *King Lear* as "the perfect fusion of psychological realism with the daring

---

"I didn't even know the Boy was going to come on stage. Until I wrote a line, 'the Boy enters.' I didn't know he was coming on stage" (139). Mann has eloquently written of Albee's need to exorcise the ghost of his mother while paradoxically at the same time needing her as his muse ("Return to the Muses").

flights of a fantastic imagination" ("Comedy of the Grotesque" 123). Similarly, in *Three Tall Women*, psychological realism lies embedded in "the daring flight of fantastic imagination" that constitutes act 2. This fantastic dramatic presentation enables Albee to embody the lived-time theme of *Three Tall Women*, which the director, Sacharow, characterizes as "how different we are at different ages in our life. The play reveals the journey we take toward aging and death and the characters examine their lives in vivid, three-dimensional tall depth" (124). All lives have shape—at least they have when seen in time from birth to death—and most of us feel a need late in life, if not before, to reconcile ourselves with the lives we have led. The play performs this reconciliation through the three stages, the three blocks of time that comprise the Tall Woman's life, entering into dialogue with one another during which the Tall Woman confronts the truth—that in her view Life did not deal her a very good hand but, by accepting this as a given by mid-life, she proceeded to play her cards as best as she could. Her development appears almost opposite to that of Lear's: from the beginning of the play she emerges, like Lear, as cantankerous, willful, stubborn in her old age, but unlike Lear, as far as we know, the Tall Woman, as we learn in act 2, needed all of those qualities to survive. Greedy, often hateful, and unforgiving, the Tall Woman, in part, drove her only son away from her. A dogged fighter for survival, she persisted in a marriage that she candidly evaluates as "bearable." She endures, surmounts the difficulties including her husband's notorious philandering plus those horrible six years during which he dies slowly of prostate cancer that metastasizes throughout his body. "It's terrible!" she exclaims, adding: "And there's nothing you can do to prepare yourself!" (105). In this visualization of the drama within the Tall Woman, she refuses to despair over her life but instead affirms the end of her life as "the greatest woe of all"; that is, the looked-for moment that will provide an appropriate finish for her life's time. She is herself—the sum total of all her "works and days."

> The happiest moment of all? . . . The happiest moment? (*To the audience now.*) Coming to the end of it, I think, when all the waves cause the greatest woes to subside, leaving breathing space, time to concentrate on the greatest woe of all—that blessed one—the end of it. (109)

As in most of Albee's dramas, there is the distinct echo of several of Samuel Beckett's plays including *Krapp's Last Tape*, where Krapp assesses his recorded memories and then welcomes the end; *Happy Days*, where Winnie tells her life story while at the same time she is symbolically trapped in that story as she is buried in sand; and *Play*, where a character asks plaintively, "All this, when will this have all been . . . just play?" (313). But the clearest reference of all is to the great speech in act 2 of *Godot*, where Vladimir describes giving birth "astride of a grave" (83). Both Beckett and Albee succeed in finding fresh metaphors for mortal life lived in time and therefore lived in the face of certain death. Beckett finds his in the gravedigger's forceps: "Down in the hole, lingeringly, the grave digger puts on the forceps. We have time to grow old" (83). Albee finds his in the breath of life:

> You take the breath in . . . you let it out. The first one you take in you're upside down and they slap you into it. The last one . . . well, the last one you let it all out . . . and that's it. You start . . . and then you stop. (*Tall Women* 13)

Like Lear, "stripped of additions and in his dotage" (Kermode 187), the Tall Woman does the hard work of self-acceptance as she, too, "discovers . . . what the evil have known from their cradles, that *in this world there is no poetic justice*" (Enid Welsford qtd. in Kermode 187). Rather than bemoan the nature of mortal life lived in such a world, the Tall Woman achieves what Erikson calls in a previously quoted passage a "meaningful interplay between beginning and end as well as some finite sense of summary and . . . a more active anticipation of dying" (Erikson, *Completed* 63). As part of this process she, like Lear, must learn that "suffering [is] a condition of the world as we inherit it or make it for ourselves" (Kermode 184).

The distinguished director, scholar, and reviewer of drama Robert Brustein once remarked that "unlike contemporary ideologists, great classical dramatists rarely adduce a single explanation for any crime" (*Dumbocracy* 150). Similarly, great drama seldom offers a single explanation for human behavior. Lear's motives remain to this day a matter of argument and controversy. The Tall Woman's motives are simple only on the surface; as soon as we begin to examine them we find that they are quite complicated. Facing "the dominant antithesis in old age . . . *integrity* vs. *despair*" (Erikson, *Completed* 61), the Tall Woman eschews despair and achieves a kind of integrity by neither regretting nor denying her life or how she spent her time, and by accepting both life and death. Unable to see herself as victim, "she watches herself battle on with a humor which makes her something more than a mere victim" (Bigsby 150). Her internal dialogue may well be, as Christopher Bigsby argues, "the only dialogue worth having" (150), but it is also the only dialogue possible for a comatose stroke victim. Within such confined and narrow straits, the Tall Woman maintains her integrity, which for Erikson consists of a kind of "informed and detached concern with life itself in the face of death itself" (61). That "informed and detached concern with life" exactly describes the Tall Woman at the end of the play. She characterizes the process as

> Going through the whole thing and coming out . . . not out beyond it, of course, but sort of to . . . one side . . . to the point where you *can* think about yourself in the third person without being crazy. . . . I suppose, that that's the way I'm *living*—beside myself, to one side. . . . there's a difference between knowing you're going to *die* and *knowing* you're going to die. The second is better; it moves away from the theoretical. (109)

The visual and verbal imagery at the end of the play also gains depth from Albee's allusion to Walt Whitman's great eulogy for the martyred president Abraham Lincoln, "When Lilacs Last in the Dooryard Bloom'd." In that poem, Whitman memorably described

> . . . the knowledge of death as walking one side of me,
> And the thought of death close-walking the other side
>   of me,
> And I in the middle as with companions, and as holding
>   the hands of companions . . . (120-22)

Echoing Whitman, A in the closing moments of the play puts her hand out and takes both B's and C's hands as she delivers her last lines (110).[14] She faces the end with the knowledge of

---

14. Mann, reviewing the various textual and personal influences on Albee's play, hears another echo in this "final tableau": it is, he maintains, "reminiscent of the ending of Chekhov's *Three Sisters*, when Olga puts her arms around Masha and Irena. Albee's ending is more positive, although it is still shadowed by earlier tragic events, giving it a complex resonance, like a Chekhov play" (8). Albee himself acknowledges the

death on one side and the thought of death on the other. The physical joining together of the three stages of the Tall Woman's life that were separated in and by time by the holding of hands emphasizes the unity of the end, the achieving of integrity. Nor does this "acknowledgement of death as the end of the journey . . . invalidate the fact of the journey," as Bigsby cogently argues. "The old woman spreads little light but in her amused contemplation of the stages of her life she does transform it into a game which is not without its pleasures and ambiguous satisfactions" (151). Albee's play, like Shakespeare's *King Lear*, becomes a play of reconciliation as the central characters at the end of life, at the end of their time, become reconciled to their life story. Albee's play then ends appropriately at this moment of death as the Tall Woman achieves an "informed and detached concern with life itself in the face of death itself" (Erikson, *Completed* 61).

Whatever the strengths or limitations of the theatre, drama as text and theatre as performance can and do deal with such large, and often unanswerable, questions such as questions of morality, metaphysics, love, religion, revolution, time, death, and suffering. When successful, as in the plays discussed in *It's Time* including *King Lear* and *Three Tall Women*, the resulting play is, as Colin Falck argues, "not merely a text along with all other texts but is also a capturing of some part of the essential nature of human life, and an insight into the nature of (humanly apprehended—but this is the only kind we can hope to know about) reality itself" (32)—a reality grounded in lived-time. This "capturing of some part of the essential nature of

---

considerable influence of Chekhov, Pirandello, and Beckett on his work in general (see Carol Rosen, "Writers and Their Work: Edward Albee," *Dramatists Guild Quarterly* [1966]: 27-39 qtd. in Mann). More specifically, Albee says speaking of contemporary playwrights, "We're all Beckett's children" (Interview 131).

human life" may emerge most clearly only in performance, as in Christopher Plummer's acting in *King Lear* (see O'Brien, Brantley) or Sacharow's direction of *Three Tall Women.* Apprehending such insights into the nature of reality becomes one of the chief rewards of going to the theatre. Robert Brustein spoke for many of us when he ironically confessed: "I persist in the delusion that at its best, and even less than its best, the stage can provide telling metaphors for the condition of our society, the quality of our ambitions, and the state of our souls" (*Dumbocracy* 4), to which I would add: and for the human being living in time.

Postscript:
On the Nature of Human Lived Time

I was made of a changing substance,
of mysterious time.
———*Jorge Luis Borges, "Heraclitus"*

I began this meditation on the nature of "mysterious time" and our experience of living in it by giving the first word to an experimental physicist, Richard Muller, who in his "*now* theory of time creation" posits a continual creation of time where "[e]very moment the universe gets a little bigger and there is a little more time, and it is this leading edge of time that we refer to as *now*" (*NOW: The Physics if Time* 302, 293; see the introduction). It may, therefore, be only appropriate to give the last—but not in any sense final—word on time as "the problem whose solution we'll never find" ("Borges at N.Y.U." 123) to the poet W. H. Auden, one of the many writers whose imaginative narratives I've discussed. As this "mosaic of what living in time is like" demonstrates: for people living in time it rarely feels like there is enough time or that more of it is continually being created. The human situation instead usually reflects our feeling that we are running short of time. This human, individual, personal experience of time taps into our common understanding of lived time that often changes as we grow, mature, and age. For example, W. B. Yeats as a young man and poet may have bravely declared, "I spit into the face of Time," yet years later realized that time "has transfigured me" in "Lamentations of the Old Pensioner" (17-18), where "trans-figured" may apply both to the changes wrought by time to the human body and to those changes occasioned by mentally contemplating time. A quite different, far less boastful

expression of the human experience of and attitude towards
time may be found in Auden's deceptively simple yet in the
same moment profoundly insightful ballad "As I Walked Out
One Evening," with which I'll end this book:

> As I walked out one evening
>   Walking down Bristol Street,
> The crowds upon the pavement
>   Were fields of harvest wheat. (1-4)

The opening four-line stanza juxtaposes urban Bristol Street in
London with its multitude of car dealerships with crowds of
mortal human beings that are metaphorically compared to
"fields of harvest wheat" implying that they are ripe for
reaping; that is, that their time has almost run out. This is the
backdrop against which a romantic lover pledges his undying
love that he boasts is so powerful that it can and will overcome
time itself and thus defy omnipresent mortality:

> The years shall run like rabbits,
>   For in my arms I hold
> The Flower of the Ages,
>   And the first love of the world. (17-20)

The lover's hyperboles are wonderfully exaggerated but still
come down to Andrew Marvell's by now familiar poetic
declaration: "though we cannot make our sun stand still, yet we
will make him run" ("To His Coy Mistress"). Of the first five
stanzas of the poem four stanzas are given over to such
hyperbolic declarations of how romantic love will overcome
time, while the remaining ten stanzas focus on just how
impossible it is for humans to overcome their time-bound lives
as every clock in the city declares, "You cannot conquer Time"
(24). The examples begin to ring true as Auden personifies time

as an intruder into our lives. Time becomes that person or thing that remains just out of our sight but hints at its disturbing presence: "Time watches from the shadow / And coughs when you would kiss" (27-28). Not only can humans not "conquer time," but time itself flies by as "the years . . . run like rabbits" or, alternatively, time appears to seep through people's hands as the unimportant, mundane, ordinary daily tasks and events take their toll: "In headaches and in worry / Vaguely life leaks away" (31-32). But whether time "runs like rabbits" or "leaks [vaguely] away," it does disappear, and it will come to an end for each individual. The incontrovertible fact of life remains that "time will have its fancy / To-morrow or to-day" (33-34). For change still is basic to the order of human life and experience—change that includes the death of all things, or as William Shakespeare put it more memorably in *Cymbeline*,

> Golden lads and girls all must
> Like chimney-sweepers, come to dust. (4.2.274-75)

Similarly, while the lover may make extravagant promises of a wonderful new life, only in fairy tales that take place in the Land of Cockaigne do beggars rather than bankers "raffle the banknotes" or the cannibalistic giant appear "enchanting to Jack" (Auden, "As I Walked Out" 45, 46). In this more commonplace world where humans live even the athletic diver's "brilliant bow" (50) made as she descends gracefully from the diving board into the water beneath does not and cannot last beyond her youth. Also with age those lovely "threaded dancers" may well stumble and fall while the verdant landscape will most years be blighted by the "appalling snow" (49, 48).[1]

---

1. John Fuller points out that "[a] phrase like 'appalling snow' is literal (the snow makes the valleys pale) and yet reinvigorates a common cliché about bad weather: the careful doubleness of the epithet manages to capture its most useful sense of dismaying" (108).

The boasts of the lover also have to be tempered by our knowledge of the transient nature of all human life and the common human feeling mid-life or later that somehow, somewhere we could have made better choices or chosen a different path, a different road to follow, and so are left to "wonder what you've missed" (54). Behind all action, thought, and decision-making is time, whose presence throughout the poem appears in the ubiquitous chiming of the clocks that mark the passing of each hour and minute.

Against such a background of time's inevitable passage and despite, or perhaps because of, the resulting mortality of human beings, any affirmation of a life lived in time represents a considerable human achievement, which is reflected in the end of the poem: "Life remains a blessing / Although you cannot bless" (65-66). Similarly Love, albeit not that romantic love of the poem's opening lines, remains the best course for human beings as they are commanded by time's passage to "love your crooked neighbor / With your crooked heart" (69-70). Like the basin of water that may be momentarily disturbed, even roiled, by human hands being plunged into and then agitating it, but when the hands are removed, the water swiftly returns to its normal placidity showing no sign of any human activity, so when "[t]he clocks had ceased their chiming, . . . the deep river" (73-74)—that river of time which we can never step into twice—flows on, continuing on its way in the forever new Now. This seemingly simple yet profound ballad, contrasting extravagant assertions of overcoming time against the reality of living and loving within time, becomes a fitting summary of this investigation and report on what living in time is like for us mortal humans.

That persistent "smell of mortality" emanating from William Shakespeare's *King Lear* and Edward Albee's *Three*

Tall Women and so vigorously fought against by Oscar Wilde's Dorian Gray and a host of others (see "The Chimera of Immortality"), while denied to Jonathan Swift's Struldbrugs and to Gaius Petronius's Sybil of Cumae remains a metaphor that mirrors the nature of human life: that our lives being mortal are lived within time and that time, whether Dorian Gray's, Lear's, or the Tall Woman's or any human being's, must come to an end. How they meet that end reflects whether their life ends in futility (Dorian Gray), in despair (Lear), or with integrity (the Tall Woman).

Perhaps an even clearer example is the late Oliver Sacks, whose life with all its pitfalls, detours, and losses, nevertheless brought him meaningful work to do, intense interaction with his fellow human beings, many of whose suffering he could alleviate, great success in his chosen profession as a neurologist as well as in his accidental profession of writer, and, finally, love (see his memoir, *On the Move: A Life*, 2016). At the very end of his life his "predominant feeling," he writes, became "one of gratitude" for the gift of life:

> I have loved and been loved, I have been given much and I have given something in return; I have read and traveled and thought and written. I have had an intercourse with the world, the special intercourse of writers and readers.
>
> Above all, I have been a sentient being, a thinking animal, on this beautiful planet, and that in itself has been an enormous privilege and adventure. (*Gratitude* 20)

In his last months, facing inoperable, fatal cancer, Sacks continued to work, writing a series of four very short but often profound essays collected in his posthumously published book, *Gratitude*, which begins with this summary sentence: "I am now face to face with dying, but I am not finished living" (v). The fourth and final essay, "Sabbath," was especially important to Sacks, and he devoted his last days to writing and rewriting it until he was satisfied that it said what he had found most important in life through his eighty-two years of living on Earth. At the end, in addition to being grateful for having been given this time (20), he became increasingly aware at the close of life that—appropriately enough—this *now* was the time "when one can feel that one's work is done, and one may, in good conscience, rest" (45). "To everything there is a season . . . a time to be born and a time to die" (Ecclesiastes 3.1-2). Accepting that time as our own, however long or short it may be, becomes the work of a human lifetime, as Oliver Sacks so beautifully demonstrates.

Figure 1: The Corpus Clock with
"The Chronophage" by John C. Taylor.
Photograph Cathy Neill (used by kind permission
of the artist)

Bibliography of Works Cited

Adams, James Luther. *Paul Tillich's Philosophy of Culture, Science, and Religion.* New York: Harper and Row, 1965.

Adorno, Theodor. "Commitment." *Aesthetics and Politics.* 1965. Trans. Francia MacDonagh. *Literature and the Modern World.* 1990. Ed. Dennis Walder. London: Oxford University Press, 1991. 89-100.

Albee, Edward. Interview by Bruce J. Mann. Mann, *Casebook* 129-44.

---. *Three Tall Women.* 1994. New York: Penguin, 1995.

Amis, Martin. "Bujak and the Strong Force or God's Dice." *Einstein's Monsters.* 1987 25-48.

---. *Time's Arrow.* 1991. London: Penguin, 1992.

Andreski, Stanislav, ed. *Herbert Spencer: Structure, Function and Evolution.* London: Michael Joseph, 1971.

Apter, Emily. *Continental Drift: From National Characters to Virtual Subjects.* Chicago: University of Chicago Press, 1999.

Arthur, David T. "Joshua V. Himes and the Cause of Adventism." Numbers and Butler 36-58.

Attebery, Brian. *Strategies of Fantasy.* Bloomington: Indiana University Press, 1992.

Auden, W. H. "As I Walked Out One Evening." *CP* 197-99.

---. *Collected Poetry of W. H. Auden.* New York: Random House, 1945.

---. *The Complete Works of W. H. Auden: Prose.* Vol. 2: 1939-1948. Ed. Edward Mendelson. Princeton: Princeton University Press, 2002.

---. *The Dyer's Hand and Other Essays.* New York: Random House, 1962.

---. *For the Time Being. W. H. Auden: Collected Longer Poems.* London: Faber, 1968. 131-97.

---. "Kairos and Logos." *CP* 11-16.

---. "King Lear." *Lectures on Shakespeare.* Ed. Arthur Kirsch. Princeton: Princeton University Press, 2000. 219-30, 384-85.

---. *The Living Thoughts of Kierkegaard.* Ed. W. H. Auden. Bloomington: Indiana University Press, 1963.

---. "The Means of Grace." *New Republic* 104 (June 1941): 776.

---. "New Year Letter." *CP* 263-316.

---. "September 1, 1939." *CP* 57-59.

---. Untitled essay. *Modern Canterbury Pilgrims.* Ed. James Pike. New York: Morehouse-Gorham, 1956. 32-43.

---. Untitled essay. *Partisan Review Special Issue: Religion and the Intellectuals.* 27.2 (February 1950): 103-42.

---. "We're Late." *CP* 26-27.

Augustine, Saint. *The Confessions of St. Augustine.* Trans. Rex Warner. New York: Mentor, 1963.

*

Baltz, Dan. "Trump Is Impeached, Again, with the Country Even More at War over His Presidency." *Washington Post* 13 Jan. 2021. Web. 13 Jan. 2021.

Barbour, Jullian. *The End of Time.* 1999. London: Phoenix, 2000.

Barr, Marleen S. "'We're at the start of a new ball game and that's why we're all real nervous': Or, Cloning—Technological Cognition Reflects Estrangement from Women." Parrinder, ed. *Learning* 193-207.

Baudrilland, Jean. *The Illusion of the End.* Trans. Chris Turner. Stanford: Stanford University Press, 1994.

Beauchamp, Gorman. "Zamiatin's *We.*" *No Place Else: Explorations in Utopian and Dystopian Fiction.* Ed. Eric S. Rabkin, Martin H. Greenberg, and Joseph D. Olander. Carbondale: Southern Illinois University Press, 1983. 56-77.

Beaumont, Keith. *Alfred Jarry: A Critical and Biographical Study.* Leicester: Leicester University Press, 1984.

Beckett, Samuel. *Act Without Words I. Complete Dramatic Works* 201-06.

---. *All that Fall. Complete Dramatic Works* 168-99.

---. *The Complete Dramatic Works.* London: Faber and Faber, 1986.

---. *Embers. Complete Dramatic Works* 251-64.

---. *Endgame. Complete Dramatic Works* 89-134.

---. *Krapp's Last Tape. Complete Dramatic Works* 213-23.

---. *Ohio Impromptu. Complete Dramatic Works* 443-48.

---. *Play. Complete Dramatic Works* 305-20.

---. *Proust.* London: Chatto and Windus, 1930.

---. *That Time. Complete Dramatic Works* 385-95.

---. *Waiting for Godot. Complete Dramatic Works* 7-87.

---. *What Where. Complete Dramatic Works* 467-76.

Benjamin, Walter. "Theses on the Philosophy of History." *Illuminations.* Trans. Harry Zohn. Ed. Hannah Arendt. 1968. New York: Schocken Books, 1969. 253-64.

Bermel, Albert. *Contradictory Characters: An Interpretation of the Modern Theatre.* 1973. Evanston, IL: Northwestern University Press, 1996.

Bernstein, Max B., Scott A. Sandford, and Louis J. Allamandola. "Life's Far-Flung Raw Materials." *Scientific American* July 1999: 26-33.

Bespaloff, Rachel. *On the Iliad.* Trans. Mary McCarthy. 1948. Harper: New York, 1962.

Bigsby, C. W. E. *Modern American Drama, 1945-2000*. Cambridge: Cambridge University Press, 2000.

Blake, Andrew. *The Irresistible Rise of Harry Potter*. London: Verso, 2002.

Bloom, Harold. *Omens of Millennium: The Gnosis of Angels, Dreams, and Resurrection*. New York: Riverhead Books, 1996.

Boland, Eavan. "The Veil Over the Future's Face." *Profession 1997* (2006):13-17.

Booker, M. Keith. *Dystopian Literature: A Theory and Research Guide*. Westport, CT: Greenwood, 1994.

Boorstin, Daniel. *The Discoverers: A History of Man's Search to Know His World and Himself.* New York: Abrams, 1983.

Borges, Jorge Luis. "Averroe's Search." Trans. James E. Irby. *Labyrinths* 180-88.

---. "Borges at N.Y.U." 1971. Interviewed by Ronald Christ, Alexander Coleman, and Norman Thomas di Giovanni. *Jorge Luis Borges: Conversations*. Ed. Richard Burgin. Jackson, MS: University of Mississippi Press, 1998. 118-37.

---. "Cambridge." Trans. Norman Thomas di Giovanni. *Praise* 20-23.

---. "Funes the Memorious." Trans. James E. Irby. *Labyrinths* 59-64.

---. "James Joyce." Trans. Norman Thomas di Giovanni. *Praise* 29.

---. *In Praise of Darkness*. Trans. Norman Thomas di Giovanni. New York: Dutton, 1974.

---. *Labyrinths: Selected Stories and Other Writings*. Ed. Donald A. Yates and James E. Irby. New York: New Directions, 1964.

---. "A New Refutation of Time." Trans. James E. Irby. *Labyrinths* 252-69.

---. "The Unending Gift." Trans. Norman Thomas di Giovanni. *Praise* 31.

Bowerstock, G. W. "The Invention of Time." Review of Paul J. Kosmin, *Time and its Adversaries in the Seleucid Empire. New York Review of Books* 7 Nov. 2019: 29-31.

Boyers, Paul. *By the Bomb's Early Light: American Thought and Culture at the Dawn of the Atomic Age.* New York: Pantheon, 1985.

Brandon, S. G. F. "Time and the Destiny of Man." Fraser, *Voices* 140-57.

Brantley, Ben. "A Fiery Fall into the Abyss, Unknowing and Unknown." Review of *King Lear. The New York Times* 5 March 2004. Web. 8 March 2004.

Bredehoft, Thomas A. "The Gibson Continuum: Cyberspace and Gibson's Mervyn Kihn Stories." *Science-Fiction Studies* 22.2 (1995): 252-63.

Broer, Lawrence R. "Hartke's Hearing: Vonnegut's Heroes on Trial." *The Vonnegut Chronicles: Interviews and Essays.* Ed. Peter J. Reed and Marc Leeds. Westport, CT: Greenwood, 1996. 179-203.

Brustein, Robert. *Dumbocracy in America: Studies in the Theatre of Guilt, 1987-1994.* Chicago: Dee, 1994.

---. *The Theatre of Revolt.* Boston: Atlantic-Little, Brown, 1964.

Buber, Martin. *I and Thou.* Trans. Ronald Gregor Smith. 1937. New York: Charles Scribner's Sons, 1962.

---. "Saga and History." *The Writings of Martin Buber.* Ed. Will Herberg. Cleveland: Meridian Books, 1956. 146-56.

Bukatman, Scott. "Amidst These Fields of Data: Allegory, Rhetoric, and the Paraspace." *Critique* 33.3 (1992): 199-219.

---. *Terminal Identity.* Durham: Duke University Press, 1993.

Buñuel, Luis. *My Last Sigh.* Trans. Abigail Israel. New York: Knopf, 1983.

de Burca, Demelza. "Dementia Appeal." London. *The Daily Mirror* 28 Apr. 2010: 23.

Burkitt, F. Crawford. *Jewish and Christian Apocalypse (The Schweich Lectures 1913).* London: Oxford UP, 1914.

Buruma, Ian. "Asia World." *The New York Review* 12 June 2003: 54-57.

Butler, Jonathan. M. "The Making of a New Order: Millerism and the Origins of Seventh-Day Adventism." Numbers and Butler 189-208.

Butler, Lance St. John. *Samuel Beckett and the Meaning of Being: A Study in Ontological Parable.* London, Macmillan, 1984.

*

Cahill, Suzanne, Eamon O'Shea, and Maria Pearce. *Dementia in Ireland 2012: Creating Excellence in Dementia Care.* DSIDC's Living with Dementia Research Programme, 2012. Web. 29 Apr. 2019.

Callender, Craig. "Is Time an Illusion?" *Scientific American* June 2010: 41-47.

Carr, Marina. "The Bandit Pen." Program notes for *Good Evening, Mr Collins* by Tom Mac Intyre. Peacock Theatre, Dublin, July 1996.

---. Interview with James F. Clarity. "A Playwright's Post-Beckett Period." *New York Times* 3 Nov. 1994: C23.

---. *The Mai.* Loughcrew: Gallery, 1995.

---. *Portia Coughlan. The Dazzling Dark.* Ed. Frank McGuinness. London: Faber, 1996. 235-309.

Carroll, Lewis [Charles L. Dodgson]. *Through the Looking-Glass.* 1871. *The Annotated Alice.* Ed. Martin Gardner. New York: World, 1963. 166-345.

Carroll, Sean. "The Cosmic Origins of Time's Arrow." *Scientific American* June 2008: 48-57.

---. *From Eternity to Here: The Quest for the Ultimate Theory of Time.* 2010. New York: Dutton, 2016.

DeCarava, Roy, and Langston Hughes. *The Sweet Flypaper of Life.* New York: Simon and Schuster, 1955.

Clark, C. M. "Deep in the Volcano." Review of Ian Kershaw, *To Hell and Back: Europe, 1914-1949. New York Review of Books* 7 Apr. 2016: 58-60.

Clarke, Arthur C. "Introduction: The Exploration of Time." Simpson vii-xix.

Clemons, Amy Lea. "Adapting Revelation: *Good Omens* as Comic Corrective." *Journal of the Fantastic in the Arts* 28.1 (2017): 86-101.

Cohler, Bertram J. "Aging, Morale, and Meaning: The Nexus of Narrative." Cole 107-33.

Cohn, Ruby. *Just Play: Beckett's Theatre.* Princeton: Princeton University Press, 1980.

Cole, Thomas R. W., Andrew Achenbaum, Patricia L. Jakobi, and Robert Kastenbaum. *Voices and Visions: Towards a Critical Gerontology.* New York: Springer, 1993.

Collins, Robert A. "Preface." *The Scope of the Fantastic—Theory, Technique, Major Authors: Selected Essays from the First International Conference on the Fantastic in Literature and Film.* Ed. Robert A. Collins and Howard D. Pearce. Westport, CT: Greenwood, 1985. xi-xii.

Cook, C., and J. Stevenson. *Longman Handbook of Modern British History 1714-1987.* Harlow: 1988.

Coveney, Peter, and Roger Highfield. *The Arrow of Time.* 1990. London: Flamingo, 1991.

Csicsery-Ronay, István, Jr. "The Sentimental Futurist: Cybernetics and Art in William Gibson's *Neuromancer.*" *Critique* 33.3 (1992): 221-40.

Cullmann, Oscar. *Christ and Time.* Philadelphia: Westminster Press, 1950.

*

Davies, Paul. *About Time.* London: Penguin, 1995.

---. *God and the New Physics.* New York: Simon and Schuster, 1983.

---. *How to Build a Time Machine.* New York: Penguin, 2002.

---. *The Last Three Minutes: Conjectures about the Ultimate Fate of the Universe.* New York: Basic Books, 1994.

Davis, Robert E. "The Instantaneous Worldwide Release: Coming Soon to Everyone, Everywhere." *Transnational Cinema: The Film Reader.* Ed. Elizabeth Ezra and Terry Rowder. London: Routledge, 2006. 73-80.

Deane, Seamus. "Joyce and Beckett." *Irish University Review* 14.1 (Spring 1984): 57-68.

Dettmar, Kevin J. J. *The Illicit Joyce of Postmodernism: Reading Against the Grain.* Madison: University of Wisconsin Press. 1996.

Deutsch, David, and Michael Lockwood. "The Quantum Physics of Time Travel." *Scientific American* March 1994: 68-73.

Dickinson, Emily. "Apparently with No Surprise." 1624. *CP* 667-68.

---. "A Bird Came Down the Walk." 328. *CP* 156.

---. *The Complete Poems of Emily Dickinson.* Ed. Thomas H. Johnson. London: Faber and Faber, 1970.

---. "Tell All the Truth." 1129. *CP* 506-07.

Disch, Thomas M. *The Dreams Our Stuff Is Made Of: How Science Fiction Conquered the World.* 1998. New York: Touchstone, 2000.

Dixon, Dougal, and John Adams. *The Future Is Wild: A Natural History of the Future.* Buffalo, NY: Firefly Books, 2003.

Doan, Ruth Alden. "Millerism and Evangelical Culture." Numbers and Butler 119-38.

Donaldson, Stephen. *Epic Fantasy in the Modern World.* Kent, OH: Kent State University Libraries, 1986.

Donne, John. "A Valediction: Forbidding Mourning." *John Donne, the Penguin Poets.* Ed. John Hayward. 1950. Harmondsworth: Penguin, 1958. 54-55.

Driver, Tom F. "Auden's View of History in *For the Time Bring.*" *Journal of the Bible and Religion* 31.1 (Jan. 1963): 3-8.

---. "Via Dolorosa: A Long Road." *Union News* (Summer 1992): 6, 15-16.

Dryden, John. *Secular Masque. John Dryden.* Ed. Douglas Grant. Harmondsworth: Penguin, 1955. 143-46.

Dubs, Kathleen E., ed. *"Now You See It, Now You Don't": Hiding and Revealing in Text and in Performance.* Piliscsaba, Hungary: Pázmány Péter Catholic University, 2006.

Dunn, Robin. "The Generative Edge." *Foundation* 32:87 (2003): 73-93.

*

Eagleton, Terry. *After Theory.* New York: Basic Books, 2003.

Ecclesiastes. The Holy Bible. Authorized or King James version. Uhrichville, OH: Barbour Publishing, 2002. 283-87.

Elias, Marilyn. "MRIs Reveal Possible Source of Woman's Super-Memory." *USA Today* 27 Jan. 2009. Web 7 Mar. 2009.

Eliot. T. S. "The Waste Land." *Collected Poems 1909-1962.* New York: Harcourt, Brace and World, 1962. 51-75.

Ellmann, Richard. *James Joyce.* Oxford: Oxford University Press, 1959.

Emerson, Ralph Waldo. "The American Scholar." *Essays and Lectures* 53–71.

———. "Circles." *Essays and Lectures* 401–14.

———. *Essays and Lectures.* Ed. Joel Porte. New York: Library of America, 1983.

———. "Self-Reliance." *Essays and Lectures* 257–82.

Erikson, Erik H. *Identity and the Life Cycle.* 1980. New York: Norton, 1994.

———. *The Life Cycle Completed.* Ext. ver. 1997. New York: Norton. 1998.

Euripides. *Medea.* Trans. Brendan Kennelly. Newcastle upon Tyne: Bloodaxe, 1991.

*

Falck, Colin. *Myth, Truth and Literature: Towards a True Post-Modernism.* 1989. 2nd ed. Cambridge: Cambridge University Press, 1994.

Fernbach, Amanda. *Fantasies of Fetishism: From Decadence to the Post-Human.* New Brunswick: Rutgers University Press, 2002.

Ferris, Timothy. *Coming of Age in the Milky Way.* New York: William Morrow, 1988.

Fiedler, Leslie. "Bloom on Joyce: or, Jokey for Jacob." In *New Light on Joyce from the Dublin Symposium.* Ed. Fritz Senn. Bloomington: Indiana University Press. 1972. 195–208.

Fischer, Joachim. "A Future Ireland under German Rule: Dystopias as Propaganda during World War I." *Utopian Studies* 18.3 (2007): 345–63.

Fitzgerald, F. Scott, *The Great Gatsby.* 1926. Harmondsworth: Penguin, 1950.

Ford, Ford Maddox. *Ladies Whose Bright Eyes.* 1953. New York: Echo Press, 1987.

Ford, George H. "Humanities and the Experiences of Time." Fraser, et al. *Time, Science, and Society* 141-48.

Frank, Tibor. "'Dogma and Science': Patterns of Victorian Unbelief." *Studies in English and American* 3. Ed. Tibor Frank and Erzsébet Perényi. Budapest: L. Eötvös University, 1977. 61-95.

Fraser, J. T. "Human Temporality in a Nowless Universe." *Time and Society* 1.2 (1992): 159-73.

---. *Of Time, Passion and Knowledge.* 1961. 2nd ed. Princeton: Princeton University Press, 1990.

---. *The Voices of Time.* 2nd ed. 1966. Amherst: University of Massachusetts Press, 1981.

---, N. Lawrence, and F. C. Harger. *Time, Science, and Society in China and the West.* Amherst: University of Massachusetts Press, 1986.

Freedman, Carl. *Critical Theory and Science Fiction.* Hanover, NH: Wesleyan UP, 2000.

Frick, Thomas. "Either/Or." *Antioch Review* (1996). Rpt. in *Tolstoy's Dictaphone.* Ed. Sven Birkerts. Minneapolis: Greywolf Press, 1996. 200-21.

Friel, Brian. *Dancing at Lughnasa.* London: Faber, 1990.

---. *Give Me Your Answer, Do!* London: Penguin, 1997.

---. *Translations.* London: Faber, 1981.

Fuller, John. *A Reader's Guide to W. H. Auden.* New York: Farrar, Strause and Giroux, 1970.

*

Gee, Henry. *Deep Time.* London: Fourth Estate, 2000.

Gibson, William. *All Tomorrow's Parties.* New York: Putnam's, 1999.

---. "The Digital Way of Life." Interview with William Gibson. *Newsweek* 21 Oct. 1996: 64.

---. "The Gernsback Continuum." *Burning Chrome*. New York: Ace, 1987. 23-35.

---. *Idoru*. 1996. New York: Berkley, 1997.

---. *Mona Lisa Overdrive*. Toronto: Bantam Books, 1988.

---. *Neuromancer*. 1984. London: Grafton, 1986.

---. *Pattern Recognition*. New York: Putnam, 2003.

Gifford, Don. *The Farther Shore*. New York: The Atlantic Monthly Press, 1990.

---. "A Memory at the Elbow: The Teaching of James Joyce's *Ulysses*." *ADE Bulletin* 76 (Winter 1983): 43-45.

---. *Zones of Re-membering: Time, Memory, and (un)Consciousness*. Ed. Donald E. Morse. Amsterdam: Rodopi, 2011.

---, and Robert J. Seidman, ed. Ulysses *Annotated: Notes for James Joyce's* Ulysses. 2nd ed. Berkeley: University of California Press, 1988.

Giraudoux, Jean. *The Madwoman of Chaillot*. Trans. Maurice Valency. *Jean Giraudoux: Four Plays, Adapted, and with an Introduction by Maurice Valency*. New York: Hill and Wang, 1958.

Gould, Stephen Jay. *Full House: The Spread of Excellence from Plato to Darwin*. New York: Three Rivers, 1996.

---. *Time's Arrow, Time's Cycle: Myth and Metaphor in the Discovery of Geological Time*. The Jerusalem-Harvard Lectures. Cambridge: Harvard University Press, 1987.

---. "Today Is the Day." *New York Times* 23 Oct. 1997. Web. 18 Apr. 2019.

Gray, John. *Black Mass: Apocalyptic Religion and the Death of Utopia*. London: Penguin, 2007.

Greene, Brian. *Until the End of Time: Mind, Matter, and Our Search for Meaning in an Evolving Universe*. London: Allen Lane, 2020.

Gribbin, John. *Alone in the Universe: Why Our Planet Is Unique.* Hoboken: J. Wiley, 2011.

Grudin, Robert. *Time and the Art of Living.* 1982. New York: Ticknor and Fields, 1988.

Gunn, James. "Science Fiction." Introduction to *The Road to Science Fiction.* Vol. 4. *From Here to Forever.* New York: Signet, 1982.

*

Hancock, P. A. "The Time of Your Life: One Thousand Moons." *Kronoscope: Journal of the Study of Time* 2.2 (2002): 135-65.

Hart, Christopher. "Byzantiums: Yeats's Myth versus W. G. Holmes's History, *The Age of Justinian and Theodora.*" *Yeats Eliot Review* 15.2 (1998): 21-26.

Hassan, Ihab. "Joyce-Beckett: A Scenario in Eight Scenes and a Voice." *New Light on Joyce from the Dublin Symposium.* Ed. Fritz Senn. Bloomington: Indiana University Press, 1972. 180-94.

Hayden, Robert. "Traveling through Fog." *Collected Poetry.* Ed. Frederick G. Laysher. New York: Liveright, 1985. 122.

Hayles, N. Katherine. *How We Became Posthuman: Virtual Bodies in Cybernetics, Literature, and Informatics.* Chicago: University of Chicago Press, 1999.

Hays, Jeffrey. "Nuclear Waste and Radioactive Contamination in Russia." *Facts and Details.* 2008. Web. 20 Apr. 2020.

Hesson, E. C., and I. M. Hesson. "Eugene Ionesco: The Fantastic and Social Estrangement." *The Spectrum of the Fantastic.* Ed. Donald Palumbo. New York: Greenwood, 1988. 195-201.

Hilborn, Robert C. "Seagulls, Butterflies, and Grasshoppers: A Brief History of the Butterfly Effect in Nonlinear Dynamics." *American Journal of Physics and Applications* 72.4 (2004): 425-27.

Hirsch, David H. *The Deconstruction of Literature: Criticism after Auschwitz*. Hanover, NH: The University Press of New England, 1991.

Holmes, Bob, and James Randerson. "Humble Clay Tablets Are Greatest Loss to Science." *New Scientist* 10 May 2003: 8.

Hopkins, Gerard Manley. "Dun Scotus Oxford." *Poems* 79.

---. *Journal for 1872*. Web. 29 March 2021.

---. *The Poems of Gerard Manley Hopkins*. 4th ed. Ed. W. H. Gardner and N. H. MacKenzie. London: Oxford University Press, 1967.

---. "Spring." *Poems* 7.

Hoyle, Fred. "The Operation." *Element 79*. New York: NAL, 1967.

Hume, Kathryn. *Fantasy and Mimesis: Responses to Reality in Western Literature*. New York: Methuen, 1984.

Huntington, John. *The Logic of Fantasy: H. G. Wells and Science Fiction*. New York: Columbia University Press, 1982.

Huxley, Aldous. *After Many a Summer*. 1939. Harmondsworth: Penguin, 1972.

*

Ibsen, Henrik. *Ghosts: In a Version by Frank McGuinness*. Trans. Frank McGuinness. London: Faber and Faber, 2010.

Ingman, Heather. *Ageing in Irish Writing: Strangers to Themselves*. London: Palgrave Macmillan, 2018.

Ionesco, Eugene. *Notes and Counter Notes*. New York: Grove Press, 1964.

Ittzés, Gábor. "'What, Then, Is Time?': A Reading of Book XI of Augustine's *Confessions*." *"What, Then, Is Time?": Responses in English and American Literature*. Ed. Tibor Fabiny. *Pázmány Papers in English and American Studies* 1 (2001): 7-28.

*

Jackson, Joe. "The Healing Touch." Interview with Frank McGuinness. *Sunday Independent* (Dublin) 21 Apr. 2002. Web. 19 Oct. 2013.

Jackson, Rosemary. *Fantasy: The Literature of Subversion.* New York: Methuen, 1981.

James, Edward. "Before the *Novum*: The Prehistory of Science Fiction Criticism." Parrinder, *Learning* 19-35.

James, William. *Principles of Psychology.* Cambridge: Harvard University Press, 1983.

Jarry, Alfred. "Preliminary Address at the First Performance of *Ubu Roi*, December 10, 1896." Trans. Simon Watson Taylor. *Selected Works* 76-78.

---. *Selected Works of Alfred Jarry.* Ed. Roger Shattuck and Simon Watson Taylor. New York: Grove Press, 1965.

---. *Ubu Roi. Tout Ubu.* Paris: Librairie Générale Française, 1962. 15-131.

Jaspers, Karl. "Tragedy Is Not Enough." Trans. E. W. Deutsch. 1952. *Tragedy: Modern Essays in Criticism.* Ed. Lawrence Michel and Richard B. Sewall. Englewood Cliffs, NJ: Prentice Hall, 1963.

Jenckes, Norma. "Postmodern Tensions in Albee's Recent Plays." Mann, *Casebook* 107-18.

Jenkins, Jerry B., and Tim LaHaye. Left Behind. A series of 16 novels. Carol Stream, IL: Tyndale House, 1995-2007.

Jewitt, David, and Amata Moro-Martin. "Intersteller Interlopers." *Scientific American* Oct. 2020: 34-41.

Jones, Malcolm, Jr. "Snapshot Century." Review of Harold Evans, *The American Century*, Knopf, 1998. *Newsweek* 22 Sept. 1998: 78-79.

Joyce, James. *Dubliners.* 1914. *Essential* 22-173.

---. *The Essential James Joyce.* Ed. Harry Levin. St. Albas, Herts: Triad, 1977.

---. *Finnegans Wake.* New York: Viking, 1939.

---. *A Portrait of the Artist as a Young Man.* 1916. *Essential* 175-365.

---. *Ulysses.* 1922. New York: Random House, 1961.

Judd, Wayne R. "William Miller: Disappointed Prophet." Numbers and Butler 17-35.

Jung, Carl Gustav. "Stages of Life." 1930. Trans. R. F. C. Hull. *The Portable Jung.* Ed. Joseph Campbell. New York: Viking, 1971. 3-22.

*

Kahler, Erich. *The Tower and the Abyss.* New York: George Braziller, 1957. Rpt. Routledge, 2017. *Google Books.* 20 June 2019.

Kaelin, Eugene. *The Unhappy Consciousness: The Poetic Plight of Samuel Beckett.* Boston: D. Reidel Publishing, 1961.

Kafka, Franz. "Investigations of a Dog." *Selected Stories of Franz Kafka.* Trans. Willis and Edwin Muir. New York: Modern Library, 1952.

Kaku, Michio. *Hyperspace: A Scientific Odyssey through Parallel Universes, Time Warps, and the Tenth Dimension.* New York: Oxford University Press, 1994.

Kastenbaum, Robert. "Encrusted Elders: Arizona and the Political Spirit of Postmodern Aging." Cole 160-83.

Kearney, Richard. "Beckett: The Demythologizing Intellect." *The Irish Mind.* Ed. Richard Kearney. Dublin: Wolfhound Press, 1985. 267-93.

Keating, Sarah. "A Cruel Patriarch." *The Irish Times* 10 Oct. 2013: Web 12 Oct. 2013.

Keats, John. "Ode to a Nightingale." *The Complete Poems.* Ed. Jack Stillinger. Cambridge: Harvard University Press, 1983.

Kemper, Hans-Georg. "Speech of Acceptance." Trans. Hans-Georg Kemper. Debrecen: Kossuth University, 11 Dec. 1999.

Kennelly, Brendan. "Introduction." *Medea: A New Version.* Newcastle upon Tyne, England: Bloodaxe, 1991.

Kermode, Frank. *Shakespeare's Language.* London: Penguin, 2000.

Kiberd, Declan. *Irish Classics.* London: Granta, 2000.

---. *Ulysses and Us.* New York: W. W. Norton, 2009.

Kierkegaard, Søren. *The Journals and Notebooks.* Vol. 4. Ed. Niels Jørgen Cappelørn, et al. Princeton, NJ: Princeton University Press, 2011.

Kinsella, W. P. "Shoeless Joe Jackson Comes to Iowa." *Shoeless Joe Jackson Comes to Iowa.* Ottawa: Oberon, 1980.

---. *Shoeless Joe.* New York: Houghton Mifflin, 1982.

Kirkwood, Tom. *Time of Our Lives: The Science of Human Aging.* New York: Oxford University Press, 1999.

Kirsch, Arthur. *Auden and Christianity.* New Haven: Yale University Press, 2005.

Knight, G. Wilson. "*King Lear* and the Comedy of the Grotesque." *Wheel of Fire* 160-76.

---. "The *Lear* Universe." *Wheel of Fire* 177-206.

---. *The Wheel of Fire.* 1930. Cleveland: Merridian, 1949.

Kott, Jan. *The Theater of Essence.* Evanston: Northwestern University Press, 1984.

Kurdi, Mária. "An Interview with Frank McGuinness." *NUA: Studies in Contemporary Irish Writing* 4.1-2: 113-32.

*

Lakoff, George, and Mark Johnson. *Philosophy in the Flesh: The Embodied Mind and Its Challenge to Western Thought.* New York: Basic Books, 1999.

Lancashire, Ian. "Ninsei Street, Chiba City, in Gibson's *Neuromancer.*" *Science Fiction Studies* 30.2 (2003): 341-46.

Lanters, José. *Missed Understandings: A Study of Stage Adaptations of the Works of James Joyce.* Amsterdam: Rodopi, 1988.

---. "Old Worlds, New Worlds, Alternative Worlds: *Ulysses, Metamorphoses* 13, and the Death of the Beloved Son." *James Joyce Quarterly* 36.3 (1999): 525-40.

Lawrence, Nathaniel. "The Origins of Time." Fraser, et al 25-38.

Lászlóffy, Csaba. *The Heretic; or, A Plague of Slugs.* Trans. from the original Hungarian by Csilla Bertha and Donald E. Morse. *Silenced Voices.* Dublin: Carysfort Press, 2008. 99-157.

LeClair, Tom. *The Art of Excess: Mastery in Contemporary American Fiction.* Urbana: University of Illinois Press, 1989.

Lee, Chris. *The Electrocution of Children.* Unpublished playscript. n. pag.

Le Guin, Ursula K. "American SF and the Other." *Science Fcition Studies* 2.3 (Nov. 1973) Web. 31 Aug. 2018.

Leman, Jennifer. "Dare Devil Dies in Failed Homemade Rocket Launch to Prove the Earth Is Flat." *Popular Mechanics* 22 Feb. 2020. Web. 31 March 2020.

Leonard, John. "Black Magic." Review of *Hocus Pocus. The Nation* 15 Oct. 1990: 421-25. Rpt. in Mustazza 301-07.

Levitt, Morton. "Editor's Introduction." *Journal of Modern Literature* 24.1 (2000): 5-6.

Levi, Primo. *The Drowned and the Saved.* Trans. Raymond Rosenthal. 1988. London: Abacus, 1989.

Lifton, Robert Jay. *The Nazi Doctors: Medical Killing and the Psychology of Genocide.* New York: Basic Books, 1986.

Liu, Melinda, and Christopher Dickey. "Unearthing the Bible." *Newsweek* 30 Aug. 2004: 43-45.

*

McCabe, Colin. *James Joyce and the Revolution of the Word.* London: Macmillan, 1979.

McGuinness, Frank. *Dolly West's Kitchen.* London: Faber and Faber, 1999.

---. *The Hanging Gardens.* London: Faber and Faber, 2013.

---. "An Irish Writer and Europe, 1999-2009." *Irish University Review* 40.1 (2010): 1-17.

---. *The Visiting Hour.* London: Faber and Faber, 2021.

McHale, Brian. "Elements of a Poetics of Cyberpunk." *Critique* 33.3 (1992): 149-75.

McInerney, Jay. "Still Asking the Embarrassing Questions." Review of *Hocus Pocus. The New York Times Book Review* 9 Sept. 1990: 12. Rpt. in Mustazza 309-11.

MacColl, Ewan."The Lag's Song." *Ewan MacColl and Peggy Seeger Songbook.* New York: Oak Publications, 1963. 80.

Mac Intyre, Tom. *Good Evening, Mr Collins.* London: Faber, 1996.

Malekin, Peter. "Knowing about Knowing: Paradigms of Knowledge in the Postmodern Fantastic." *State of the Fantastic: Studies in the Theory and Practice of Fantastic Literature and Film.* Ed. Nicholas Ruddick. New York: Greenwood, 1992. 41-48.

Mallett, Ronald L., and Bruce Henderson. *Time Traveler: A Scientist's Personal Mission to Make Time Travel a Reality.* New York: Thunder's Mouth Press, 2006.

Malmgren, Carl D. *Worlds Apart: Narratology of Science Fiction.* Bloomington: Indiana University Press, 1991.

Manlove, C. N. *The Impulse of Fantasy Literature.* Kent, OH: Kent State University Press, 1983.

Mann, Bruce, ed. *Edward Albee: A Casebook*. New York: Routledge, 2003.

---. "*Three Tall Women*: Return to the Muses." Mann, *Casebook* 8.

Martin, George R. R. *A Dance with Dragons: Book Five of A Song of Ice and Fire*. 2011. New York: Harper, Voyager, 2012.

Massing, Michael. "The Unseen War." *The New York Review* 29 May 2003: 16-19.

Meany, Helen. "The Hanging Gardens: Review." *Guardian* 11 Oct. 2013:

Mihálycsa, Erika. "'Petits pas. Nulle part. Obstinément': Writing Finitude, Writing On." *Hungarian Journal of English and American Studies* 26.1 (Spring 2020): 175-200.

Miller, Arthur. *Death of a Salesman*. 1949. New York: Penguin, 1977.

Miller, J. Hillis. "Time in Literature." *Deadalus* (Spring 2003): 86-97.

Mistichelli, Bill. "History and Fabrication in Kurt Vonnegut's *Hocus Pocus*." Mustazza 313-25.

Mitchison, Rosalind. "Right to be Pleased." Review of *The Scottish Enlightenment. TLS* 2 Jan. 1998: 9.

Morrison, Toni. "Nobel Lecture." Web. 7 Aug. 2006.

Morse, Donald. "The Ditches of Hell: Csaba Lászlóffy's *The Heretic; or, A Plague of Slugs*." *Theatre Journal* 43 (1991): 209-18.

---. *The Novels of Kurt Vonnegut: Imagining Being an American*. Westport, CT: Praeger, 2003.

---. "Review of *NOW: The Physics of Time* written by Richard A. Muller." *Kronoscope* 18.1 (2018): 86-88.

---. "'Sleepwalkers along a precipice': Staging Memory in Marina Carr's The Mai." *Hungarian Journal of English and American Studies* 2.2 (1996): 111-22.

Muilenburg, James. "The History of the Religion of Israel." *The Interpreter's Bible*. Vol. 1. New York: Abington/ Cokesbury, 1952. 330-33.

Muller, Richard. *NOW: The Physics of Time*. New York: Norton, 2016.

Murray, Christopher. "Beckett Productions in Ireland: A Survey." *Irish University Review* 14.1 (Spring 1984): 103-25.

---. *Twentieth Century Irish Drama: Mirror up to Nation*. Manchester: Manchester University Press, 1997.

Murry, J. Middleton. Review of *Ulysses. National Atheneum* 31 (22 Apr. 1922): 124-25.

Mustazza, Leonard, ed. *The Critical Response to Kurt Vonnegut*. Westport, CT: Greenwood, 1994.

Niebuhr, Reinhold. *The Nature and Destiny of Man: A Christian Interpretation*. 2 vol. New York: John Knox Press, 1964.

Niebuhr, H. Richard. *The Meaning of Revelation*. New York: Macmillan, 1941.

Niffenegger, Audrey. *The Time Traveler's Wife*. 2004. London: Vintage, 2005.

Novak, Amy. "Virtual Poltergeists and Memory: The Question of Ahistoricism in William Gibson's *Neuromancer* (1984)." *Hungarian Journal of English and American Studies* 6.1 (2000): 55-78.

Numbers, Ronald L., and Jonathan M. Butler. *The Disappointed: Millerism and Millenarianism in the Nineteen Century*. Knoxville, TN: University of Tennessee Press, 1993.

---. "Introduction." In Numbers and Butler. xv-xxiv.

*

O'Brien, Geoffrey. "Lear for Real." Review of *King Lear* by William Shakespeare, dir. by Jonathan Miller, Vivian Beaumont Theater, Lincoln Center, New York, 11 Feb.-18 Apr. 2004. *New York Review of Books* 25 March 2004: 22-24.

O'Faolain, Seán. *And Again?* 1979. Harmondsworth: Penguin Books, 1982.

O'Kelly, Emer. "Genius from McGuinness." *Sunday Independent* 13 Oct. 2013: 19.

O'Malley, Michael. *Keeping Watch: A History of American Time.* Washington, DC: Smithsonian Institution Press, 1990.

O'Neill, Eugene. *The Iceman Cometh.* 1940. New York: Vintage, 1957.

O'Toole, Fintan. "The Irish Family: Proceed with Caution." Review of Frank McGuinness, *The Hanging Gardens. Irish Times* 26 Oct. 2013. Web. 29 Apr. 2019.

*

Palmer, Christopher. "*Mona Lisa Overdrive* and the Prosthetic." *Science Fiction Studies* 31 (2004): 227-42.

Park, David. "Laws of Physics and Ideas of Time." *The Study of Time II.* Ed. J. T. Fraser and Nathaniel Lawrence. New York: Springer-Verlag, 1975.

Parrinder, Patrick. "Introduction." *Learning from Other Worlds* 1-16.

---. *Shadows of the Future: H. G. Wells, Science Fiction, and Prophecy.* Syracuse: Syracuse University Press, 1995.

---, ed. *Learning from Other Worlds: Estrangement, Cognition and the Politics of Science Fiction and Utopia.* Liverpool: Liverpool University Press, 2000.

Patel, Vibhuti. "The Spaces Between." Review of Richard Serra's Museum of Modern Art Exhibit, *Richard Serra Sculpture: Forty Years. Newsweek* 25 June 2007: 64.

Peake, Charles. *James Joyce: The Citizen and the Artist.* Stanford: Stanford University Press, 1977.

Perényi, Eleanor. *More Was Lost.* New York: New York Review of Books, 1946.

Petronius. *The Satyricon*. Trans. William Arrowsmith. New York: Signet, 1958.

Pew Research Center for Religion and Life. Web. 29 Apr. 2019.

Phillips, Robert. "Fiction Chronicle." *Hudson Review* 44 (1991): 133-41.

Pierce, John J. *Foundations of Science Fiction: A Study in Imagination and Evolution*. Westport, CT: Greenwood, 1987.

Pinter, Harold. *Mountain Language*. London: Methuen, 1989.

---. *One for the Road*. London: Methuen, 1985.

Postlewait, Thomas. "Self-Performing Voices: Mind, Memory, and Time in Beckett's Drama." *Twentieth Century Literature* 24.4 (Winter 1978): 473-91.

Potts, Timothy. "Looking for the Hanging Gardens." Review of Stephanie Dalley, *The Mystery of the Hanging Gardens of Babylon: An Elusive World Wonder Traced. New York Review of Books* 26 Sept. 2013: 77-80.

Pound, Ezra. *ABC of Reading*. Norfolk, CT: New Directons, 1934.

Puce, Jill. *The Mystic Spiral: Journey of the Soul*. 1974. London: Thames and Hudson, 1985.

*

Racoma, Bernadine. "March 25 Was the New Year Once Upon a Time." *Day Translations*. Web. 22 Apr. 2019.

Reed, Peter. "A Conversation with Kurt Vonnegut, 1982." *The Vonnegut Chronicles: Interviews and Essays*. Ed. Peter J. Reed and Marc Leeds. Westport, CT: Greenwood, 1996. 3-14.

Rees, Martin. "Our Place in the Universe: How Astronomers Revealed a Much Bigger and Stranger Cosmos Than Anyone Suspected." *Scientific American* Sept. 2020: 56-62.

Replogle, Justin. "Auden's Religious Leap." *Wisconsin Studies in Contemporary Literature* 7 (Winter-Spring 1966): 47-75.

Rice, Thomas J. "Subtle Reflections of/upon Joyce in/by Borges." *Journal of Modern Literature* 24.1 (2000): 47-62.

Roche, Anthony. *Contemporary Irish Drama: From Beckett to McGuinness.* Dublin: Gill and Macmillan, 1994.

---. "An Interview with Frank McGuinness." *Irish University Review* 40.1 (2010): 18-25.

---. "Women on the Threshold: J. M. Synge's *The Shadow of the Glen,* Teresa Deevy's *Katie Roche* and Marina Carr's *The Mai.*" *Irish University Review* 25.1 (1995): 143-62.

Ronsley, Joseph. "Leopold Bloom: The Manly Man." *Conflicting Identities: Essays on Modern Irish Literature.* Ed. Robbie B. H. Goh. Singapore: Uni Press, 1997. 99-119.

Rosenfield, Israel. *The Invention of Memory: A New View of the Brain.* New York: Basic Books, 1988.

Rovelli, Carlo. *The Order of Time.* Trans. Erica Segree and Simon Carnell. 2018. London: Penguin, 2019.

Rowe, David L. "Millerites: A Shadow Portrait." Numbers and Butler 1-16.

Ruddick, Nicholas. "Introduction." Wells, *Time Machine* 9-45.

---. "Putting the Bits Together: Information Theory, *Neuromancer,* and Science Fiction." *Journal of the Fantastic in the Arts* 3.4 (1994): 84-92.

---. "The Search for Quantum Ethics: Michael Frayne's *Copenhagen* and Other Recent British Science Plays." *Hungarian Journal of English and American Studies* 6.1 (2000): 119-37.

---. "The Spatial-Temporal Context: The Fourth Dimension." Wells, *Time Machine* 212-23.

Ryan, Alan. "The Power of Positive Thinking." *New York Review of Books* 50.1 (16 Jan. 2003). Web. 27 Apr. 2020.

*

Sacharow, Lawrence. "Directing *Three Tall Women.*" Mann, *Casebook* 119-28.

Sacks, Oliver. *Gratitude.* New York: Knopf, 2015.

---. *The Man Who Mistook His Wife for a Hat.* 1985. London: Picador, 2011.

---. *Musicophilia: Tales of Music and the Brain.* 2008. Rev. ed. London: Picador, 2011.

---. *On the Move: A Life.* New York: Vintage, 2016.

Samuelson, Robert. "We Should Know by Now That Progress Isn't Guaranteed—and Often Backfires." *Washington Post* 27 Apr. 2020: 128, 295. Web. 27 Apr. 2020.

Schulz, Joseph H., and Robert H. Binstock. *Aging Nation.* Westport: Praeger, 2006.

Schwarz-Bart, André. *The Last of the Just* [Le dernier des justes]. Trans. Stephen Becker. New York: Atheneum, 1960.

Shakespeare, William. *King Lear.* Ed. Alfred Harbage. 1958. New York: Penguin, 1970.

---. "Song." *Cymbeline. The Complete Works of Shakespeare.* London: Spring Books, 1958. 800.

Shattuck, Roger. "Introduction." Jarry, *Selected Works of Jarry* 9-20.

Simmons, Dan. *The Fall of Hyperion.* New York: Bantam Books, 1990.

---. *Hyperion.* New York: Bantam Books, 1989.

Simpson, George Gaylord. *The Dechronization of Sam Magruder.* New York: St. Martin's, 1996.

Smith, Russell. "The New Newspeak." *The New York Review of Books* 29 May 2003: 19.

Snyder, Gary. "Entering the Fiftieth Millennium." *Profession 1997* 35-40.

Sophocles. *Oedipus Rex. The Oedipus Cycle.* Trans. Dubley Fitts and Robert Fitzgerald. New York: Harcourt Brace, 1949.

"Speculative and Pessimistic." Review of *The Time Machine. New York Times* 23 June 1895: 27. Rpt. in Wells, *The Time Machine* 262-63.

Steiner, George. *The Death of Tragedy.* 1961. New Haven: Yale University Press, 1996.

Stoker, Bram. *Dracula.* 1897. New York: Penguin, 1992.

Suvin, Darko. "SF and the Novum." *The Technological Imagination: Theories and Fictions.* Ed. Teresa de Lauretis. Madison: Coda Press, 1980. 141-58.

Swift, Jonathan. *Gulliver's Travels.* Ed. Peter Dixon and John Chalker. 1967. London: Penguin, 1985.

Synge, John M. *Riders to the Sea. J. M. Synge: Plays.* Ed. Ann Saddlemyer. 1969. New York: Oxford University Press, 1980. 1-14.

*

Taylor, Mark C. *After God.* Chicago: University of Chicago Press, 2007.

Tennyson, Alfred Lord. "Locksley Hall." *The Poems and Plays of Alfred Lord Tennyson.* New York: Modern Library, 1938. 169-75.

Teres, Gustav. "Time, Computations and Dionysius Exiguus." *Journal of the History of Astronomy* (1984): 177-88.

Thoreau, Henry David. *Walden. Walden and Civil Disobedience.* Ed. Sherman Paul. Boston: Houghton Mifflin, 1960. 1-227.

Tillich, Paul. *The Interpretation of History.* Trans. N. A. Rasetzki and Elsa L.Talmey. New York: Charles Scribner's Sons, 1936.

---. *The Religious Situation.* New York: Meridian, 1956.

Tolstoy, Leo. *Anna Karenina.* Trans. Richard Pevear and Larissa Volokhonsky. London: Penguin, 2000.

Torres, Phil. *Bulletin of the Atomic Scientists* 18 Aug. 2017. Web. 15 Aug. 2018.

Twain, Mark. *A Connecticut Yankee in King Arthur's Court.* Ed. Bernard L. Stein. 1889. Berkeley: University of California Press, 1979.

*

Vonnegut, Kurt. *Breakfast of Champions.* 1973. New York: Dell, 1991.

---. *Cat's Cradle.* 1963. New York: Dell, 1970.

---. *Deadeye Dick.* 1982. New York: Dell, 1985.

---. *Fates Worse Than Death: An Autobiographical Collage of the 1980s.* 1991. New York: Vintage, 1992.

---. *Galápagos.* New York: Dell, 1985.

---. *God Bless You, Mr. Rosewater, or Pearls Before Swine.* 1965. New York: Dell, 1970.

---. *Hocus Pocus.* 1990. New York: Berkley, 1991.

---. *Jailbird.* 1979. New York: Dell, 1980.

---. *Mother Night.* 1961. New York: Dell, 1966.

---. *Palm Sunday: An Autobiographical Collage.* 1981. New York: Dell, 1984.

---. *The Sirens of Titan.* New York: Dell, 1959.

---. *Slapstick, or Lonesome No More.* 1976. New York: Dell, 1989.

---. *Slaughterhouse-Five.* 1969. New York: Dell, 1991.

---. *Timequake.* New York: Putnam, 1997.

*

Walls, Laura Dassow. *Emerson's Life in Science: The Culture of Truth.* Ithaca: Cornell University Press, 2003.

Ward, Peter. "What Will Become of *Homo Sapiens?*" *Scientific American* Jan. 2009: 54–59.

Watts, Isaac. "Our God, Our Help." 1708. *Poetry Foundation.* Web. 5 June 2021.

Weiss, Dennis M. "Digital Ambivalence: Utopia, Dystopia, and the Digital Cosmos." *The Utopian Fantastic*. Ed. Martha Bartter. Westport: Praeger, 2004. 67-79.

Wells, H. G. "The Extinction of Man: Some Speculative Suggestions." *Pall Mall Gazette* 39 (25 Sept. 1894): 3. Rpt. in Wells, *Time Machine* 181-83.

---. "The Man of the Year Million: A Scientific Forecast." *Pall Mall Gazette* 57 (6 Nov. 1893): 3. Rpt. in Wells, *Time Machine* 176-81.

---. "On Extinction." *Chamber's Journal of Popular Literature, Science, and Art* 10 (30 Sept. 1893): 623-24. Rpt. in Wells, *Time Machine* 173-76.

---. *The Time Machine*. 1895. Ed. Nicholas Ruddick. Toronto: Broadview, 2001.

Wertenbaker, Timberlake. *After Darwin*. London: Faber, 1998.

"The Whiffenpoof Song." 1907. Web. 8 Apr. 2019.

White, Donald W. *The American Century: The Rise and Decline of the United States as a World Power*. New Haven: Yale University Press, 1996.

White, Hayden. *The Content of the Form: Narrative Discourse and Historical Representation*. Baltimore: The Johns Hopkins University Press, 1987.

Whitrow, G. J. *Time in History: Views of Time from Prehistory to the Present Day*. 1988. New York: Oxford University Press, 1989.

Wiesel, Elie. "In the Footsteps of Shimon Dubnov." *Modern Language Studies*. Special Holocaust Literature Issue 16.1 (Winter 1986): 100-10.

Wilde, Oscar. *An Ideal Husband*. 1895. Ed. Julie Nord. Mineola, NY: Dover, 2000.

---. *The Picture of Dorian Gray*. 1891. Harmondsworth: Penguin, 2006.

Wilder, Thornton. *Our Town. Our Town, The Skin of Our Teeth, The Matchmaker.* 1958. London: Penguin, 1962: 15-91.

Williams, Paul. "Nuclear Criticism." *The Routledge Companion to Science Fiction.* Ed. Mark Bould, et al. London: Routledge, 2009. 246-55.

Williams, Tennessee. *The Glass Menagerie.* 1945. Harmondsworth: Penguin, 1955.

Worth, Katherine. *The Irish Drama of Europe from Yeats to Beckett.* London: University of London, 1978.

*

"Y2K Bug." *Encyclopedia Britannica.* Web. 9 Sept. 2018.

Yeats, W. B. "The Circus Animals' Desertion." *Collected Poems* 392.

---. *Collected Poems of W. B. Yeats.* 1933. London: Macmillan, 1971.

---. "The Lamentation of the Old Pensioner." *Collected Poems* 52.

---. *The Land of Heart's Desire.* 1894. *The Collected Plays of W. B. Yeats.* New York: Macmillan, 1960.

---. *Letters of W. B. Yeats.* Ed. Allan Wade. New York: Macmillan, 1955.

---. "The Second Coming." *Collected Poems* 210-11.

---. "The Stolen Child." *Collected Poems* 20-21.

Index

Acker, Kathy 45n

Adams, John 144n

Adorno, Theodor 118–19

Agassiz, Louis 142

Albee, Edward
>   *The Goat or Who Is Sylvia?* 265
>   *Three Tall Women* 28–29, 265–75, 281
>   *Who's Afraid of Virginia Woolf?* 265
>   *Zoo Story* 265

American Civil War 35, 131, 134

Amis, Martin 25
>   *Time's Arrow* 100, 104–22

apocalypse 25, 61, 125, 128–44, 265

Attebery, Brian 97

Auden, W. H. 23, 29, 180, 225, 253, 257, 260, 269
>   "As I Walked Out One Evening" 278–80
>   *For the Time Being: A Christmas Oratorio* 26, 166, 168–69,
>   171–73, 175–79, 233
>   *The Dyer's Hand* 176
>   *The Living Thoughts of Kierkegaard* 173

Augustine, St. 19–20, 97, 122, 242–43

Auschwitz 107, 110–11, 118–19, 161

Back to the Future 85

Barbour, Julian 18

Baudrillard, Jean 38

Beckett, Samuel 23, 26
>   *Act without Words I* 114, 180, 183–84, 195
>   *Act without Words II* 180–81, 195, 197
>   *All that Fall* 180, 183
>   *Embers* 181, 189–90
>   *Endgame* 180, 182, 193, 264

Happy Days 180, 195, 271

Krapp's Last Tape 121, 181, 185, 188, 197, 264, 271

Malone Dies 192

Not I 195

Play 181–82, 188, 190, 193, 195, 264, 271

Proust 180

That Time 181

Waiting for Godot 180, 182, 190, 192–95, 197, 264, 271

What Where 180, 197

Benjamin, Walter 120

Bentley, Eric 269

Bespaloff, Rachel 53n

Big Bang 58–60, 116

Bigsby, Christopher 272, 274

Binstock, Robert H. 222

Blake, Andrew 94n

Boland, Eavan 23

Book of Job 28, 260–61

Boorstin, Daniel 54, 199

Borges, Jorge Luis 19, 22, 78, 121n, 197, 199, 251, 277

Bradbury, Ray 23, 84

Brady, Matthew 35

Bredehoft, Thomas A. 52

Broer, Lawrence 162n

Bronowski, Jacob 119

Brustein, Robert 265, 267, 272, 275

Bukatman, Scott 44n, 52

Buñuel, Luis 218, 233

Burnett, Thomas 129n

Burns, Joan Simpson 86n

Burridge, Kenelm 139

Butler, Jonathan M. 138–39

Butler, Lance St. John 184, 189, 193, 196

butterfly effect 84–85

INDEX

Callender, Craig 18

Carr, Marina 19, 23

    The Mai 27, 200–17

    Portia Coughlan 207n

Carroll, Lewis (Charles L. Dodgson)

    Through the Looking-Glass, and What Alice Found There 25, 77, 170

Carroll, Sean 77–79, 94

Cervantes, Miguel

    Don Quixote 159

Chekhov, Anton

    Three Sisters 273

Clark, C. M. 74

Clarke, Arthur C. 56n, 86, 92

    Childhood's End 90

Clay, E. R. 32

Cohn, Ruby 191

Csicsery-Ronay, István 42

D Day 36

Dante Alighieri 107, 112n, 188

    Divina Commedia 130

Darby, John Nelson 124

    The Rapture 124–25, 141, 145

Darwin, Charles 81, 134–35, 150–51, 156

    On the Origin of Species 80

Davies, Paul 84, 87, 91, 96, 132, 143–44

Debs, Eugene Victor 157

deep time 59, 134, 136–37, 147

Defoe, Daniel 113n

dementia 27–29, 200–34

Des Pres, Terrence 112n

Dickinson, Emily 23, 127, 139–40, 142

dispensationalists 141n

Dixon, Dougal 144n
Donaldson, Stephen 115
Donne, John
    "A Valediction: Forbidding Mourning" 89
Dostoevsky, Fyodor 108
Driver, Tom F. 100, 171
Dryden, John 75

Eagleton, Terry 260
Einstein, Albert 83, 90
Eliot, T. S.
    "The Waste Land" x, 254n
Emerson, Ralph Waldo 63, 65, 74, 139–12
    "The American Scholar" 122, 163
    "On Nature" 121
    "Self-Reliance" 127
Erikson, Erik H. 233, 236, 239, 243, 246, 250, 252, 272
Euripides 211, 216–17

Falck, Colin 274
Fernbach, Amanda 47
Feynman, Richard 83
Fiedler, Leslie 246–47
Fitzgerald, F. Scott 121
Ford, Ford Maddox
    Ladies Whose Bright Eyes 98
Ford, George H. 22
Frank, Tibor 80n
Fraser, J. T. 22n, 107, 123
Freedman, Carl 40n
Frick, Thomas 38n
Friel, Brian 202n, 208n, 227
Frost, Robert 128n
Fuller, John 280n

Genesis, Book of 135

genocide 108

Gibbon, Edward 126

Gibson, William 23, 40, 52–53
 All Tomorrow's Parties 39, 42, 44–45, 48
 Burning Chrome 45–46
 Idoru 45
 Mona Lisa Overdrive 41, 45, 47, 50–51
 Neuromancer 45, 48, 51
 Pattern Recognition 40

Gifford, Don 31, 35, 109–10, 132, 164, 241, 244

Giraudoux, Jean 262–63

Gizot, François 126

Gnosticism 138

Gould, Stephen Jay 72, 135, 143, 151–53

Graham, Billy 124

grandfather paradox 85, 88

Great Disappointment 138–40, 145

Greene, Brian 123, 165, 253

Gribbin, John 61n

Gulf War (1990) 36, 108

Gunn, James 144

Hancock, P. A. 46n

Hare, David 263

Hartke, Vance 157

Hayden, Robert 199

Hayles, N. Katherine 49n

Heidegger, Martin 184, 193

Heraclitus 19, 45, 53, 243, 277

Hercules 169

Hirsch, David H. 110

Holmes, William Gordon 126

Homer
    Odyssey 49
Hopkins, Gerard Manley 32
Hugo, Victor 225
Hume, Kathryn 125n
Hutton, James 134, 147
Huxley, Aldous 98

Ibsen, Henrik 214
    Ghosts 229–30, 233
Ionesco, Eugène 209, 264
Ittzés, Gábor 97n

Jackson, Rosemary 51
James, William 39, 109
    saddleback of time 23, 31, 34, 41, 51, 53
Jannings, Emil 187
Jarry, Alfred 69
    Ubu Roi 66, 68, 72
Jaspers, Karl 232
Jenkins, Jerry 25, 124, 129, 141, 143, 145
Johnson, Dr. (Samuel Johnson) 260
Johnson, Mark 21
Joyce, James 21, 23, 32, 202n
    Dubliners 236, 238, 252
    Finnegans Wake 42, 94, 236, 248–53
    A Portrait of the Artist as a Young Man 236, 238
    Ulysses 21, 28, 33–34, 61, 96, 235–52
Jung, Carl Gustav 236, 239

Kafka, Franz 183–84
Kahler, Erich 107
Kelvin, Lord (William Thomson) 80

INDEX

Kennelly, Brendan 215n

Kermode, Frank 259–60

Kertész, Imre 74

Kierkegaard, Søren 166, 173, 242

King, Martin Luther, Jr. 158

Kinsella, W. P. 23, 27, 200

Kirkwood, Tom 239n

Knight, G. Wilson 269

Kopp, Sheldon 245

Kremer, Johann Paul 111n

Kubrick, Stanley 163

Kurdi, Mária 230

LaHaye, Tim 25, 124, 129, 141, 143, 145

Lakoff, George 21

Lanters, José 240n

Lapore, Jill 16

Lascaux cave 64

Lászlóffy, Csaba 109n

Lawrence, Nathaniel 21, 167, 200

Le Guin, Ursula K. 93

LeClair, Tom 235, 247

Lee, Chris
    The Electrocution of Children 66, 69, 71–72

Levi, Primo 110, 115n

Levitt, Morton 240

Lifton, Robert Jay 115n

Lyell, Charles 135

McCabe, Colin 236n

McGuinness, Frank 19, 223
    Dolly West's Kitchen 225
    Factory Girls 224n

Gates of Gold 224n
   The Hanging Gardens 200, 219–27, 230
   The Visiting Hour 224n
McHale, Brian 49
McPhee, John 59, 135
Mac Intyre, Tom 207–08
MacColl, Ewan x, 16
Mallet, Ronald R. 84
Mamet, David 265
Manlove, Colin 210
The March of Time 36
Martin, George R. R. 19
Marvell, Andrew 278
Marx, Karl 125
Mengele, Joseph 117n
Michelangelo Buonarroti 130
Miller, Arthur 264
Miller, J. Hillis 22
Miller, William 131, 133–34, 137–39, 143, 145
Mitchell, David 15
Möbius strip 181, 190
Montesquieu, Charles de 269
Morrison, Toni 218
Muller, Richard 17
   now theory of time creation 18, 277
Murry, John Middleton 235

Nebuchadnezzer 220
Nero 257
Newcomb, Simon 92
Niebuhr, H. Richard 167, 174, 178, 194
Niebuhr, Reinhold 130, 167
Niffenegger, Audrey 23
   The Time Traveler's Wife 25, 86–95

Novak, Amy 47

O'Faolain, Seán 114, 120–21
    And Again? 100–02, 104
O'Kane, John 215
O'Kelly, Emer 230
O'Neill, Eugene
    The Iceman Cometh 204, 265
    A Long Day's Journey into Night 263
Oates, Joyce Carol 15

Park, David 21
Parrinder, Patrick 40n, 83
Pascal, Blaise 269
Peake, Charles 249
Perényi, Eleanor 186
Perlmutter, Saul 17
Petronius 28, 253–54, 257–58, 281
Pierce, John 41
Pinczés, István 68
Pinter, Harold 109n, 263
Pirandello, Luigi 266
Plummer, Christopher 275
Pope Gregory 166
Postlewait, Thomas 185
Price, George McCready 136–37

Ronsley, Joseph 241
Rose Center for Earth and Space 59
Rosenfield, Israel 205

Sacharow, Lawrence 266, 270, 275
Sacks, Oliver 156n, 218, 281–82

Samuelson, Robert 146
Schulz, James H. 222
Schwarz-Bart, André 251
Scotus, Dun 32
Serra, Richard iv, 94–96
SETI 61n
Shakespeare, William 235, 239
    Coriolanus 263
    Cymbeline 279
    Hamlet 263
    Henry IV 28, 261
    King Lear 28, 259–62, 269, 274, 281
    Othello 263
Shepard, Sam 263
Simmons, Dan 48n
Simpson, George Gaylord
    The Dechronization of Sam Magruder 25, 91–92, 96
simulacrum 45n
Snow, C. P. 153
Snyder, Gary 64
Sophocles 105, 211
Spencer, Herbert 126, 135
Stein, Gertrude 47, 93
Steiner, George 259
Stoker, Bram 120
    Dracula 98
Stoppard, Tom 263
Suvin, Darko 39
Swift, Jonathan 28, 257–58, 281
    Gulliver's Travels 255
Synge, J. M. 210

Taylor, E. B. 126
Taylor, John 94

INDEX

Taylor, Mark 138
television 37–38, 119
Tennyson, Alfred Lord 126
Teres, Gustav 55n
Thoreau, Henry David 62–63, 127, 138–42, 148
    Walden 31, 139, 235
Tillich, Paul 167–68, 173, 175, 180
time travel 25, 83, 86–89, 91
Tír na nÓg 50, 52
Tolkien, J. R. R. 94
Truman, Harry 73
Trump, Donald 137
Twain, Mark (Samuel Langhorne Clemens) 120
    A Connecticut Yankee in King Arthur's Court 98

Ussher, James 132, 143, 145

Vietnam War 36, 157–58
Vonnegut, Kurt 19, 23, 26, 91, 95, 120
    Cat's Cradle 152
    Deadeye Dick 153–55, 164
    Fates Worse than Death 117n, 160
    Galápagos 149–151, 159
    Hocus Pocus 147, 157, 159, 162, 164
    Jailbird 158
    Mother Night 158, 225n
    The Sirens of Titan 148, 164
    Slapstick 156
    Slaughterhouse-Five 25, 86–87, 99, 108–09, 116, 146, 159
    Tralfamador 87, 100, 109n, 148

Wallace, Henry 72
War in Iraq 37, 43–44

Ward, Peter 81n
Watson, Lyall 236
Watts, Isaac 258
Wells, H. G. 23, 91
    "The Extinction of Man" 81
    "On Extinction" 81, 86
    The Time Machine 25, 80–82, 93
    War of the Worlds 81
Wheeler, John 31
White, Donald W. 73n
White, Hayden 97, 122
Whitehead, Alfred North 31
Whitman, Walt
    "When Lilacs Last in the Dooryard Bloom'd" 273
Whitrow, G. J. 128
Wiesel, Elie 111n
Wigglesworth, Michael
    The Day of Doom 123
Wilde, Oscar 28, 204, 254
    The Picture of Dorian Gray 256, 258, 281
Wilder, Thornton
    Our Town 99, 103, 121
Williams, Tennessee 209
    The Glass Menagerie 201–02
    Sweet Bird of Youth 263
Wolf of Time 218, 221, 226, 233
World War I 68, 72, 108
World War II 26, 36–37, 64, 68, 86, 108, 116, 153–54,
    159

Y2K 56–57
Yeats, W. B. 49–53, 73, 229, 277
    The Land of Heart's Desire 50